HOW TO
REGISTER
YOUR OWN
COPYRIGHT

HOW TO REGISTER YOUR OWN COPYRIGHT

Fourth Edition

———

Mark Warda
Attorney at Law

SPHINX® PUBLISHING
AN IMPRINT OF SOURCEBOOKS, INC.®
NAPERVILLE, ILLINOIS

Fourth Edition, 2002

Published by: **Sphinx® Publishing, An Imprint of Sourcebooks, Inc.®**

<u>Naperville Office</u>
P.O. Box 4410
Naperville, Illinois 60567-4410
630-961-3900
Fax: 630-961-2168
http://www.sourcebooks.com
http://www.sphinxlegal.com

This publication is designed to provide accurate and authoritative information in regard to the subject matter covered. It is sold with the understanding that the publisher is not engaged in rendering legal, accounting, or other professional service. If legal advice or other expert assistance is required, the services of a competent professional person should be sought.

From a Declaration of Principles Jointly Adopted by a Committee of the American Bar Association and a Committee of Publishers and Associations

This product is not a substitute for legal advice.

Disclaimer required by Texas statutes

Library of Congress Cataloging-in-Publication Data
Warda, Mark.
   How to register your own copyright / Mark Warda.-- 4th ed.
      p. cm.-- (Legal survival guides)
   Includes index.
   ISBN 1-57248-200-1 (alk. paper)
   1. Copyright--United States--Popular works. 2. Copyright--United States--Forms. I. Title. II. Series.

KF3004.Z9 W373 2002
346.7304'82--dc21
                                                    2001057812

Printed and bound in the United States of America.

VHG Paperback — 10 9 8 7 6 5 4 3 2 1

CONTENTS

Using Self-Help Law Books

Before using a self-help law book, you should realize the advantages and disadvantages of doing your own legal work and understand the challenges and diligence that this requires.

THE GROWING
TREND

Rest assured that you won't be the first or only person handling your own legal matter. For example, in some states, more than seventy-five percent of the people in divorces and other cases represent themselves. Because of the high cost of legal services, this is a major trend and many courts are struggling to make it easier for people to represent themselves. However, some government offices are not happy with people who do not use attorneys and refuse to help them in any way. For some, the attitude is, "Go to the law library and figure it out for yourself."

We write and publish self-help law books to give people an alternative to the often complicated and confusing legal books found in most law libraries. We have made the explanations of the law as simple and easy to understand as possible. Of course, unlike an attorney advising an individual client, we cannot cover every conceivable possibility.

COST/VALUE
ANALYSIS

Whenever you shop for a product or service, you are faced with various levels of quality and price. In deciding what product or service to buy, you make a cost/value analysis on the basis of your willingness to pay and the quality you desire.

When buying a car, you decide whether you want transportation, comfort, status, or sex appeal. Accordingly, you decide among such choices as a Neon, a Lincoln, a Rolls Royce, or a Porsche. Before making a decision, you usually weigh the merits of each option against the cost.

When you get a headache, you can take a pain reliever (such as aspirin) or visit a medical specialist for a neurological examination. Given this choice, most people, of course, take a pain reliever, since it costs only pennies; whereas a medical examination costs hundreds of dollars and takes a lot of time. This is usually a logical choice because it is rare to need anything more than a pain reliever for a headache. But in some cases, a headache may indicate a brain tumor and failing to see a specialist right away can result in complications. Should everyone with a headache go to a specialist? Of course not, but people treating their own illnesses must realize that they are betting on the basis of their cost/value analysis of the situation. They are taking the most logical option.

The same cost/value analysis must be made when deciding to do one's own legal work. Many legal situations are very straight forward, requiring a simple form and no complicated analysis. Anyone with a little intelligence and a book of instructions can handle the matter without outside help.

But there is always the chance that complications are involved that only an attorney would notice. To simplify the law into a book like this, several legal cases must often be condensed into a single sentence or paragraph. Otherwise, the book would be several hundred pages long and too complicated for most people. However, this simplification necessarily leaves out many details and nuances that would apply to special or unusual situations. Also, there are many ways to interpret most legal questions.

Therefore, in deciding to use a self-help law book and to do your own legal work, you must realize that you are making a cost/value analysis. You have decided that the money you will save in doing it yourself outweighs the chance that your case will not turn out to your satisfaction. Most people handling their own simple legal matters never have a problem, but occasionally people find that it ended up costing them more to have an attorney straighten out the situation than it would have if they had hired an attorney in the beginning. Keep this in mind while handling your case, and be sure to consult an attorney if you feel you might need further guidance.

LOCAL RULES   The next thing to remember is that a book which covers the law for the entire nation, or even for an entire state, cannot possibly include every procedural difference of every jurisdiction. Whenever possible, we provide the exact form needed; however, in some areas, each county may require unique forms and procedures. In our state books, our forms usually cover the majority of counties in the state, or provide examples of the type of form which will be required. In our national books, our forms are sometimes even more general in nature but are designed to give a good idea of the type of form that will be needed in most locations. Nonetheless, keep in mind that your state or county may have a requirement, or use a form, that is not included in this book.

CHANGES IN   You should not necessarily expect to be able to get all of the informa-
THE LAW   tion and resources you need solely from within the pages of this book. This book will serve as your guide, giving you specific information whenever possible and helping you to find out what else you will need to know. This is just like if you decided to build your own backyard deck. You might purchase a book on how to build decks. However, such a book would not include the building codes and permit requirements of every city, town, county, and township in the nation; nor would it include the lumber, nails, saws, hammers, and other materials and tools you would need to actually build the deck. You would use the book as your guide, and then do some work and research involving such matters as whether you need a permit of some kind, what type and grade of wood are available in your area, whether to use hand tools or power tools, and how to use those tools.

Before using the forms in a book like this, you should check with your secretary of state or local government office to see if there are any local rules of which you should be aware, or local forms you will need to use. Often, such forms will require the same information as the forms in the book but are merely laid out differently or use slightly different language. They will sometimes require additional information.

Besides being subject to local rules and practices, the law is subject to change at any time. The courts and the legislatures of all fifty states are constantly revising the laws. It is possible that while you are reading this book, some aspect of the law is being changed.

In most cases, the change will be of minimal significance. A form will be redesigned, additional information will be required, or a waiting period will be extended. As a result, you might need to revise a form, file an extra form, or wait out a longer time period; these types of changes will not usually affect the outcome of your case. On the other hand, sometimes a major part of the law is changed, the entire law in a particular area is rewritten, or a case that was the basis of a central legal point is overruled. In such instances, your entire ability to pursue your case may be impaired.

Again, you should weigh the value of your case against the cost of an attorney and make a decision as to what you believe is in your best interest.

INTRODUCTION

While nearly everyone has created some work that deserves copyright protection, few people know the process for registering and protecting a copyright. It is the purpose of this book to explain the law of copyright in simple language and provide step-by-step instructions for registration of a copyright.

This book answers most basic questions about copyright protection. In the event that your case is in some way complicated or does not fit within the explanations in this book, you should seek further information from the Copyright Office or from an attorney specializing in copyright law. The address and phone numbers of the Copyright Office are contained in Appendix A of this book.

Copyright law offers protection to a wide range of works. Although written works are well known to be copyrightable due to their obvious copyright notice, copyright protection is also available for such things as photographs, sculptures, musical compositions, and other sounds and choreographic works.

Unlike some types of protection, such as patents, which can only be awarded to the first producer of the work, copyright is available to anyone who creates an original work. If two people create identical works independently and without copying each other, both are entitled to protection. However, the one who registered first would be in a much better position should a legal battle result.

A change in rules by the copyright office allows us to provide master forms that may be photocopied and used for filing registrations. Previously, they required the registrations to be on original forms that had to be obtained from their office. In using these forms, the instructions in Chapter 7 should be followed carefully.

For those who would like to do further research into the law, we have included court case citations. These cases can be looked up in a law library or some public libraries. For example, *Broadcast Music, Inc. v. Claire's Boutiques, Inc.*, 754 FSupp 1324 (1990). This case is found in Volume 754 (the first number listed), Page 1324 (the second number listed) of the set of books called *Federal Supplement*, available at most law libraries. (The year the case was heard is listed in the parentheses.)

Congratulations on becoming the creator of a new work and best wishes in your career!

COPYRIGHT, GENERALLY 1

Before registering your copyright, you should understand the basic rights and procedures of copyright law.

LEGAL RIGHTS

A *copyright* is a legal monopoly. It is a grant of exclusive rights, guaranteed by the United States government, to a work of authorship.

The five exclusive rights granted by a copyright are as follows:

1. the exclusive right to **reproduce the work**;

2. the exclusive right to **prepare derivative works** such as translations and abridged versions;

3. the exclusive right to **distribute copies** of the work to the public by sale or rental;

4. the exclusive right to **perform the work** publicly such as for music, plays, dances, pantomimes, and motion pictures; and,

5. the exclusive right to **display the work** publicly such as for paintings, sculptures, or photographs.

A copyright only protects you from others who may *copy* your work. If someone independently creates the same work, without knowing of your work, both of you can obtain a copyright of your works. Of course, it would be up to a court to decide if the works were created independently or if one of you copied the other.

The basic law concerning copyrights is the Copyright Act of 1976 (United States Code, Title 17.) This was amended by the Copyright Amendments Act of 1992 (amending Section 304 of Title 17), the Sonny Bono Copyright Term Extension Act of 1998 (amending Chapter 3 of Title 17), and the Digital Millennium Copyright Act of 1998 (this includes the WIPO Copyright and Performances and Phonograms Treaties Implementation Act of 1998, the Online Copyright Infringement Liability Limitation Act, the Computer Maintenance Competition Assurance Act, the Vessel Hull Design Protection Act, and six additional provisions). You can find the United States Code at most law libraries and some public libraries. You can find the copyright act on the Internet at the following website:

http://www.loc.gov/copyright/title17

LIMITATION ON RIGHTS

There are some limitations to these exclusive rights, such as the rights of others to *fair use* of the work or to obtain a *compulsory license* (the right to use the work as long as payment is made). Fair use includes such things as copying small excerpts, quoting parts in reviews and critiques, making parodies, and use by educators. A compulsory license is the right of someone to make copies of phonorecords if they pay a royalty that is set by law. Chapter 4 explains these limitations in more detail.

INTELLECTUAL PROPERTY

There are several types of intellectual property and copyright only offers protection to a few of them. For creations such as inventions and names, other types of protections must be used. The following are the different types of protections available for intellectual property.

COPYRIGHT   A *copyright* is protection given to "original works of authorship" such as written works, musical works, visual works, or performance works. But one cannot copyright titles, names, slogans, or works not fixed in tangible form. A copyright gives the author and his or her heirs the exclusive right to his or her work for the life of the author plus fifty years. Copyrights are registered with the Register of Copyrights at the Library of Congress. Examples of copyrightable works are books, paintings, songs, poems, plays, drawings, sculptures, and films. A more detailed explanation is contained in Chapter 2.

TRADEMARK

A *trademark* is a name or symbol used to identify goods or services. It can consist of letters, numerals, packaging, labeling, musical notes, colors, or a combination of these. A trademark lasts indefinitely if it is used continuously and renewed properly. Trademarks are registered in the United States Patent and Trademark Office.

PATENT

A *patent* is protection given to new and useful inventions and designs. A work must be completely new and "unobvious" to be entitled to a patent. (Unobvious is a legal term that can only be explained by reading the patent legal cases.) A patent is granted to the first inventor who files for the patent. Once an invention is patented, no one else can make use of it, even if they discovered it independently after a lifetime of research.

The term for a patent for inventions is twenty years, and for designs is fourteen years. Patents cannot be renewed. The application must clearly explain how to make the invention so that when the patent expires it will be available for others to freely make and use. Patents are registered in the United States Patent and Trademark Office.

TRADE SECRET

A *trade secret* is information or a process that provides a commercial advantage that is protected by keeping it a secret. Examples of trade secrets may be a list of successful distributors, a formula, such as for Coca-Cola, or some unique source code in a computer program. Trade secrets are not registered anywhere. They are protected by the fact that they are not disclosed. They are protected for as long as they are kept secret.

UNPROTECTABLE

Some things are just *unprotectable*. Such things as ideas, systems, and discoveries are not protected by any law. If you have a great idea, such as selling packets of hangover medicine in bars, you cannot stop others from doing the same thing. If you invent a new medicine, you can patent it; if you choose a distinctive name for it, you can trademark it; and if you create a unique picture for the package, you can copyright it.

Nonetheless, your basic business idea of selling hangover medicine in bars cannot be protected.

It is important to consider all of these types of protection before deciding which one to rely on for protection of your work. For a formula such as Coca-Cola, trade secret protection would be better than a patent since a patent would have expired after only twenty years. For some computer programs, a patent might be better than a copyright since it would keep others from developing the process independently. The shorter period of protection offered by a patent would not matter since computer software evolves so rapidly. While the name of a book cannot be copyrighted (see Chapter 3), you may trademark a name that distinguishes your book from others.

CREATION OF RIGHTS

A copyright, that is, the exclusive right to a work, is automatic upon the creation of a work. Nothing need be done at the creation of a work to give you the copyright. A work is considered "created" when it is "fixed in a medium," such as written down or recorded. No copyright can be had for a work that is just a thought and not yet fixed in a medium. (To avoid confusion with information you may have heard, the law prior to passage of the 1976 Copyright Act held that there was no copyright until the work was published with a copyright notice. This has changed.)

PROTECTION OF RIGHTS

Until March 1, 1989, a copyright notice had to appear on a published work before it could be protected. If a work was published without such notice, the copyright was lost and the work was in the public domain for anyone to use. However, in 1989, the United States joined the Berne Convention, an international agreement that allows a work to be protected even if it has no notice on it. Therefore, works originally published in the United States after March 1, 1989 are protected even if no copyright notice appears on them.

NOTE: *In copyright law, the word* publish *means to distribute copies to the public. This does not necessarily have to be done by a commercial "publisher." Making several photocopies of your manuscript and loaning, selling, or giving them out can be considered publishing a work.*

WORKS PUBLISHED
BEFORE 3/1/89

If a work was published (see above definition) prior to March 1, 1989, it must have been published with the copyright notice to be entitled to protection. If it was published without the copyright notice, you may have lost the right to copyright your work.

WORKS PUBLISHED
AFTER 3/1/89

As stated above, no notice is required by law to copyright a work, whether or not it has been published. However, as a practical matter, it is best to put a copyright notice on all copies of a work. Believe it or not, some people may not be aware that the law changed. Therefore, they may believe that any work without a copyright notice is in the public domain. Rather than pay your lawyer tens of thousands of dollars to convince them otherwise, you should always put the notice on your work.

NOTICE OF COPYRIGHT

The notice that was required on all works published prior to March 1, 1989, and which it is advisable to use now, is the three parts as follows:

1. the symbol ©, the word "copyright," or the abbreviation "copr.";

    - to protect international rights, it was necessary to use the symbol © rather than the word.

      NOTE: *Some people use (c) but the law does not recognize this as a copyright symbol and it is not known if a court would accept it as valid.*

    - for phonorecords, the symbol ℗ (P in a circle) is used instead of the word copyright or the ©.

      NOTE: *The word* phonorecord *is defined in the Copyright Act as any material object that records sounds (other than a motion picture or audiovisual work). This includes records, tapes, compact discs and any method that might be invented in the future to record sounds.*

2. the year of *first* publication of the work. Where a pictorial, graphic, or sculptural work is reproduced on postcards, greeting cards, stationery, jewelry, toys or other useful articles, the year may be omitted; and,

3. the name of the copyright owner or a recognizable abbreviation of the owner's name.

Thus, a correct notice would be as follows:

© 1991 John Doe

or

Copyright 1991 John Doe

The notice should be affixed to the copies in such a way as to give reasonable notice of the claim of copyright. That means that in motion pictures or other audiovisual works, the notice should be with or near the title, cast, credits, or similar information, or at the beginning or end of the work. On machine readable works, the notice should be with or near the title, user's terminal, continuous display, printouts, containers for the work, or at the end of the work.

For works on which it is impractical to affix a notice, it is acceptable to use a tag attached to the goods that will stay with them while they pass through commerce.

MANDATORY DEPOSIT OF COPIES

The copyright law also requires that within three months of publication of a work, two copies of the best edition of that work must be deposited with the Copyright Office. The best edition of a work is usually the best quality edition printed (such as hardback rather than paperback). Usually, this means sending them in with the registration form.

WORKS THAT CAN BE COPYRIGHTED

Only *original works of authorship* may be copyrighted. This means that the original creator of the work or his agent (see Chapter 6) is the only one who may obtain a copyright. You cannot take someone else's work and obtain a copyright.

TYPES OF WORKS

The following types of works are allowed protection under the copyright law:

> *Literary Works*—This can include novels, non-fictional works, poems, articles, essays, directories, advertising, catalogs, speeches, and computer programs.

> *Musical Works*—This category includes both the musical notation and the accompanying words.

> *Dramatic Works*—This type includes plays, operas, scripts, screenplays, and any accompanying music.

> *Pantomimes and Choreographic Works*—Popular dance steps are not included in this type of work.

> *Pictorial, Graphic, and Sculptural Works*—Works included are sketches, drawings, cartoons, paintings, photographs, slides, greeting

cards, architectural and engineering drawings, maps, charts, globes, sculptures, jewelry, glassware, models, tapestries, fabric designs, and wallpapers.

Motion Pictures and Other Audiovisual Works—These include movies, videos, and film strips.

Sound Recordings—This includes recorded music, voice, and sound effects. Thunder, animal noises, and other sounds of nature may be copyrighted by the persons who record them.

Compilations—You can put together a collection of existing materials and the collection as a whole can be copyrighted. Some examples would be a book of poems written about trees or a list of the best cancer doctors in the U.S.

> **Example 1**: In the collection of poems you could not use poems that were copyrighted by someone else without first obtaining their permission. However, you could use old poems where the copyright has expired. Your copyright on the collection would not give you exclusive rights to each individual poem, only to the collection as a whole. But if someone else collected the same poems independently, they could also copyright their work.

> **Example 2**: In the list of doctors you could not stop someone else from also putting together a similar list. If you put together a list of all the cancer doctors in the U.S., someone could freely copy it because it is a collection of mere facts. By selecting what you call the "best" ones, you can stop others from copying your list, which is based on opinion, not mere facts.

Derivative Works—Works such as the *Mona Lisa* or the *Venus de Milo* are in the public domain and may be copied by anyone. However, if someone paints a new version of the *Mona Lisa*, or takes a photograph of the *Venus de Milo*, those works may be copyrighted if they took some creativity. An exact photograph of the *Mona Lisa* or an exact replica of the *Venus de Milo* are not protectable, but derivations that took creativity (the changes to the painting and the angle and lighting in the photograph) are protectable.

Architectural Works—Previously, it was not possible to copyright a building, only the plans used to build it. This led to some interesting lawsuits in which people who copied others' buildings would only be guilty if it could be proved that they copied the copyrighted plans. The Architectural Works Copyright Protection Act of 1990 now allows the buildings themselves to be copyrighted. This was done to bring the United States into compliance with the Berne Convention, which it signed in 1989.

It has not been illegal to make pictures or photographs of buildings that are in public view. However, in a recent case, a photographer was forbidden to sell posters of a photograph he took of the Rock and Roll Hall of Fame. This opinion has been criticized and may not be followed by other courts.

Semiconductor Chip Mask Works—The Semiconductor Chip Protection Act of 1984 provides protection for the designs of semiconductor chips. Although the protection is somewhat different from a regular copyright, the process and forms are very similar to that for copyrights and the procedure is administered by the Copyright Office. For more information, obtain *Circular 100* and *Circular 96*, Part 211 from the Copyright Office.

Vessel Hulls—The Vessel Hull Design Protection Act of 1998 made possible the copyrighting of the designs of boats. Protection lasts for ten years.

ASPECTS OF THE WORK PROTECTED

While verbatim copying of a work is clearly a violation of copyright laws, not all aspects of a work are protected from copying.

Originally, only verbatim copying was considered infringement, but in recent years courts have found paraphrasing and copying of the "total concept and feel" of a work to be infringement. There is no black and white answer as to what similarities are allowed and what constitutes infringement. Paraphrasing of small portions of a work is allowed, but if substantial portions are paraphrased, there is infringement.

Below are some cases that give examples of what has been allowed by the courts and what has been found to be infringement. Further guidance on what is and is not protectable is contained in the next chapter.

INFRINGEMENT

The following are examples of some cases where a court found infringement:

    📖 A court ordered Topps Chewing Gum, Inc. to stop making Garbage Pail Kids trading cards which "derisively depict dolls with features similar to Cabbage Patch Kids dolls in rude, violent, and frequently noxious settings." (*Original Appalachian Artworks v. Topps Chewing Gum, Inc.*, 642 F.Supp. 1031 (N.D.Ga. 1986).)

    However, the parties eventually settled and Topps was allowed to make the cards for two more years.

    📖 "McDonaldland" TV commercials which copied the "total concept and feel" of the "H. R. Pufnstuff" children's television show were found to be infringing. The court noted that McDonald's chose to duplicate the concept of the most popular children's show rather than use an original and unproven approach. (*Sid & Marty Krofft Television, Inc. v. McDonald's Corp.*, 562 F.2d 1157 (9 Cir. 1977).)

    📖 An author of a biography of Hans Christian Anderson sued an author of a new biography. Since the first author knew the Danish language and spent years researching original Danish documents, and the second author knew no Danish and merely read earlier books and copied some of the letters as well as themes and structure, the court found infringement. (*Toksvig v. Bruce Pub. Co.*, 181 F.2d 664 (7th Cir. 1950).)

📖 When Sambo's Restaurant made a "Dancing Seniors" commercial as parody of Dr. Pepper's "Be a Pepper" commercial, Dr. Pepper sued and Sambo's was ordered to stop running the commercial and to pay a financial settlement to Dr. Pepper Co. (*Dr. Pepper Co. v. Sambo's Restaurant's Inc.*, 517 F.Supp. 1202, (N.D.Tx. 1981).)

📖 Because Judge Kimba Wood was convinced that a toy company had copied the patterns for Fisher-Price's "Shmooshee" dolls, she issued an injunction ordering the company to stop making them. (*Quaker Oats Co. v. Mel Appel Ent., Inc.*, 703 F.Supp. 1054 (S.D.N.Y. 1989).)

📖 When judges were considering whether the motion picture "Debbie Does Dallas" infringed the Dallas Cheerleaders' uniforms, and although they were considering both copyright and trademark law, the judges could not seem to get over the "depravity" of the film and found that use of the uniform "hardly qualifies as parody or any other form of fair use." (*Dallas Cowboys Cheerleaders, Inc. v. Pussycat Cinema, Ltd.*, 604 F.2d 200 (2d Cir. 1979).)

NO INFRINGEMENT   The following are examples of cases where a court did not find infringement:

📖 A year after Alberto-Culver invented the first "feminine deodorant spray," Andrea Dumon, Inc. decided to market a competing product called "Personal Spray" using a similarly designed can. The trial court found that the similarities of the packages were not enough to amount to infringement but that copying the phrase "most personal sort of deodorant" was infringement. The appeals court, however, ruled that it was not protectable since the phrase was a "short phrase or expression." (*Alberto-Culver Company v. Andrea Dumon, Inc.*, 466 F.2d 705 (C.A. 7th 1972).)

    The author of a musical play, *Lokey from Maldemar*, sued Steven Spielberg, claiming that *E.T.—The Extra Terrestrial* infringed her work. The author provided the court with a list of numerous similarities between the works, but these were found to be "random similarities scattered throughout the works." There was found to be no substantial similarity between "sequences of events, mood, dialog and character." Two courts ruled that there was not even enough of an issue for there to be a trial and the case was dismissed. (*Litchfield v. Spielberg*, 736 F. 2d 1352 (C.A. 9th 1984).)

The court found that the author's suit was based "partly upon a wholly erroneous understanding of the extent of copyright protection; and partly upon that obsessive conviction, so common among authors and composers, that all similarities between their works and any others that appear later must inevitably be ascribed to plagiarism."

    The author of two books that theorized that John Dillinger, Public Enemy No. 1, was not killed in a shoot-out with the FBI at the Biograph Theater in Chicago, as is commonly believed, sued CBS for using a similar plot on its show *Simon and Simon*. Because the books purported to explain facts, and not fiction, the court ruled that CBS had a right to use the same theories in its show. (*Nash v. CBS, Inc.*, 899 F.2d 1537 (7th Cir. 1990).)

    A writer published a children's book based upon an old folk tale and later a magazine published a story with a very similar plot. Although the concept was the same the court found that the "feel" was different in the mood and characterization so there was no infringement. (*Reyher v. Children's Television Workshop*, 433 F.2d 87 (2d Cir. 1987).)

Works That Cannot Be Copyrighted 3

Until a work has been written down on paper or made into some other form that can be seen and/or held, it is not copyrightable. Some examples of works not yet fixed in tangible form are stories that have not been written down, dances that have not been notated or recorded, or speeches or lectures that have not been written down or recorded.

Titles, Names, Mottos, or Slogans

Book titles, company names, group names, pen names, pseudonyms, product names, phrases, mottos, slogans, catchwords, advertising expressions, bumper stickers, and the like may not be copyrighted. If they are part of a creative design or logo, the design or logo can be copyrighted, but you cannot stop someone from using the basic words in another way.

NOTE: *Some of these may be registered as trademarks.*

Ideas, Methods, Procedures, and Systems

Copyright only protects the form of expression of an idea—not the idea itself. If you come up with a great way to make a million dollars, a process for tripling corn yield or a system for eliminating paying income tax, you can write and copyright a book and no one can copy the words in your book. However, others can use your ideas or write their own books about your ideas.

In some cases, a method or procedure could be patented. In many cases, an idea, method, procedure, or system could be protected by keeping it a trade secret.

PLOTS AND THEMES

The basic plot of a story cannot be protected, only the words in which the story is told. One famous theme is the love story of Romeo and Juliet. It has been retold in many other ways, the most popular of which was *West Side Story*. Each version of the story can be copyrighted, but you cannot keep someone from using the theme in another story.

SCÈNES À FAIRE

Scenes or incidents that are indispensable to a certain type of story are called *scènes à faire*.

Example: Someone writing about the Hindenburg disaster in 1937, would probably use scenes of Germans in beer-halls singing "Deutschland Über Alles" and giving the "Heil Hitler" salute. Since these are so necessary to the story, the first writer could not stop future writers about the Hindenburg from using the same scenes.

HISTORICAL EVENTS

Similarly, historical facts cannot be copyrighted. If you write a story about your experiences in World War II, you cannot stop others from writing about the same incidents, as long as they do not copy your exact words.

COMMON INFORMATION

No one may copyright the basic information for calendars, height and weight charts, rulers, or other such lists of information. If you design a creative form of calendar or ruler, you can copyright your design but not the information.

MERE FACTS

A collection of facts is not copyrightable. For many years, the courts held that collections of facts that took time and labor to collect, such as lists of certain persons' names and addresses, were entitled to copyright protection. This was known as the "sweat of the brow" doctrine. But in 1991, the United States Supreme Court unanimously held that collections of mere facts cannot be copyrighted.

📖 The case by which the Supreme Court made that decision was *Feist Publications, Inc. v. Rural Telephone Services, Co., Inc.*, 111 S.Ct. 1282 (1991). Feist was a publisher of an alternative phone book, and it copied the names and addresses from Rural's directory. Rural sued and won in two lower courts but the Supreme Court reversed the decisions, saying that a collection of names and addresses took no creativity to compile or to alphabetize, and that copyright was only for works that took some *creativity*.

This can cause a problem for businesses that make money by compiling facts. It can take a lot of time and effort to gather facts, and they can be quite valuable. Some businesses pay thousands of dollars for information that helps them make greater profits. However, if the first recipient of the information can copy it, and sell it for less, the originator may not be able to recoup the cost of gathering the material.

Because of this problem, businesses that sell information should consider protections other than copyright. One type of protection is the licensing of the use of the information. By making each user of the information agree not to disclose it to others, one could hold that user liable for such disclosure. If the information were treated as a trade secret, then unauthorized users could be charged with theft of a trade secret.

In some areas of the country, this entitles the victim to triple the damages found by the jury. This would not be practical for directories sold to libraries, but it would be useful for information distributed to limited numbers of users. See Chapter 12 for more information on alternative protections.

    📖 If a person writes a work of fiction based on historical facts, the fictional elements are copyrightable, but the historical facts can be used by others. However, if a work is advertised and promoted as fact, but contains fiction, the author loses the right to protect the fictional parts. (*Houts v. Universal City Studios, Inc.* 603 F.Supp.26 (C.D.Cal 1984).)

HOT NEWS   Some facts are more valuable when they first become available than later in time. During World War I, Associated Press had reporters in Europe covering the fighting and sending back reports that were sold to newspapers around the country.

    📖 One company, International News Service, operated by the Hearst newspapers, had no reporters, but they read AP's stories and rewrote them taking just the facts. Thus, they could sell the same stories with almost no cost, while AP was paying its reporters substantially for their coverage. In a lawsuit between them, the Supreme Court created the *Hot News* doctrine to protect facts that one party has spent a lot of time and money to gather and that are time-sensitive.

The National Basketball Association tried to use the same theory to keep a company from sending basketball scores to fans over pagers while games were in progress. The federal court of appeals disagreed and said that the scores were not protected by copyright law and that such use was not *misappropriation* (an improper or unlawful use of money or property), as the NBA had also claimed. The court said that the hot news rule did not apply since the NBA did not gather the news at great cost like the AP's reporters.

FUTURE
DEVELOPMENTS

Companies that deal in databases are unhappy with the fact that they are not protectable under copyright law. Some are urging Congress to overturn the Supreme Court decision and others are pushing an international treaty to protect databases.

A diplomatic conference in Geneva, Switzerland, failed to take action on the proposed database treaty, but the European Union has new laws for protecting databases in their countries. Whether the U.S. adopts this stance will probably not be answered for years. The best way to protect such works for now is by licensing them— rather than selling them— and putting strict controls in the license. See Chapter 12.

Lists of Ingredients

The text of a recipe may be copyrighted, but not a mere list of ingredients. This means that someone else may copy your recipe as long as they rewrite the instructions in their own words.

Blank Forms and Record Books

Any form that is relatively blank such as a check, diary, address book, or columnar pad may not be copyrighted. Where there is some creativity in a form, such as a lengthy legal form, the text may be copyrighted. However, such works as legal forms are provided less protection than other works because no one is to have a monopoly on a legal process, and there are a limited number of ways to word a legal document.

There have been a few cases in which courts have held forms to be copyrightable. These have been instances where the forms included some instructional material or were creatively designed for computer use. For guidance, you could read two cases on the subject, *Edwin K. Williams & Co. v. Edwin K. Williams & Co. - East*, 542 F.2d 1053 (9th Cir. 1976) and *Harcourt, Brace & World, Inc. v. Graphic Controls Corp.* 329 F.Supp. 517. (S.D.N.Y. 1971)

If you try to copyright a form, the copyright office might accept it under its *rule of doubt*. Under this rule, they will accept works even if they do not believe they are registrable. If they refuse your registration, you could explain why you feel your work contains creativity and ask them to register it under their rule of doubt.

GOVERNMENT PUBLICATIONS

Works of the United States Government may not be copyrighted, and anyone may copy them freely. Some people reprint government publications and sell them at a profit. Copyrighted works may contain works of the government, but the copyright only applies to the other material in the book. For example, you may freely copy the forms and circulars in the back of this book.

LAWS AND COURT OPINIONS

As early as 1834, the United States Supreme Court ruled that statutes and judicial opinions cannot be copyrighted. The rationale is that the citizens are authors of the law and are therefore its owners regardless of who drafts the words. The policy is that citizens must have free access to the laws that govern them. Therefore, all statutes and court opinions are in the public domain.

   📖 In 1982, the state of Georgia tried to copyright its laws and give one company the exclusive right to publish them. A United States District Court did an excellent analysis of the law in ruling against the state. (*State of Georgia v. Harrison Co.*, 548 F. Supp. 110 (N.D.Ga. 1982).)

Later, the parties settled the case and the court vacated its opinion, but it still provides useful background analysis and citations of Supreme Court rulings.

Many states are putting their statutes on the Internet. Some are claiming that the statutes are copyrighted. The state of Idaho passed a law purporting to copyright its statutes. Considering past Supreme Court rulings, this law is probably invalid.

A more complicated question comes up when a copyrighted work, such as a building code, is adopted by a government body and made into law. While the rationale still exists that people should have free access to their laws, the other factor is that groups would have no incentive to create standards if they would lose their copyright upon adoption.

No court has yet ruled that a copyrighted work of this sort loses its copyright upon adoption as law. However, courts have made efforts to allow others to use the work in spite of upholding the copyright.

📖 In a case where the American Medical Association's standards were adopted by Medicare, a court ruled that because the AMA's licensing agreement said that the government could not use any other system, it had misused its copyright and a competitor could copy the work. (*Practice Management Information Corp. v. American Medical Association*, (C.D.Cal. 1997).)

This made sense because to rule otherwise would have given the AMA a monopoly on publishing materials about the federal Medicare system standards.

RELIGIOUS REVELATIONS

If governmental laws should be freely available for everyone to use, what about spiritual revelations? Can a church copyright the works of celestial beings? Yes, said the U.S. Court of Appeals for the 9th Circuit in 1997.

    📖 While the facts of religious beliefs cannot be copyrighted, the expression of those facts as written by humans can be. (*Urantia Foundation v. Maaherra*, Case No. 95-17093 (CA 9th 1997).)

Therefore, if you want to spread a religion without using the copyrighted works of the founders, you must take only the facts, and put them in your own form of expression. (*Oliver v. St. Germain Foundation*, 41 F.Supp. 296 (S.D.Cal. 1941).)

TYPE FACES

The design of a type face has never been entitled to protection in the U.S. Some argue that protection is needed or else no one will design any more fonts. However, every year new ones appear even without protection.

Recently, some courts have ruled that while the font design is not entitled to protection, the computer code that causes a printer to print it can be protected. Some have argued that this allows font designers to protect that which is not legally protectable, but others answer that the font can still be copied by writing a different code. Again, expect this area of law to remain in flux.

UTILITARIAN OBJECTS

If an object is designed merely to work in a certain way, such as a pair of scissors, its design cannot be copyrighted. This is because such works should be covered by patents, and you cannot use a copyright to get longer protection than patents offer. What can be copyrighted is any decoration on the object that does not add to the function but is merely ornamental.

WORKS OF OTHERS YOU CAN USE 4

In certain instances, it is permissible to use and copy the works of others. Sometimes, you may copy even copyrighted works if you carefully follow the rules. The basic rules for use of the works of others are explained in this chapter.

WHEN YOU OWN A COPY OF A WORK

It should first be explained that ownership of a copy of a work does not confer any rights to the copyright on the work. If someone writes you a letter, that person owns the copyright to the letter the moment they write it down. You own the letter, and you may sell it, but you cannot reproduce it or enjoy any of the other five exclusive rights of the copyright owner that are listed on page 1.

If you buy a painting, you can display it, but you do not have the right to make copies of it. If you buy a record or video cassette, you can listen to or watch it yourself, but you cannot play it in public or make copies of it.

WORKS IN THE PUBLIC DOMAIN

All works that are in the *public domain* can be copied by anyone in any quantity. Works in the public domain include works that have never been copyrighted, works in which the copyright has expired, works created by the United States government, and state laws and court opinions. The following copyrighted works are now in the public domain:

- any work copyrighted before 1923;

- any work copyrighted before January 1, 1964 of which the copyright was not renewed; and,

- any work that was published (see definition on page 5) in the United States before March 1, 1989 without a copyright notice (unless the author made a special effort to retrieve all copies).

The recent law that extended the length of copyrights by twenty years will mean that works published in 1923 and later will not start entering the public domain until 2018, unless a pending lawsuit results in the law being declared unconstitutional.

The rules for future works are as follows:

- works published between 1964 and 1977 enter the public domain ninety-five years after their date of copyright;

- on works published January 1, 1978 or later, the copyright lasts for the life of the author plus seventy years. If the work was authored by a corporation or the author is anonymous or pseudonymous, the copyright lasts until ninety-five years from publication, or 120 years from creation, whichever is shorter;

- if a work was created before January 1, 1978 but not published, its copyright lasts for the life of the author plus seventy years or until December 31, 2002, whichever is greater; and,

● if a work was created before January 1, 1978 and is published before December 31, 2002, the copyright lasts for the life of the author plus seventy years or to December 31, 2047, whichever is greater. (This means that old manuscripts or diaries that are discovered should be published by December 31, 2002 or else they cannot be copyrighted.)

As you can see, there is a lot of material in the public domain that you may freely reproduce (and sell if you wish). Such classics as the works of Shakespeare, Dickens, Mark Twain, and Tolstoy are now in the public domain and you are free to publish your own edition.

NOTE: *Recent translations are not in the public domain.*

Warning: Works such as sound recordings and films may have more than one copyright. The words, the sound, and the scenes each may be copyrighted separately. Therefore, even if the copyright in, for example, a film has expired, the underlying book or music may still be protected. So reproducing a film in the public domain may violate the other copyrights.

📖 In one case a company that had dubbed some Chinese films into Cambodian, but neglected to register the copyrights was still able to win an infringement suit against a video rental store because they had the rights to the original Chinese film versions. (*Gamma Audio & Video, Inc. v. Ean-Chea*, 11 F.3d 1106 (1st Cir. 1993).)

PUBLIC PERFORMANCES

As a rule, you cannot perform any copyrighted work in public without obtaining the permission from the copyright owner (and paying royalties). However, the Copyright Act contains several exceptions where performance or display is allowable. These are:

- face-to-face systematic teaching in a nonprofit educational institution (all types of works);

- instructional broadcasting (only nondramatic literary and musical works);

- religious services (only nondramatic literary and musical works);

- nonprofit performances, where there is no admission fee or payment to promoters, organizers or performers and the copyright owner has not objected (only nondramatic literary and musical works);

- reception of broadcasts in a public place, if there is no charge, the equipment is not a commercial type, and there is no further transmission (all types of works). See the section on "Playing of Broadcasts," page 30, for more on this;

- agricultural and horticultural fairs run by governmental or nonprofit bodies (only nondramatic musical works);

- retail businesses selling records, tapes, compact disks, and sheet music (only nondramatic musical works);

- noncommercial broadcasts to the deaf or blind (only nondramatic literary works);

- noncommercial broadcasts to the blind or visually handicapped (only dramatic literary works published at least ten years previous); and,

- social functions by veterans' or nonprofit fraternal organizations that are not open to the general public (only nondramatic literary and musical works).

FAIR USE OF COPYRIGHTED WORKS

The copyright law that was passed in 1976 contains a provision that one may make *fair use* of copyrighted works. This is merely an acknowledgment of what the courts had decided under the previous laws. However, the task of determining just what constitutes fair use has been called "the most troublesome in the whole law of copyright." Since anyone can file a lawsuit at any time for little reason and a small filing fee, you should check your position before taking a chance and copying someone's work. A consultation with an experienced copyright attorney would be well worth the investment.

Under copyright law, there are four main factors to be looked at in determining whether a particular use is legal or not:

1. whether the copying is for commercial or educational purposes (a commercial use is less likely to be fair);

2. whether the work copied is fact or fiction (factual works may be used more freely than fictional works);

3. the amount of material copied (the less the better); and,

4. the effect on the potential market for the original work (if the new work does not take customers from the original work, that is better.)

The remainder of this section will give examples of fair and unfair use.

PARODY   It is legal to copy part of a work in a *parody*, which is a work that makes fun of another work. Some examples of parody of copyrighted works are *MAD Magazine* and the songs of "Weird Al" Yankovic.

 📖 The owner of the copyright of the song "Oh, Pretty Woman" by Roy Orbison sued 2 Live Crew for their song "Pretty Woman" about a "big, hairy woman, a bald headed woman and a two-timin' woman." The federal district court called it fair use as parody. (*Acuff-Rose Music, Inc. v. Campbell*, 754 F.Supp. 1150 (M.D.Tenn. 1991).)

The case eventually was taken to the U.S. Supreme Court which unanimously agreed. 510 U.S. 569,114 S.Ct. 1164, 127 L.E2d 500 (1994).

LIMITED USE

Limited Use is a use of a copyright work that is small enough to be allowed by copyright law. While the percentage of a work used is considered in determining if the use is fair, there is no hard and fast rule as to what percentage is legal. It depends upon the nature of the work. In some cases, copying several pages has been considered fair use, while in others, copying a few words has been ruled to be infringement.

    📖 Copying three hundred out of 200,000 words (15/100ths of one percent) was held to be illegal since what was copied was the "heart of the work." (*Harper & Row, Publishers, Inc. v. Nation Enterprises*, 471 U.S. 539 (1985).)

In another case, copying 4.3% of a work was considered fair use. (*Maxtone-Graham v. Burtchaell*, 803 F2d 1253 (USCA 2nd Cir 1986).)

POLITICAL USE

If copies of a work are being used for some political cause, this may be characterized as fair use.

    📖 A conservative group used photocopies of an artist's work in a pamphlet arguing against funding of the National Endowment for the Arts. The artist sued, but the court ruled that such a pamphlet was entitled to great protection and that those accepting federal funds must accept the rights of others to protest such expenditures. (*Wojnarowicz v. American Family Ass'n.*, 745 F. Supp. 130 (S.D.N.Y. 1990).)

UNPUBLISHED WORKS

There is not as great a right to use *unpublished works* as there is for published works. Three cases in the 1980s held that copyright infringement exists when even small amounts of unpublished materials are used. Biographers and the press then pointed out that this will make it very difficult to write biographies. Arthur Schlesinger has said that if he were writing his three volume *The Age of Roosevelt* today, he would be two volumes short.

In 1992, the copyright law was amended to allow copying of unpublished matter as fair use, if such use is fair under the four standard fair use factors mentioned on the previous page.

LIBRARIES AND ARCHIVES

Libraries are allowed much greater rights to make copies of copyrighted materials for their own use. If the library is open to the public, it may make isolated copies of works for archiving and research if the copy includes a copyright notice and if it is not done to make a profit.

The copyright office has a twenty-eight page brochure available explaining the rights of libraries to copy materials. Ask for *Circular 21*. See page 75 of this book for the address and phone number. Also, *Librarian's Guide to the New Copyright Law* is available from the American Library Association, 50 East Huron Street, Chicago, IL 60611.

The most important part of the law as far as librarians are concerned, is that a notice regarding the copyright law should be posted next to photocopy machines. If this is done, the library is not liable for violations committed by patrons.

EDUCATIONAL USE

Copying of copyrighted material is more likely to be considered fair use if it is for an educational purpose, especially nonprofit *educational use*.

📖 Teachers have been allowed to copy material out of textbooks to distribute to their students. However, a copy shop that copied chapters from text books to sell to students as course materials was held liable for $510,000 in damages. (*Basic Books, Inc. v. Kinko Graphics Corp.*, 758 FSupp 1522 (S.D.N.Y. 1991).)

Circular 21, mentioned in the previous section, also explains the rights of educators to copy materials.

This issue was revisited in 1994-1996 when a Michigan district court judge held that a copy shop in Ann Arbor could copy portions of books under certain circumstances, and a panel of the Sixth Circuit Court of Appeals agreed. However, the publishers asked the entire Sixth Circuit to review the decision and it agreed.

In the final decision, eight judges decided to reverse the ruling and four judges *dissented*, or disagreed. This means that when educational coursepacks are made by a copy service, they must contact the publishers or the Copyright Clearance Center for permission and pay the required royalty.

INCIDENTAL USE If a copyrighted work is used *incidentally* (in a background of a work), the use is usually considered fair.

> **Example**: A television broadcast of a county fair that included a scene of a band playing a copyrighted song, or the use of copyrighted photographs in the background of a movie scene would not violate the copyright of the owner of the song or the photographs.

PERSONAL USE There is no specific exemption in the law for *personal use*. But because the constitutional purpose of copyright law is to promote the "progress of Science and useful Arts," courts have ruled that making copies for personal use is a kind of fair use. See the section on home videotaping later in this chapter.

However, in a recent case, a court held Texaco liable for making in-house photocopies of newsletters.(*American Geophysical Union v. Texaco*, 60 F.3d 913 (2d Cir.), *cert. dismissed*, 116 S.Ct. 592 (1995).) Some commentators have felt that this case has gone too far and given too much weight to the factor of whether copying costs a publisher money. The U.S. Supreme Court declined to hear an appeal of the case, but years earlier in a copyright case, Chief Justice Warren Burger admitted from the bench that he occasionally photocopied material for his own use or to share with colleagues.

USE WITH PERMISSION

Of course, you can use another's copyrighted work if you obtain permission ahead of time. Often, the copyright owner will require a fee for such use. When requesting permission for use, you should always get it in writing and you should include "subsequent editions" of your work in the request so that you do not have to request permission again if you revise it and issue a new edition.

You will usually be asked to pay for the right to use someone's work. The fee may range from $10 to $100 per page or more. In most cases, you need to go through the publisher, which often has its own form to be used for such permissions. It usually takes several months to get permission. It is not an easy process. You are better off finding public domain material to use, or else writing the material yourself whenever possible.

In 1978, a group of publishers formed the Copyright Clearance Center "CCC" to ease the process of selling licenses to copy material. Because this system makes obtaining of permission easier, courts have seemed less likely to allow copying as fair use.

COMPULSORY LICENSE

There is a provision in the copyright law dating back to the days of the player piano that allows persons to copy certain works without permission if they pay a set royalty to the copyright owner. The law allows this in these circumstances:

- phonorecords (See definition on page 5);

- juke boxes;

- cable systems making secondary transmissions; and,

- noncommercial public broadcasters.

For more information about this, you should obtain copies of both the Copyright Act and the regulations covering compulsory licenses. The following information pamphlets are available from the Copyright Office:

Circular 73
Circular 96, Section 201.17
Circular 96, Section 201.18
Circular 96, Section 201.19

The sections of Circular 96 are actually sections of the Code of Federal Regulations (C.F.R.). To find them on the Copyright Office's website, you need to download Chapter 201 of the Code of Federal Regulations. (see Appendix A for more information.)

SOUND RECORDINGS MADE BEFORE FEBRUARY 15, 1972

Prior to February 15, 1972, one could not copyright a recording of sounds in the United States. The underlying words and music could be copyrighted, but not the sounds. Therefore, making copies of sound recordings that were recorded before February 15, 1972, which are of works not covered by copyright (Mozart, Beethoven, etc.) would not violate the copyright law. This is why some CDs of classical music can be obtained so inexpensively. However, some states have passed laws protecting such works.

Under the General Agreement on Tariffs and Trade (GATT), those from countries that offer protection to pre 1972 sound recordings are allowed to regain the copyrights to them in the U.S., if they are still under protection in their home country. This means that much music that was in the public domain and freely copied by many record companies is now illegal to copy. Litigation is pending on the legality of this treaty.

PLAYING OF BROADCASTS

For many years, anyone who played a radio in a commercial establishment would run the risk of being visited by enforcers from the musicians' unions, ASCAP and BMI, requiring payment of a royalty. There were many court cases ruling whether, based on the size of the establishment and the type of receiver, any royalty was owed.

However, the issue was settled in 1998 by an amendment to the Sonny Bono Copyright Term Extension Act. This amendment allows many types of establishments to provide music or television broadcasts. Some of these establishments are:

- food or drinking establishments of under 3,750 square feet;

- establishments other than food or drinking establishments of under two thousand square feet; and,

- establishments that have no more than six speakers of which no more than four are in one room.

For more specifics of the law, review Title II of the Sonny Bono Copyright Term Extension Act. One place to obtain it is at:

http://www.loc.gov/copyright/title17/

Home Videotaping

Of course, the copyright holders of video productions such as films and television shows would like to make some extra money off the taping of their programs on home video cassette recorders. In fact, they sued the manufacturers of the devices claiming that the sale of these devices made the manufacturers "contributing infringers." (This is like arresting camcorder makers as contributing pornographers.)

The California district court threw the case out, but the United States Court of Appeals reversed that decision. The United States Supreme Court agreed to review the case and groups from all over the country filed briefs.

In support of consumers' rights were the American Library Association, the Consumer Electronics Group, General Electric Co., the National Retail Merchants Association, Sears, Roebuck and Co., TDK Electronics Co., Ltd., Pfizer Inc., and others. Opposed to home taping were the Association of American Publishers, Inc., the Authors League of America, Inc., CBS Inc., the AFL-CIO, and others.

At least seventeen state Attorneys General also filed briefs in the case. When the dust settled, the Supreme Court held that home taping of copyrighted programs for later use was "fair use" under the copyright laws and was not infringement. (*Sony Corporation of America v. Universal City Studios, Inc.*, 464 U.S. 417, 104 S. Ct. 774, 78 L. Ed.2d 574 (1984).)

RENTAL OF COPYRIGHTED WORKS

Historically, a person who purchases a copy of a work had the unlimited right to sell or rent it to others. This is called the *first sale doctrine*. There are some who are arguing that this is not fair to authors, that every time a book or record is sold, a royalty should be paid to the author. Others argue that this would be a nightmare for used bookstores and flea market vendors and that it is just as ridiculous as giving General Motors a royalty whenever a used car is sold.

Another argument being used against the first sale doctrine is that books and records used to be fragile, but now electronic media can last much longer than similar items in the past. But actually the opposite seems to be true. Eight track tapes and old style floppy disks are already obsolete while books from the 1700s are still very useable.

Powerful interests in the record and computer industries have already persuaded Congress to limit this right. In 1984, the record industry was able to secure the passage of the Record Rental Amendment of the Copyright Act. This forbids the rental of sound recordings. In 1990, the computer industry went to Congress and got the Computer Software Rental Amendments Act passed, which forbids the rental of computer programs.

One interesting loophole in these laws is that they exempt nonprofit libraries. This provides the necessary protection to your local city library, but it would probably allow anyone to set up a record or computer program library as long as it was "nonprofit." Nonprofit usually means that the members make no profit on their shares. (However, there is no set limit on how high the officers and employees salaries can be as evidenced by many nonprofit groups.)

THE RIGHT TO PUBLICITY

Just because you have created a photograph of someone and therefore own the copyright to the photograph does not give you unlimited rights to use the photograph. In recent years, courts have recognized a *right to publicity*, which is part of the right to privacy. This means that if you take a picture of a film star or famous musician, you do not have the right to make posters or T-shirts out of the picture. The First Amendment to the Constitution guarantees your right to use the picture in a magazine or other news media, but you cannot otherwise use it commercially.

The law of publicity is included in the statutes in some states, and in others it is part of the common law, which is decided by the courts. Therefore, the law is different in each state. Some states do not recognize the right to publicity and some require that a person exploit his likeness during his lifetime before his heirs can claim rights to it.

TRADEMARK RIGHTS

As mentioned in the last chapter, a title cannot be copyrighted. However, it can be trademarked, and some have tried to use trademark law to keep others from successfully using a *public domain work*.

    The John Wayne film *McLintock* entered the public domain when its copyright was not renewed. One company that bought the home video rights sued another company distributing the film arguing that the title was a trademark and was being infringed. The court ruled that it would not allow trademark law to protect an expired copyright. (*Maljack Productions, Inc. v. Goodtimes Home Video Corp.*, 81 F.3d 881, (9th Cir. 1996).)

However, the court also said that others could be forbidden to use it in cases where the title had acquired a "secondary meaning." (The test is whether the public is being deceived.)

Trademark law can also protect fictional characters. Under Section 43(a) of the Lanham Act (the trademark law) the costumes, physical features, names, and nicknames of characters can be protected. However, physical abilities and personality traits cannot.

"Moral" Rights

A relatively recent concept in copyright law is that of *moral rights*. This is the theory that an artist has put part of himself or herself into his or her work and that after the work is sold, some rights of the artist remain. This concept developed in France and is completely counter to the English-American theory that property rights are important and that a purchaser of an item acquires all rights to it.

Under this French theory, a purchaser of a work of art would not be allowed to make a change to the work and the artist would always have his or her name associated with the work. There are several facets to the rights, some of which have been adopted by the different jurisdictions to varying degrees.

Example: In France an artist has no right to transfer or waive his or her rights. But in other countries, artists have been given these options.

Things that could be forbidden by an artist would be colorization of a black and white film, or modification of a sculpture to fit new surroundings. Under the moral rights theory, no one other than the artist has the right to change the artist's work, even if the work has been sold.

VARA   In 1990, the United States passed the Visual Artists Rights Act (VARA), which gives some of these rights to American artists. This act protects paintings, drawings, prints, sculptures, or photographs produced for exhibition after June 1, 1991.

The work must be either a single piece or have no more than two hundred signed and numbered copies. It does not include advertising materials, applied art, audio visual works, books, electronic publications, motion pictures, posters, or works for hire.

The work also must be of recognized statute in the art community to be protected. The protection lasts for the lifetime of the author and only the artist may assert a VARA claim.

The impact of this law is that owners of sculptures and other works of art may be liable to artists for damaging or improperly displaying them. In some cases, buildings may not be demolished until arrangements have been made with the creator of any art work installed in them.

Violation of the act can result in damages of between $500 and $20,000, or if the violation was willful, up to $100,000. Attorney's fees and court costs can also be awarded and in one case an artist was awarded $20,000 and his attorney, $131,252.55.

Some of the questions not answered by the act are what an owner of a work can do if he cannot sell or give away the work. Can it be put in storage? Does it have to be left on display until the artist dies?

Example: Several artists created a work on vacant land and when the owner attempted to develop the land, it was sued by the artists to protect their work. Sensibly, the court ruled that VARA does not apply if a work is installed without permission.

Besides this federal law, some states and municipalities have laws protecting artists moral rights, most notably California and New York.

RESALE ROYALTIES

A concept even further removed from American thinking is *artist resale rights*, also developed in France. This is the theory that artists deserve some of the profits from their works that normally go to the collectors or investors who originally bought the works. To enforce such rights, laws are passed that require art works to be registered with a body that keeps track of them and each time a work is sold a commission must be paid to the artist.

The rationale behind this law is that artists are not fairly compensated for their works at the time of creation and that they should get a share of the profits that an investor will make in the work. The other side of the argument is that artists are paid exactly what their works are worth at the time and that those who risk their money on the works of unknown artists should be fully rewarded for their contributions to the art scene.

In the U.S., this concept is only enforced in California, where there is a state law granting resale rights to California artists. Under this law, an artist is entitled to be paid five percent of the sales price of any work of fine art sold in California or by a California resident. The law even applies if the seller does not make a profit on a work, so that a buyer of California art could lose money on a work when paying the royalty to dispose of the work.

One might expect that such a law would drive art galleries out of the state and cause art buyers to avoid works of California artists. There have been efforts to repeal the law but it is still on the books.

REASONS TO REGISTER YOUR COPYRIGHT 5

A copyright automatically exists from the moment of creation of a work (fixing it in a tangible medium). However, registration of the work with the United States Copyright Office is important. The cost of registration is low and the procedure is simple.

DAMAGES AND ATTORNEY'S FEES

If your work is registered before someone infringes it (or within three months of publication), you can receive a monetary *award* set by the copyright law and payment of your attorney's fees. If you do not register and you must pay your own attorney's fees for a federal lawsuit, it might not be worth suing someone for infringement.

EVIDENCE

Your registration certificate is *prima facie* evidence of the validity of your copyright. This means that the burden is on the person infringing to prove that he has some right to the work.

The registration also provides a permanent record of your claim to the work. If your certificate is ever lost or destroyed you can get a duplicate.

Your copyright certificate is tangible evidence of your rights in a work. If you plan to sell a collection of your work at a future date, you can provide copyright certificates that provide physical evidence that the purchaser is getting something. Also, in the event of your death, it will be an estate asset, which can be passed on to your heirs or beneficiaries.

CORRECTION OF ERRORS

Your application will be reviewed by the copyright office, which may bring errors that may be corrected to your attention.

Additionally, if you released copies of your work without the proper copyright notice, or if the name is listed incorrectly, the registration will help overcome these problems.

MONEY

For recorded musical works, registration allows you to collect compulsory royalty payments from persons who may make use of your works. Your work may also be discovered by someone searching the copyright registration which may result in a business opportunity.

PEOPLE WHO CLAIM AND REGISTER COPYRIGHTS 6

Immediately upon the creation of a work in a fixed form, a copyright exists for the author or creator of the work. An author or creator can register the copyright as soon as it is created, or can wait until it is published.

HEIRS

The rights to a person's creative work pass to the beneficiaries of their will at death, or if they have no will, to their heirs at law. These people may register the copyright if it has not previously been registered and may sell or license it. An exception to this is where a spouse makes a claim against the estate of a decedent as explained below.

A person inheriting creative works from a deceased person should receive an assignment of copyright form from the person's estate. This paper transfers the rights in the work and will be necessary to register, license, or sell the copyrights.

SPOUSES

In nine states, property acquired during a marriage is considered community property, which means both spouses have a right to it. This means that if a person creates a copyrightable work during a marriage in one of those states, his or her spouse may claim an interest in that work.

The nine community property states are Arizona, California, Idaho, Louisiana, Nevada, New Mexico, Texas, Washington, and Wisconsin. Most other states use an *equitable distribution* of assets in a divorce and a copyright may or may not become part of the settlement.

Upon the death of an author, a spouse in any state may claim a right to a copyright that has been left by will to someone else under certain circumstances. The usual situation where a spouse can make a claim is where he or she has not been left a certain percentage of the estate (between thirty percent and one-half depending upon the state).

If you want to avoid the situation where your spouse is awarded your copyright, you should use a prenuptial agreement or a marital agreement.

EMPLOYERS

Where a work is created by an employee in the scope of his or her employment, the employer is considered to be the author and owner of the copyright.

BUYERS OF CREATIVE WORKS

When a person pays someone to create a work, the rights obtained depend upon the relationship of the parties. If the creator of the work is an *independent contractor*, then he or she retains the copyright and the buyer only gets limited rights to the work. If the relationship is one of a *work-made-for-hire*, the buyer owns the copyright and all rights to the work.

What type of relationship exists between a buyer and creator depends upon the terms of the agreement between them. Unfortunately, such agreements are not always put in writing so there is often disagreement as to who owns the rights to a work. Many of these disagreements have gone to court and different courts have given different answers as to who should own the copyright.

In 1989, the United States Supreme Court decided a case that answered many questions.

📖 An artist who created a work and an organization that commissioned and paid for the work both filed claims for a copyright on the work. The court ruled that one should look to state common law principles to decide if a person is an employee or an independent contractor.

This means that if the person paying for the work controls such things as how the work is created, when the artist works, where the work is done, and other things which employers typically control, then the person is considered an employee for determining who owns the copyright. However, if the creator of the work works independently with little supervision or control, then he or she is an independent contractor and the owner of the copyright. (*Community for Creative Non-Violence v. Reid*, 490 U.S. 730; 109 S. Ct. 2166, 104 L. Ed. 2d 811 (1989).)

These are the same factors that one looks for in determining if a person is an employee or an independent contractor for tax withholding and social security purposes.

To avoid questions and legal problems in this area, an agreement should be signed by both parties spelling out who is to own the copyright. A WORK MADE-FOR-HIRE AGREEMENT is in Appendix H. (see form 22, p.195.) An INDEPENDENT CONTRACTOR AGREEMENT is also included in Appendix H of this book. (see form 24, p.199.) Sample filled-in agreements can be found in Appendix G.

INDEPENDENT
CONTRACTORS

If you are the creator of works such as articles or artwork, then it is in your interest to work as an *independent contractor*. This way you retain the copyright and the purchaser only obtains the rights for which he purchased the work.

Example: If you provided artwork for a book cover, the publisher paying you would normally only obtain the rights to the artwork for that book cover (unless a written agreement stated otherwise). If the publisher later wanted to use the artwork to make postcards or mugs, it would have to pay you additional for those rights. Also, you would be able to sell the original and copies of the work to others.

WORKS MADE-
FOR-HIRE

Works made-for-hire are a category of copyrighted works in which the person paying for the work obtains all rights under the copyright. If you are purchasing artwork, written works, or other copyrightable materials from creators, it is in your interest to make your relationships with such people work-for-hire relationships. This way you obtain all rights and do not have to pay again for the same work if you want to use it for other purposes. As explained above, if you commission artwork for a book cover, you would not be able to use it on other products unless you pay the artist again for it.

There are nine types of works that are specifically allowed to be works made-for-hire even if created by nonemployees. These are:

1. contributions to collective works such as newspapers and magazines;

2. supplementary works such as forewords, illustrations and indexes;

3. translations;

4. instructional manuals;

5. tests;

6. answers for tests;

7. atlases;

8. compilations; and,

9. parts of audiovisual works such as motion pictures.

The only way for other types of works to be considered works made for hire is if the author or artist is considered an employee. One important consideration in whether a person is an employee is whether the hiring party has the right to control the location, hours, materials, and methods used by the creator of the work. However, one thing that has been taken into consideration is whether the person is given employee benefits and whether social security or taxes have been withheld. To be sure you will be able to claim the copyright, this should be done.

In fact, in California the law states that someone who commissions a work made for hire must pay workers' compensation, unemployment insurance, and unemployment disability insurance. California appears to be the only state with such a law. Rather than protect artists, as it was intended to do, it will likely lead to California artists losing commissions to artists in other states. There is a WORK MADE-FOR-HIRE EMPLOYMENT AGREEMENT in Appendix H. (see form 23, p.197.) A filled-in sample is in Appendix G.

ASSIGNMENT OF COPYRIGHT

To avoid the liability for social security taxes, unemployment insurance and the like, you can commission a work to someone as an independent contractor and then have them assign the copyright to you. An ASSIGNMENT OF COPYRIGHT is included in Appendix H of this book. (see form 26, p.203.)

One drawback of having a person create a work as an independent contractor and then assign the copyright is that the copyright law provides that anyone assigning their copyright can get it back after thirty-five years. This right is absolute and they cannot waive it even if you pay them extra. For more information, see Chapter 10.

This will not matter for most works since they will be valueless after thirty-five years, but where a company spends considerable funds keeping a work marketable, the sudden loss of rights would be a problem.

At the very minimum, you should have an agreement with the creator that you have the exclusive right to the work at least in the field you are using it.

Example: If you commission someone to take photographs for your book, be sure that your agreement prohibits them from selling the rights to publishers of competing books.

JOINT WORKS

Where a copyrightable work is created by two or more persons, the ownership of the copyright can be owned in several ways depending on the intent of the parties.

COLLABORATION   Where two or more people create a work with the intention that it be a *collaborative* work and that one copyright cover the work as a whole, it is considered a collaboration and the creators become joint owners of the copyright.

Example: If two people go on a trip with the intention that one writes about the trip and the other takes photographs. To confirm that this is the understanding of the parties, a written agreement should be signed.

A COLLABORATION AGREEMENT form is contained in Appendix H. (see form 25, p.201.) There is a filled-in sample in Appendix G on page 129. If the parties do not wish to create a collaborative work, (for example if the photographer wants to sell the photos to others) then the parties should not sign a COLLABORATION AGREEMENT but should copyright their works separately.

COLLECTIVE
WORK   If two people created their works separately, such as one person wrote a book on gardening and another person took photographs of plants that the author of the book later decides to use in the book, the book is considered a collective work. Each party should obtain a copyright to their contribution to the work.

DERIVATIVE
WORK   If the material of an existing work is made into a new work but is used in a different way than originally created, the resulting work is a *derivative* work.

Example: A film that is based on a novel is a derivative work. If parts of a previously-written musical score are used in the film, the resulting film is a derivative work based upon both the novel and the music. The creator of the film is entitled to a copyright. If the novel and the music are still under copyright, the creator of the film needed to get their permission (and pay for a license) before using their works.

Nearly every work created is derivative of something that came before. A biology text is derivative of all other works of biology. But for copyright purposes, a work is only considered derivative if it uses substantial amounts of existing works.

ASSIGNEES

The creator of a copyrightable work may assign his rights in the work to another person and that person, the assignee of the creator, may claim and register the work. An **ASSIGNMENT OF COPYRIGHT** form is included in Appendix H. (see form 26, p.203.)

MINORS

Minors may claim a copyright in works they create. However, state laws usually restrict their business dealings and require a guardian to handle their business affairs.

OWNERS OF THE WORK

The owner of a work (for example, a book, letter, painting, video tape) usually does not have any right to the copyright unless he or she has an assignment of copyright from the creator. (see page 60.) A person who inherits a work from someone who created it should receive an assignment of the copyright in the work from the estate.

REGISTERING YOUR COPYRIGHT 7

To register a copyright, a simple application form must be filed with the copyright office along with the filing fee and one or two copies of the work. The first step is to decide which application form to use. Next, you should read the instruction sheet accompanying the form to be sure your work qualifies.

APPLICATION FORMS

The following are the different forms available:

- **FORM TX FOR NONDRAMATIC LITERARY WORKS. FORM TX** applies for written works that are not plays or other "performing arts." This includes most works that consist of text. If a written work also includes some pictures, and the person who made these pictures is one of the copyright claimants, these can be included in the copyright obtained with **FORM TX.**(see form 1, p.137.)

- **SHORT FORM TX FOR NONDRAMATIC LITERARY WORKS.** The **SHORT FORM TX** is for written works which have one author, are not made for hire, and do not contain material previously published. (see form 2, p.141.)

- FORM SE FOR A SERIAL. FORM SE is used for works such as newspapers, magazines, annuals and newsletters, which are intended to continue publication indefinitely. (see form 3, p.143.)

- SHORT FORM SE FOR A SERIAL. SHORT FORM SE applies to serials which are to be copyrighted as a collective work (without names of individual authors).(see form 4, p.147.)

- FORM SE/GROUP — FOR SERIALS. FORM SE/GROUP is for registering several issues of a publication on one application. Before using this form, you must have given the copyright office two complimentary subscriptions to the publication and received a letter of confirmation. (see form 5, p.149.)

- FORM PA FOR A WORK OF THE PERFORMING ARTS. FORM PA applies to musical and dramatic works, pantomimes, choreographic works, motion pictures, and other audiovisual works. (see form 7, p.153.)

- SHORT FORM PA FOR A WORK OF THE PERFORMING ARTS. The SHORT FORM PA is used for performing arts works which have one author, are not made for hire, and do not contain material previously published. (see form 8, p.157.)

- FORM VA FOR A WORK OF THE VISUAL ARTS. FORM VA applies to pictorial, graphic and sculptural works. (see form 9, p.159.)

- SHORT FORM VA FOR A WORK OF THE VISUAL ARTS. SHORT FORM VA is for visual works that have one author, are not made for hire and do not contain material previously published. (see form 10, p.163.)

- FORM SR FOR A SOUND RECORDING. FORM SR is used for recordings of sounds on records, tapes, discs or other medium. FORM SR differs from FORM PA in that FORM PA is for registration of the notation on paper of a work and FORM SR is for the performance. One person can own the rights to a musical composition and another can own the copyright to his or her performance of the work. (see form 11, p.165.)

- FORM CON. CONTINUATION SHEET. This form is used to provide additional material for forms CA, PA, SE, SRC, TX, and VA. (see form 17, p.185.)

- FORM MW FOR MASK WORKS. FORM MW applies to semiconductor chip mask works. (see form 18, p.187.)

- FORM D-VH VESSEL HULLS. FORM D-VH is used for designs of ship hulls. (see form 28, p.207.)

- FORM CA. FOR SUPPLEMENTARY INFORMATION. This form is used for correcting errors or changes on an application. (see form 15, p.177.)

The Copyright Office used to require that only forms from their office be used, but now there are several ways to get forms.

FORMS **This book.** The forms for most types of copyright registrations are contained in Appendix H of this book. You can photocopy them, or carefully tear them out. If you photocopy them, they must be copied two-sided, head to head on good paper. Also, be sure they are centered on the page.

The Internet. The forms are available in PDF format on the Copyright Office's website:

http://www.loc.gov/copyright/forms

They must either be printed on a laser printer or an ink jet printer, which is set to make them full size. A dot matrix printer is not acceptable to the copyright office.

The PDFs for some of the forms allow you to type in the information on the screen and print them out completed.

By mail or phone. You can call or write for copies of the copyright forms. The number is 202-707-9100. This number is an answering machine that is in operation twenty-four hours a day. You can leave your name and address and the names or numbers of the forms or publications you need, and they will be sent out within a few days. The mailing address is:

Register of Copyrights
Copyright Office
Library of Congress
Washington, DC 20559

COMPLETING THE FORMS

There are line-by-line instructions provided by the Copyright Office for the forms. These are well written and easy to understand. There are some sample filled-in forms to give you further guidance in Appendix G. If there is something that you do not understand, they have information specialists available by phone to help. That number is 202-707-3000.

FILING FEES

The filing fee for most applications is $30. Vessel hulls and mask works are presently $75; however, the vessel hull fee may change whenever the new regulations are released. Other fees may change July 1, 2001 and 2002.

The fee is considered a filing fee and not a registration fee, so if the application is rejected for any reason, the fee is not refundable.

COPIES OF THE WORK

If the work has not yet been published, one complete copy or phonorecord must be submitted. If the work was first published in the United States on or after January 1, 1978, then two copies of the best edition of the work must be submitted.

If the work was first published in the United States before January 1, 1978, one copy of the work as first published must be submitted. If the work was first published outside of the United States, one copy of the work as first published must be submitted.

An explanation of what is the *best edition* of a literary work is included as Appendix B of this book.

SPECIAL DEPOSIT EXCEPTIONS

The copyright office has made some exceptions to the basic rules for deposits.

LARGE WORKS
For works that exceed ninety-six inches in any dimension, you must deposit a drawing, transparency, or photograph (preferably 8 x 10 inches).

LIMITED AUDIENCE WORKS
For nondramatic literary works such as speeches, sermons, lectures, tests and answers, only one copy is necessary.

COMPUTER PROGRAMS
For computer programs, it is possible to send in only "identifying portions" of the work. This is usually the first twenty-five pages and the last twenty-five pages of the program printed out on paper along with the page containing the copyright notice. For special rules regarding computer programs, see Appendix C of this book.

VISUAL & THREE-DIMENSIONAL WORKS
For works such as sculptures, "identifying material" such as a photograph of the work must be submitted instead of physical copies. An explanation of what must be deposited for a work of the visual arts is included as Appendix D of this book.

PERFORMING ARTS WORKS
For motion pictures that are published, musical compositions that are rented and not sold, and published instructional multi-media kits, only one copy need be deposited. For unpublished motion pictures, identifying material can be sent instead of a complete copy. The identifying material can be a description of the motion picture and a copy of the sound track or an enlargement of one frame from each ten-minute portion of the work.

SOUND RECORDINGS
For sound recordings, the visual or written material included with the recording must also be included with the deposit.

It must be remembered that a sound recording includes two separate works, the underlying composition and the actual rendition of the sounds. Each of these can be copyrighted separately or they can be copyrighted together. To copyright them together, use FORM SR. To copyright them separately, use FORM SR for the sound and either FORM TX or FORM PA for the underlying work.

SENDING IT IN

To obtain all of the benefits of copyright registration as explained in Chapter 5, you must register your copyright in a *timely* manner. This means that your application must be filed within three months of the first publication of the work, or at least prior to infringement. For unpublished works, it must be filed prior to infringement to gain the benefits. The application, filing fee, and copies must be enclosed in the same envelope and sent to the Register of Copyrights at the following address:

> Register of Copyrights
> Copyright Office
> Library of Congress
> Washington, DC 20559

RECEIVING YOUR CERTIFICATE

The Copyright Office will not acknowledge receipt of your application. If you wish to receive proof of receipt, you should send it by certified mail, return receipt requested. Because of the volume of mail received by the Copyright Office (700,000 applications a year), it may be up to three weeks before your receipt is returned. Your actual certificate of registration will take several weeks longer, sometimes as long as sixteen weeks.

EXPEDITED SERVICE

If you have a special reason for needing your certificate (such as a pending lawsuit) you can request expedited service. There is a special $500 handling fee for this, in addition to the normal filing fee. With special handling your application will be processed within about a week. To request special handling, you can use the form included on page 193 of this book and send it to:

Special Handling
Library of Congress
Department 100
101 Independence Avenue, S.E.
Washington, DC 20540

LENGTH OF A COPYRIGHT 8

The length of a copyright depends upon when the work was created and is subject to change by Congress.

WORKS CREATED AFTER JANUARY 1, 1978

As of January 1, 1978, the term of the copyright was for the life of the author plus fifty years. This was extended in 1998 to seventy years by the Sonny Bono Copyright Term Extension Act. For works prepared by two or more authors, the term is the life of the last surviving author plus seventy years. For works made for hire, and for anonymous and pseudonymous works (unless the identity is disclosed in Copyright Office records), the term is for ninety-five years from publication or 120 years from creation, whichever is shorter.

These rules can be used creatively to obtain the longest term.

Example: A very elderly person who published a work and expects it to be valuable to his heirs for a long time could publish it under a pseudonym in order for the copyright to last ninety-five years. Or he could get his grandchild to contribute to the work and then the copyright would last until seventy years after the grandchild died.

WORKS CREATED BEFORE JANUARY 1, 1978

There are special rules for works that were created prior to January 1, 1978, depending on whether they were published, whether they were copyrighted, and whether the copyright was renewed.

If you created a work before this date, but did not publish it, or published it after this date then it is protected for your life plus seventy years.

PROTECTING YOUR COPYRIGHT

Your rights to your creative work are automatic upon creation of the work in a tangible form. You do not have to do anything to obtain these rights. However, registration of your work for the mere cost of $30 will provide legal notice of your claim, additional rights, and all of the other benefits detailed in Chapter 5.

COPYRIGHT NOTICE

Prior to March 1, 1989, a copyright notice had to be placed on all copies of a work that were distributed to the public. If your work was distributed before that date without a notice, you can save your work from the public domain by registering it within five years of publication and making a reasonable effort to add a copyright notice to all copies that were distributed without the notice.

For works published after March 1, 1989, the copyright notice is not legally necessary, but as a practical matter, it is best to use the notice. It will be many years before the general public learns that copyright notices are no longer necessary and that all works have copyright protection whether or not there is a notice. Many authors and editors have learned that they can freely use anything that does not have a copyright notice on it. It will be a long time before this habit is unlearned.

RENEWAL

Copyrights no longer have to be renewed. They have one term, which is the life of the author plus seventy years. Works first copyrighted between January 1, 1964 and December 31, 1977 were automatically renewed by an amendment to the copyright law passed in 1992. However, renewing copyrights registered between those dates gives the owner important additional rights including the right to sue and to receive higher damages. The form for renewal is FORM RE and is contained in Appendix H. (see form 12, p.169.)

CORRECTIONS

If, after your copyright has been issued, you discover an error, you should take the effort to correct it. If you end up in court the error could cause you to lose your case. Depending upon the type of error there are different methods for correcting it:

OBVIOUS ERRORS

If the error is obvious, such as a missing information or transposed numbers in a date, you can write to the copyright office and ask that it be corrected. If it is something that they should have caught, there will be no charge to correct it.

CORRECTIONS AND AMPLIFICATIONS

If the error involves incorrect or incomplete information on the application, you will need to file FORM CA, APPLICATION FOR SUPPLEMENTARY COPYRIGHT REGISTRATION that is included in Appendix H. (see form 15, p.177.) There is a filled-in sample form in Appendix G.

CHANGES

If you changed your name or address, or if you changed the title of the work (without changing the contents), you should also file FORM CA. If you transfer the ownership of the copyright to someone else, you should record the transfer document at the copyright office. This is explained in Chapter 10. If you revise your work and publish a new edition, you need to file a new copyright registration, not FORM CA.

TRANSFERRING A COPYRIGHT 10

There are times when you may wish to sell or license your copyright to others. This chapter explains how that can be done.

LICENSES

As discussed in Chapter 1, a copyright consists of a "bundle of rights" including the rights to reproduce, distribute, perform, display, and make derivative works. In many cases, each of these rights can be licensed or sold separately. They can also be divided up into different geographic areas or time periods.

Example: You can sell the first right to publish an article to one magazine, then sell the right to publish it later to other magazines. You can sell the right to translate it into Spanish for the U.S. market to one publisher and sell the right to the Spanish version for South America to another publisher.

The sale of these different rights are called *licenses*. Licenses can be exclusive, such as if you sell all rights to your book to a publisher, or non-exclusive, or as in when you sell hard-cover rights to one publisher, paperback rights to another, and movie rights to a producer.

A **Copyright License Agreement** is included in Appendix H. (see form 27, p.205.) A filled-in sample form is in Appendix G. However, most publishers to whom you would sell a work will have their own forms which contain boilerplate language they prefer to use. Some of these terms are negotiable but others are not. If you do not use an agent, you should read a book or two on how to negotiate a contract with a publisher.

Assignment

While licenses transfer separate parts of your rights in a copyright, an *assignment* of the copyright transfers all rights. Such an assignment must be in writing and should be recorded with the Copyright Office. An **Assignment of Copyright** form for a copyright assignment is included in Appendix H. (see form 26, p.203.) See Appendix G for filled-in sample.

Basically, an assignment of a copyright transfers all rights to the work forever—but there is one exception. Because the drafters of the Copyright Law wanted to protect authors from their own bad decisions, they put a provision in the copyright law that gives authors who transfer their copyrights the right to take them back after thirty-five years. This means that even if you sold all rights to your work, you can come back thirty-five years later and demand it back. To make sure you are not talked out of this right, it is not possible to legally waive it. No matter what you sign or agree to, you can terminate the agreement and get the rights back.

If you are a business buying copyrights, you must keep this in mind if you have a long term plan for the work.

Example: A company like Disney, which keeps its works alive for decades, would always want to have the work created by employees rather than independent artists since they would not want to lose the rights after spending millions of dollars building up the value of the work.

This procedure is explained in much greater detail in the section titled "Revocation" beginning on the next page.

OTHER TRANSFERS

Besides voluntary licenses and assignments, copyrights can be transferred by a court such as in a bankruptcy or divorce. They can also be transferred by a will upon a person's death. If a person does not have a will, they would be transferred to whomever the state laws give the author's property.

RECORDATION

Whenever a copyright is transferred the transfer should be registered with the copyright office. This is done by sending a copy of the written instrument (with original signatures or a certified copy) to the Copyright Office. You should include a DOCUMENT COVER SHEET (included in Appendix H) and a self-addressed, stamped envelope for return of your document. (see form 20, p.191.) A filled-in sample is in Appendix G on page 125.

The filing fee at time of publication of this book is $50 for the first work and $15 for each additional ten works included on the same assignment document. All of this should be sent to the following address:

> Documents Unit, Cataloging Division
> Library of Congress
> Washington, D.C. 20559

REVOCATION

An author who has assigned his copyright has a right to *revoke* the assignment and take the rights back under certain circumstances.

PRE-1978
WORKS

The amendments to the Copyright Act in 1978 and 1998 added a total of thirty-nine more years to the life of most copyrights. Rather than give this bonus to the purchasers of the rights, Congress allowed the original creators of the works to have those rights returned to them.

Authors of pre-1978 works can have the copyright to their works returned to them during the five year period beginning seventy-six years from the date the work was first published. For more information, see the Copyright Office's *Circular 96*, section 201.10. On their website, this is only available by downloading Code of Federal Regulations, Title 37, Chapter 201.

POST-1977
WORKS

Additionally, the new copyright law allows authors who assign their works after December 31, 1977, to revoke the assignment thirty-five years from the date of publication or forty years from the date of transfer, whichever occurs first. To effectuate a revocation, a notice must be sent to the *assignee*, or the current owner, during the final five years of the time period.

The revocation can be exercised by the author or if he or she is dead, by his or her spouse or children. If he or she has no surviving spouse or child, then the right to revoke is lost. It cannot be sold or given by will.

The law is somewhat complicated in this area. If you have transferred a valuable copyright, you should consult with a copyright attorney about your best options.

INTERNATIONAL COPYRIGHTS 11

This section is intended to answer the most basic questions about international copyright protection. If you seriously plan to market overseas or see a likelihood of infringement from overseas, you should consult an attorney specializing in international copyright law.

The best way to select a competent attorney is upon the advice of a friend; but if you do not know anyone who has used a copyright specialist, you could consult your local phone directory. Sometimes copyright specialists are listed under "Attorneys–Patent, Trademark & Copyright Law." Because such specialists are not available in every town, you may have to travel to a large city to find one.

As a rule, if your creative work is copyrighted in the United States, you are protected in most countries of the world. Some types of works do not have the same protections, and some countries do not honor copyrights. But most works are protected in most countries.

The biggest difference in protection of copyrights is between developed countries and developing countries. Since developed countries (especially the United States) are the sources of most of the world's copyrighted material, developing countries have little incentive to pass laws protecting creators in developed countries from exploitation by their citizens. Some developing countries have industries that make considerable profit from exploitation of foreigners' copyrights.

The following sections explain which rights are available under the different treaties. The treaties are occasionally amended and different countries' status may change, so if you have a concern about a particular country, you should do further research. The Treatise Nimmer on Copyright (see Appendix F) is kept up to date as is the Library of Congress' web page. (see Appendix A.)

INTERNATIONAL AGREEMENTS

There are several international agreements covering copyrights. Your rights in other countries is determined by whether the country has passed one or more of these treaties. The following is a summary of the treaties and Appendix F lists which treaties were passed by each country.

BERNE
CONVENTION

The Berne Convention was first adopted in 1886, but the United States did not join until 1989. Therefore, the rights offered by this treaty do not apply to works published in the United States before March 1, 1989.

Under the Berne Convention, a work receives copyright protection without the formalities of having a copyright notice on it or being registered with the copyright office. Joining this convention was what prompted the change in U.S. law on these matters.

UNIVERSAL
COPYRIGHT
CONVENTION

The Universal Copyright Convention-Geneva was adopted by the United States in 1955, so it offers protections to works that are older than what is necessary for protection under the Berne Convention. However, the UCC requires that a copyright notice be included on a work in order to obtain protection.

The Universal Copyright Convention was revised in Paris and is called the UCC-Paris. For the U.S., it was effective as of July 10, 1974.

WTO
AGREEMENT

The World Trade Organization (WTO) Agreement under the General Agreement on Tariffs and Trade (GATT) is the latest treaty to cover copyrights. Some countries that did not sign the Berne and UCC agreements have signed the WTO Agreement, but it is too early to tell if it will be successful in protecting copyrights.

The WTO Agreement requires signing countries to comply with the main provisions of the Berne Convention. This will require some developing nations to pass new laws to provide this protection.

BILATERAL TREATIES

Some countries, which have not adopted the international conventions, protect copyrighted works of Americans under bilateral treaties. Three of these are Indonesia, Singapore, and Taiwan.

COUNTRIES OFFERING NO PROTECTION

A few countries offer no copyright protection. At the time of completion of this manuscript, those countries are: Afghanistan, Bhutan, Ethiopia, Iran, Iraq, Nepal, Oman, San Marino, Tonga, and Yemen (San'a). However, these countries may adopt one of the copyright treaties in the future; so if you have a special interest in one of these countries, you should check whether their status has changed.

UNCLEAR POLICY

The copyright office lists several countries as having unclear policies regarding the protection of copyrights. If you need to protect your work in any of these, you should contact a lawyer in that country. These are: Comoros, Jordan, Kiribati, Nauru, North Korea, São Tomé and Príncipe, Seychelles, Somalia, Sudan, Syria, Tuvalu, Vanuatu, Western Samoa, and Yemen (Aden).

Newly Independent States

Where a country has not signed any convention and does not have a treaty with the United States, there is still a chance for protection. Some countries have been honoring conventions signed before their independence. To check on an individual country, you should contact their trade representative at that country's embassy. Another possibility for protection is the fact that some countries that are not signatories to the conventions will give copyright protection to authors if the author's country gives protection to their citizens.

Other Treaties

There are a few other treaties that affect copyrights in certain types of works, such as satellite signals and phonograms (sound recordings). These treaties are listed under the countries in Appendix F.

Local Law

Some countries have different laws regarding certain aspects of copyright law.

Example: The artwork, text, and source code for computer programs is generally considered copyrightable, but the object code, ROM, and other aspects of a program may not be in some countries.

For specific questions about specific countries, you should check with counsel in those countries.

OTHER PROTECTIONS 12

As explained in the text, some things cannot be protected by copyright law. However, other laws may help you protect your creative work. These other protections are explained in this chapter.

LICENSES

If you own valuable information that you wish to distribute at a profit, you have an alternative to selling a copy outright. You can license the work under your own terms. This is what owners of databases started doing when the Supreme Court ruled that mere data could not be copyrighted. They now provide the information to customers under license agreements, which specify how the information can be used.

This is an excellent way to protect data that you have compiled. However, when using a license to protect work that you copyrighted because if you attempt to extend the scope of your copyright you might lose your copyright.

This is what happened to the American Medical Association. They created a list of numerical categories for medical conditions and licensed it to the U.S. government. The license agreement forbid the government from using any competing system. Because of this, a court said they lost their copyright.

As explained in Chapter 3, this was a good decision because otherwise one company would have had a monopoly on a system used by the government. If the licensee was a private party the case might have gone the other way unless there was a violation of anti-trust laws.

Shrink-Wrap Licenses

If you have ever bought a computer software program, you are familiar with *shrink-wrap licenses*. These are the statements on the packaging of the software that say that by opening or using the product you agree to the terms of the license.

In 1996, a Federal Court of Appeals held that such agreements can be enforceable. In *ProCD v. Zeidenberg*, a person had purchased a CD containing ninety-five million phone numbers and made it available to the public over the Internet. Since the Supreme Court held that phone listings are usually not copyrightable, the company sought protection by arguing that Zeidenberg violated the license on the package. The district court held that such a license was not enforceable since the purchaser could not even know about the terms until after he purchased the product and opened the box.

However, the Court of Appeals reversed the decision and said such a license was enforceable. It compared the shrink-wrap license to such things as insurance policies, airline tickets, and electronic devices where all the terms of the transaction are not known until after the product is purchased. The consumer's remedy is to return the product for a refund if he does not agree to the terms.

If you use a shrink wrap license on your product, be sure to word it carefully. Where a license says you agree to the terms by "breaking this seal" (on the envelope), customers might avoid liability by peeling the seal off, or cutting the other end of the envelope. Better wording would be "by using this product you agree..." or "purchasers of this product agree." Also, be sure to give the purchaser the option to return the product for a refund if they do not agree to the terms.

TRADEMARK LAW

Some things that cannot be protected by copyright law can be protected by trademark.

Example: Titles of books and films and advertising slogans cannot be copyrighted, but if used on a product to distinguish it from others, they may be registered as trademarks.

TRADE SECRETS

Trade secret law offers valuable protections for some types of works.

Example: If a company has valuable information that gives it a commercial advantage, such as a customer list or operating procedures, it may keep this as its trade secret rather than try to copyright it. This would offer more protection than a copyright because lists of companies and procedures can be rewritten in a different way to avoid infringement but convey the same information.

To protect property as a trade secret, a company must make a serious effort to keep it a secret. It must only be available to certain persons and it is best if those persons are required to sign an agreement not to disclose it.

Until recently, trade secret law was based on state statutes and was different in each state. But in 1996, Congress passed the Economic Espionage Act, which covers the whole country and imposes criminal penalties on those who steal trade secrets.

PRACTICAL SOLUTIONS

Even if copyright law protects your work, as a practical matter, you may not be able to do anything about copying.

Example: If you publish a newsletter, it is likely that subscribers to it will make copies and pass them on to others without your knowledge.

Some businesses factor this into their price and charge enough to make a profit from the copies actually purchased. Others keep their price low so that photocopying will not be worthwhile.

Another solution is to produce material that cannot be copied. Printing a newsletter on dark paper or with a colored pattern behind it may make photocopying impossible. Sellers of audio tapes with subliminal messages regularly state on the packages that the subliminal messages do not carry over to copies. Whether this is true or not, it may deter copying.

If you wish to post material on the Internet and do not want people to be able to copy it easily, you can post it as a graphic rather than text. Text on a web page can be easily copied into a word processor or into email. However, if you convert the text into a graphic, or a few graphics, it will make the text harder for users to manipulate.

Glossary

A

assignee. Person to whom a copyright has been transferred.

author. Person who created a copyrightable work.

C

collaboration. Work done by two or more authors of the same copyrightable material.

common law. Laws which are determined in court cases rather than statutes.

compilation. A collection of copyrighted works.

compulsory license. The right of a person to use a copyrighted musical work as long as a statutory fee is paid to the copyright owner.

copyright. Legal protection given to "original works of authorship."

D

damages. The financial value of the violation of legal rights.

derivative work. A creative work based upon a previously copyrighted work.

F

fair use. Limited use of a copyrighted work which is allowed by law.

H

heir. Person who inherits the property of a person who died.

I

incidental use. Use of a copyrighted work in the background of another work, in which it is unimportant to the context.

independent contractor. A person who works from him- or herself, rather than as an employee.

infringement. Violation of the rights of a copyright holder.

intellectual property. Legal rights to the products of the mind, such as writings, musical compositions, formulas and designs.

J

joint work. Copyrightable work made by two or more persons.

L

license. A grant of the right to legally use a copyrighted work.

M

mandatory deposit. The requirement that copies of a copyrighted work be sent to the copyright office within three months of publication.

moral rights. A recent theory that artists have some enduring rights in works they create and sell.

O

original works of authorship. Works created by a person, rather than copied from others.

P

parody. A humorous imitation of a work.

patent. Protection given to inventions, discoveries, and designs.

personal use. Use of a copyrighted work for other than commercial purposes.

plot. The main story line of a work.

privacy. The right of a person not to have private facts disclosed to the public.

public domain. The body of all works not protected by copyright law.

publish. To distribute copies of a work to the public or perform a work in public.

R

revocation. The right of a copyright owner to take back a copyright that has been sold to a publisher.

royalty. Payment to the owner of a copyright for the use of a work.

S

scénes á faire. Scenes or incidents which are indispensable to the telling of a certain type of story.

shrink-wrap license. A license to use a product which is triggered by the opening of the packaging of the product.

T

tangible form. A form that can be seen or held.

theme. The subject of a written work.

title. The name of a work such as a book or film.

trade secret. Commercially valuable information or process which is protected by being kept a secret.

trademark. A name or symbol used to identify the source of goods or services.

W

work for hire. A work made by a person who grants all rights in the work to the person who paid for it.

Appendix A
For Further Information

The Copyright Office has many brochures available covering most aspects of copyright law and regulations.

Both the brochures and copies of copyright forms are available at no charge and you may request them by phone, fax, mail or download them over the Internet. The Internet address is:

http://lcweb.loc.gov/copyright.

The fax-on-demand number is 202-707-2600. The phone number is 202-707-9100. This number is an answering machine that can take your order twenty-four hours a day. Leave your name and address and the numbers and quantities of the forms you need, and you will usually have them in a few days. If you prefer to make a written request, the address is:

Register of Copyrights
U. S. Copyright Office
Library of Congress
Washington, D.C. 20559

They also have phone lines available for answering questions, but they prefer that you read the brochures before calling. The number for an information specialist is 202-707-3000.

APPLICATION FORMS

For Original Registration

Form PA:
for published and unpublished works of the performing arts (musical and dramatic works, pantomimes and choreographic works, motion pictures and other audiovisual works)

Short Form PA:
to register published and unpublished works of the performing arts, including dramas, music, and lyrics. Audiovisual works, including motion pictures, must be registered on the standard forms.

Form SE:
for serials, works issued or intended to be issued in successive parts bearing numerical or chronological designations and intended to be continued indefinitely (periodicals, newspapers, magazines, newsletters, annuals, journals, etc.)

Short Form/SE and Form SE/Group:
Specialized SE forms for use when certain requirements are met

Form SR:
for published and unpublished sound recordings

Form TX:
for published and unpublished nondramatic literary works

Short Form TX:
to register published and unpublished nondramatic literary works, including fiction and non-fiction, books, short stories, poems, collections of poetry, essays, articles in serials, and computer programs.

Form VA:
for published and unpublished works of the visual arts (pictorial, graphic, and sculptural works)

Short Form VA:
to register published and unpublished works of the visual arts, including pictorial, graphic sculptural, and architectural works.

For Renewal Registration

Addendum to Form RE:
for all works published between January 1, 1964 and December 31, 1977

Form RE:
for claims to renewal copyright in works copyrighted under the law in effect through December 31, 1977 (1909 Copyright Act)

For Corrections and Amplifications

Form CA:
for supplementary registration to correct or amplify information given in the Copyright Office record of an earlier registration.

For Continuations

Form CON:
Universal continuation sheet for use with all forms **except** Form MW, Short Form PA, Short Form SE, Form SE/Group, and Form RE

Form GATT/CON:
for continuation of Form GATT and Form GATT/GRP

Form RE/CON:
for continuation of Form RE

Other Forms for Special Purposes

Document Cover Sheet:
for Recordation of Documents

Form GD/N:
for Group/Daily Newspapers

Form GR/CP:
an adjunct application to be used for registration of a group of contributions to periodicals in addition to an application Form TX, PA, or VA

Form MW:
for published and unpublished mask works

CIRCULARS

Registration

For Overall Information

Copyright Basics—**Circular 1**

Copyright Fees—**Circular 4**

For More Specific Registration Information:

Antedated Notice—**Circular 3s**

Blank Forms and Other Works Not Protected by Copyright—**Circular 32**

Cartoons and Comic Strips—**Circular 44**

Computing and Measuring Devices—**Circular 33**

Copyright Claims in Architectural Works—**Circular 41**

Copyright Notice—**Circular 3**

Copyright Protection Not Available for Names, Titles, or Short Phrases—**Circular 34**

Copyright Registration for Multimedia Works—**Circular 55**

Copyright Registration for Computer Programs—**Circular 61**

Copyright Registration for Motion Pictures Including Video Recordings—**Circular 45**

Copyright Registration for Automated Databases—**Circular 65**

Copyright Registration for Derivative Works—**Circular 14**

Copyright Registration for Musical Compositions—**Circular 50**

Copyright Registration of Musical Compositions and Sound Recordings—**Circular 56a**

Copyright Registration for Serials on Form SE—**Circular 62**

Copyright Registration for Secure Tests—**Circular 64**

Copyright Registration for Works of the Visual Arts—**Circular 40**

Copyright Registration for Sound Recordings—**Circular 56**

Extension of Copyright Terms—**Circular 15t**

Federal Statutory Protection for Mask Works—**Circular 100**

Group Registration for Daily Newspapers—**Circular 62c**

Group Registration for Daily Newspapers—**Circular 62b**

How to Open and Maintain a Deposit Account in the Copyright Office—**Circular 5**

Ideas, Methods, or Systems—**Circular 31**

Renewal of Copyright—**Circular 15**

Deposit Requirements for Registration of Claims to Copyright in Visual Arts Material—**Circular 40a**

Supplementary Copyright Registration—**Circular 8**

Works-Made-for-Hire Under the 1976 Copyright Act—**Circular 9**

Mandatory Deposit

"Best Edition" of Published Copyrighted Works for the Collections of the Library of Congress—**Circular 7b**

Mandatory Deposit of Copies or Phonorecords for the Library of Congress—**Circular 7d**

Copyright Law

Copyright Law of the United States of America—**Circular 92.** Copies can be purchased from the Superintendent of Documents. See order form page 16.

Copyright Basics—**Circular 1**

Duration of Copyright—**Circular 15a**

Licensing

Compulsory License for Making and Distributing Phonorecords—**Circular 73**

How to Make Compulsory License Royalty Payments Via Electronic Transfer of Funds—**Circular 74**

The Licensing Division of the Copyright Office—**Circular 75**

International Copyright

Highlights of Copyright Amendments Contained in the Uruguay Round Agreements ACT (URAA). (GATT Circular)—**Circular 38b**

International Copyright Conventions—**Circular 38c**

International Copyright Relations of the United States—**Circular 38a**

Services of the Copyright Office

The Copyright Card Catalog and the Online Files of the Copyright Office—**Circular 23**

The Effects of Not Replying Within 120 Days to Copyright Office Correspondence—**Circular 7c**

How to Investigate the Copyright Status of a Work—**Circular 22**

How to Open and Maintain a Deposit Account in the Copyright Office—**Circular 5**

Limitations on the Information Furnished by the Copyright Office—**Circular 1b**

Obtaining Access to and Copies of Copyright Office Records and Deposits—**Circular 6**

Publications on Copyright—**Circular 2**

Recordation of Transfers and other Documents—**Circular 12**

Special Handling—**Circular 10**

Miscellaneous

United States Copyright Office (overview)—**Circular 1a**

Reproduction of Copyrighted Works by Educators and Librarians—**Circular 21**

THE REGULATIONS OF THE COPYRIGHT OFFICE: CIRCULARS BASED ON THE *CODE OF FEDERAL REGULATIONS*

All Copyright Office circulars based on the *Code of Federal Regulations* begin with the prefix 96, followed by the appropriate section or part number(s). When ordering, be sure to give the section or part number, indicated below in **boldface** type.

Communications with the Copyright Office; Information Given by the Copyright Office—Circular 96, **Sections 201.1 and 201.2,** 37 CFR

Recordation of Transfers and Certain Other Documents—Circular 96, **Section 201.4**, 37 CFR

Corrections and Amplifications of Copyright Registrations; Applications For Supplementary Registrations—Circular 96, **Section 201.5**, 37 CFR

Payment and Refund of Copyright Office Fees—Circular 96, **Section 201.6**, 37 CFR

Cancellation of Completed Registrations—Circular 96, **Section 201.7,** 37 CFR

Recordation of Agreements Between Copyright Owners and Public Broadcasting Entities—Circular 96, **Section 201.9**, 37 CFR

Notices of Termination of Transfers and Licenses Covering Extended Renewal Term—Circular 96, **Section 201.10**, 37 CFR

Satellite Carrier Statements of Account Covering Statutory Licenses for Secondary Transmissions for Private Home Viewing—Circular 96, **Section 201.11**, 37 CFR

Recordation of Certain Contracts by Cable Systems Located Outside of the Forty-Eight Contiguous States—Circular 96, **Section 201.12**, 37 CFR

Notices of Objection to Certain Noncommercial Performances of Nondramatic Literary or Musical Works—Circular 96, **Section 201.13**, 37 CFR

Warnings of Copyright for Use by Certain Libraries and Archives—Circular 96, **Section 201.14**, 37 CFR

Statements of Account Covering Compulsory Licensing for Secondary Transmissions by Cable Systems—Circular 96, **Sections 201.17**, 37 CFR

Notice of Intention to Obtain a Compulsory License for Making and Distributing Phonorecords of Nondramatic Musical Works—Circular 96, **Section 201.18**, 37 CFR

Royalties and Statements of Account Under Compulsory License for Making and Distributing Phonorecords of Nondramatic Musical Works—Circular 96, **Section 201.19**, 37 CFR

Methods of Affixation and Positions of the Copyright Notice on Various Types of Works—Circular 96, **Section 201.20**, 37 CFR

Advance Notices of Potential Infringement of Works Consisting of Sounds, Images, or Both—Circular 96, **Section 201.22**, 37 CFR

Transfer of Unpublished Copyright Deposits to the Library of Congress—Circular 96, **Section 201.23**, 37 CFR

Warning of Copyright for Software Lending by Nonprofit Libraries—Circular 96, **Section 201.24**, 37 CFR

Visual Art Registry—Circular 96, **Section 201.25**, 37 CFR

REcordation of Documents Pertaining to Computer Shareware and DOnation of Public Domain Computer Software—Circular 96, **Section 201.26**, 37 CFR

Initial Notice of Distribution of Digital Audio Recording Devices or Media—Circular 96, **Section 201.27**, CFR 37

Statements of Account for Digital Audio Recording Devices or Media—Circular 96, **Section 201.28,** 37 CFR

Access to, and Confidentiality of Statements of Account, Verification Auditor's Reports and Other Verification Information Filed in the Copyright Office for Digital Audio Recording Devices or Media—Circular 96, **Section 201.29**, CFR 37

Verification of Statements of Account Circular 96, **Section 201.30**, 37 CFR

Procedures for Copyright Restoration for Certain Motion Pictures and Their Contents in Accordance with the North American Free TRade Agreement—Circular 96, **Section 201.31**, 37 CFR

Fees for Copyright Office Special Services—Circular 96, **Section 201.32**, 37 CFR

Procedures for Filing Notices of Intent to Enforce a Restored Copyright Under the Uruguay Round Agreements Act—Circular 96, **Section 201.33**, 37 CFR

Initial Notice of Digital Transmission of Sound Recordings Under Statutory License—Circular 96, **Section 201.35**, 37 CFR

Reports of Use of Use of Sound Recordings Under Statutory License—Circular 96, **Section 201.36**, 37 CFR

Designated Collection and Distribution Organizations for Records of Use of SOund Recordings Under Statutory License—Circular 96, **Section 201.37**, 37 CFR

Material Not Subject to Copyright—Circular 96, **Section 202.1**, 37 CFR

Copyright Notice—Circular 96, **Section 202.2**, 37 CFR

Registration of Copyright—Circular 96, **Section 202.3**, 37 CFR

Effective Date of REgistration—Circular 96, Section 202.4, 37 CFR

Pictorial, Graphic, and Sculptural Works—Circular 96, **Section 202.10**, 37 CFR

Architectural Works—Circular 96, Section 202.11, 37 CFR

Restored copyrights—Circular 96, Section 202.12, 37 CFR

Renewals—Circular 96, **Section 202.17**, 37 CFR

Deposits of Published Copies or Phonorecords for the Library of Congress; Deposit of Copies and Phonorecords for Copyright Registration; Deposit of Identifying Material Instead of Copies—Circular 96, **Section 202.19, 202.20, 202.21**, 37 CFR

Acquisition and Deposit of Unpublished Television Transmission Programs—Circular 96, **Section 202.22**, 37 CFR

Full-term Retention of Copyright Deposits—Circular 96, **Section 202.23**, 37 CFR

Freedom of Information Act: Policies and Procedures—Circular 96, **Part 203**, 37 CFR

Privacy Act: Policies and Procedures—Circular 96, **Part 204**, 37 CFR

Mask Work Protection—Circular 96, **Part 211**, 37 CFR

Copyright Arbitration Royalty Panels; Rules and Regulations—Circular 96, Parts 251-260, 37 CFR, Chapter II

THE COPYRIGHT LAW

The copyright Office operates in accordance with the Copyright Act, the statute that defines the powers and responsibilities of the Register of Copyrights.

Copyright Act of 1976 (as of September 1996). Title 17 of the United States Code. Public Law 94-553 (90 Stat. 2541) was passed by the 94th Congress at S.22 and signed into law on October 19, 1976. It became effective January 1, 1978; available as Circular 92. Copies can be purchased from the Superintendent of Documents. See order form page 16.

TO ORDER COPYRIGHT PUBLICATIONS

Unless a price is specified, Copyright Office publications are FREE of charge. Order by writing to:

Library of Congress
Copyright Office
Publication Sections, LM-455
101 Independence Avenue, S.E.
Washington, D.C. 20559-6000

Requestors may also order application forms or circulars at any time by telephoning the Forms and Publications Hotline (202) 707-9100. The TTY number is (202) 707-6737. Orders will be recorded automatically and filled as quickly as possible. See page 2 for new Copyright Internet and Fax-on-Demand services.

FACTSHEETS (SL'S AND FORM LETTER)

Fee Changes..SL 4
Get It Quick Over the Net............................SL 10
New Terms for Copyright Protection ....SL 15
Satellite Network Television Factsheet
International Copyright FL100
Pseudonyms...FL101
Fair Use FL102
Useful Articles...FL103
Music FL105
Poetry FL106
Photographs FL107
Games FL108
Books, Manuscripts, and Speeches.............FL109
Visual Arts...FL115
Dramatic Works: Scripts, Pantomimes &
Choreography FL119
Recipes..FL122

Phone Numbers of the Copyright Office

Public Information Number: 202-707-3000

Forms and Circulars Hotline: 202-707-9100

Reference & Bibliography Section: 202-707-6850

Certifications & Documents Section: 202-707-6787

Copyright General Counsel's Office: 202-707-8380

Documents Unit: 202-707-1759

Licensing Division: 202-707-8150

For In-Depth Research

If you wish to do further research into the law of copyright, the most thorough reference work is the multi-volume *Nimmer on Copyright*, by Melvin B. Nimmer (Matthew Bender, 1978). It is updated regularly so it is always up to date. It is available in most law libraries.

APPENDIX B
SCHEDULE OF COPYRIGHT
OFFICE FEES

In order to register a copyright, registration fees must be paid. The following is a list of applicable fees. Payment should be in the form of a check, money order, or bank draft made payable to: Register of Copyrights. Electronic transfers and credit card payments are not acceptable.

Copyright Office Fees
Effective through June 30, 2001[1]

Copyright Registration Fees

Basic Registrations: (Fee to accompany an application and deposit for registration of a claim to copyright)

Form TX	$ 30
Short Form TX	$ 30
Form VA	$ 30
Short Form VA	$ 30
Form PA	$ 30
Short Form PA.	$ 30
Form SE	$ 30
Short Form SE	$ 30
Form SR	$ 30
Form GATT	$ 30

Form GR/CP (This Form is an adjunct to Forms VA, PA, and TX. There is no additional charge.)

Renewal Registrations: (For works published or registered before January 1, 1978)

Form RE	$ 45
Addendum to Form RE	$ 15

Group Registrations: (Fee to register a group of related claims, where appropriate)

Form SE/Group (minimum fee $30) (serials)	$ 10 /serial issue
Form G/DN (daily newspapers and newsletters)	$ 55
Form GATT/Grp (minimum fee $30) (restored works)	$ 10 /restored work

Supplementary Registrations: (Fee to register a correction or amplification to a completed registration)

Form CA	$ 65

Miscellaneous Registrations:

Form D-VH (vessel hulls)	$75**
Form MW (mask works)	$75

Special Services Related to Registration (Optional Services)

Special Handling for Registration of Qualified Copyright Claims:
(Fee to expedite processing of qualified claims)

Special handling fee (per claim)	$ 500
Additional fee for each (non-special handling) claim using the same deposit	$ 50

Other Fees Associated with Registration:

Full-term retention of published copyright deposit	$ 365
Secure test processing	$ 60 /hour
Appeal fees (for claims previously refused registration)	
First appeal	$ 200
Additional claim in related group (each)	$ 20
Second appeal	$ 500
Additional claim in related group (each)	$ 20

[1]Some of these fees went into effect on July 1, 1999; they will be considered again in 2002. Others went into effect on July 1, 1998; they will be considered again in 2001.

Continued on back ▶

Other Copyright Service Fees

Recordation of Documents Relating to Copyrighted Works
(Fee to make a public record of an assignment of rights or other document)

Recordation of a document containing no more than one title ....$ 50

Additional titles (per group of 10 titles) ....$ 15

Recordation of NIE containing no more than one title ....$ 30

Additional titles (each) ....$ 1

Special Handling of Recordation of Documents ....$ 330

Reference and Bibliography Reports on Copyrighted Works
(Fee for searching copyright records and preparing an official report)

Preparation of a report from official records ....$ 65 /hour

Surcharge for Expedited Reference and Bibliography Reports...............................$ 125 / 1st hour

$ 95 /each add'l hour

Certification and Documents Services: Preparing Copies of Copyright Office Records
(Fees for locating, retrieving, and reproducing Copyright Office records)

Search fee for locating and/or retrieving records ....$ 65 /hour

Additional certificate of registration ....$ 25

Certification of Copyright Office records ....$65 /hour

Inspection of Copyright Office records ....$ 65

Copying fee (minimum $15) .... variable fee depending on format & size

Surcharge for Expedited Certification and Documents Services

Locating and/or retrieving in-process records ....$ 75 /hour

Additional certificate of registration ....$ 75 /hour

Certification of Copyright Office records ....$ 75 /hour

Copy of assignment or other recorded document ....$ 75 /hour

Copy of any other Copyright Office record ....$ 95 / 1st hour

$75 / each add'l hour

Miscellaneous Fees

Receipt for deposit without registration (Section 407 deposit) ....$ 4

Online Service Provider Designation ....$20 ★

Notice to Libraries and Archives ....$50 ★★

$ 20 /each add'l title

Notice of Intention to obtain compulsory license to make and distribute phonorecords..............$12

★It is anticipated that the fee will increase when final regulations are announced later in 1999.

★★ This fee may change when final regulations are announced later in 1999.

Please check the Copyright Office Website at **www.loc.gov/copyright** or call (202) 707-3000 for the latest fee information.

Appendix C
The "Best Edition" of a Literary Work

The following excerpt, *"Best Edition" of Published Copyrighted Works for the Collections of the Library of Congress*, is taken from Volume 62, No. 191 of the *Federal Register* for Thursday, October 2, 1997 (p. 51603). It lists the various specifications for submitting works for copyright registration. Additional copies are available from the United States Copyright Office as *Circular 7b*.

The copyright law (title 17, United States Code) requires that copies or phonorecords deposited in the Copyright Office be of the "best edition" of the work. The law states that "The 'best edition' of a work is the edition, published in the United States at any time before the date of deposit. that the Library of Congress determines to be most suitable for its purposes." (For works first published only in a country other than the United States, the law requires the deposit of the best edition **first** published.)

When two or more editions of the same version of a work have been published, the one of the highest quality is generally considered to be the best edition. In judging quality, the Library of Congress will adhere to the criteria set forth below in all but exceptional circumstances.

Where differences between editions represent variations in copyrightable content, each edition is a separate version and "best edition" standards based on such differences do not apply. Each such version is a separate work for the purposes of the copyright law.

The criteria to be applied in determining the best edition of each of several types of material are listed below in descending order of importance. In deciding between two editions, a criterion-by- criterion comparison should be made. The edition that first fails to satisfy a criterion is to be considered of inferior quality and will not be an acceptable deposit. Example: If a comparison is made between two hardbound editions of a book, one a trade edition printed on acid-free paper, and the other a specially bound edition printed on average paper, the former will be the best edition because the type of paper is a more important criterion than the binding.

Under regulations of the Copyright Office, potential depositors may request authorization to deposit copies or phonorecords of other than the best edition of a specific work (e.g., a microform rather than a printed edition of a serial), by requesting "special relief" from the deposit requirements. All requests for special relief should be in writing and should state the reason(s) why the applicant cannot send the required deposit and what the applicant wishes to submit instead of the required deposit.

I. PRINTED TEXTUAL MATTER

A. *Paper, Binding, and Packaging:*
 1. Archival-quality rather than less permanent paper.
 2. Hard cover rather that soft cover.
 3. Library binding rather than commercial binding.
 4. Trade edition rather than book club edition.
 5. Sewn rather than glue-only binding.
 6. Sewn or glued rather than stapled or spiral-bound.
 7. Stapled rather than spiral-bound or plastic-bound.
 8. Bound rather than looseleaf, except when future loose leaf insertions are to be issued. In the case of looseleaf materials, this includes the submission of all binders and indexes when they are part of the unit as published and offered for sale or distribution. Additionally, the regular and timely receipt of all appropriate looseleaf updates, supplements, and releases including supplemental binders issued to handle these expanded versions, is part of the requirement to properly maintain these publications.
 9. Slip-cased rather than nonslip-cased.
 10. With protective folders rather than without (for broadsides).
 11. Rolled rather than folded (for broadsides).
 12. With protective coatings rather than without (except broadsides, which should not be coated).

B. *Rarity:*
 1. Special limited edition having the greatest number of special features.
 2. Other limited edition rather than trade edition.
 3. Special binding rather than trade binding.

C. *Illustrations:*
 1. Illustrated rather than unillustrated.
 2. Illustrations in color rather than black and white.

D. *Special Features:*
 1. With thumb notches or index tabs rather than without.
 2. With aids to use such as overlays and magnifiers rather than without.

E. *Size:*
 1. Larger rather than smaller sizes. (Except that large-type editions for the partially-sighted are not required in place of editions employing type of more conventional size.)

II. PHOTOGRAPHS

A. Size and finish, in descending order of preference.
 1. The most widely distributed edition.
 2. 8 x 10-inch glossy print.
 3. Other size or finish.

B. Unmounted rather than mounted.

C. Archival-quality rather than less-permanent paper stock or printing process.

III. MOTION PICTURES

The formats under "film" and "video formats" are listed in descending order of preference.

A. Film
 1. Preprint material with special arrangement.
 2. 35 mm positive prints.
 3. 16mm positive prints.

B. Videotape formats
 1. One-inch open reel tape.
 2. Betacam SP.
 3. D-2.
 4. Betacam.

5. Videodisc
6. Three-quarter-inch cassette.
7. One-half-inch cassette.

IV. OTHER GRAPHIC MATTER

A. *Paper and Printing:*
1. Archival quality rather than less-permanent paper.
2. Color rather than black and white.

B. *Size and Content:*
1. Larger rather than smaller size.
2. In the case of cartographic works, editions with the greatest amount of information rather than those with less detail.

C. *Rarity:*
1. The most widely distributed edition rather than one of limited distribution.
2. In the case of a work published only in a limited, numbered edition, one copy outside the numbered series but otherwise identical.
3. A photographic reproduction of the original, by special arrangement only.

D. *Text and Other Materials:*
1. Works with annotations, accompanying tabular or textual matter, or other interpretative aids rather than those without them.

E. *Binding and Packaging:*
1. Bound rather than unbound.
2. If editions have different binding, apply the criteria in I.A.2-I.A.7, above.
3. Rolled rather than folded.
4. With protective coatings rather than without.

V. PHONORECORDS

A. Compact digital disc rather than a vinyl disc.

B. Vinyl disc rather than tape.

C. With special enclosures rather than without.

D. Open-reel rather than cartridge.

E. Cartridge rather than cassette.

F. Quadraphonic rather than stereophonic.

G. True stereophonic rather than monaural.

H. Monaural rather than electronically rechanneled stereo.

VI. MUSICAL COMPOSITIONS

A. *Fullness of Score:*

1. *Vocal music:*
   a. With orchestral accompaniment—
   i. Full score and parts, if any, rather than conductor's score and parts, if any. (In cases of compositions published only by rental, lease, or lending, this requirement is reduced to full score only.)
   ii. Conductor's score and parts, if any, rather than condensed score and part, if any. (In cases of compositions published only by rental, lease, or lending, this requirement is reduced to conductor's score only.)
   b. Unaccompanied: Open score (each part on separate staff) rather than closed score (all parts condensed to two staves).

2. *Instrumental music:*
   a. Full score and parts, if any, rather than conductor's score and part, if any. (In cases of compositions published only by rental, lease, or lending, this requirement is reduced to full score only.)
   b. Conductor's score and parts, if any rather than condensed score and parts, if any. (In cases of compositions published only by rental, lease, or lending, this requirement is reduced to conductor's score only.)

B. *Printing and Paper:*
1. Archival-quality rather than less-permanent paper.

C. *Binding and Packaging:*
1. Special limited editions rather than trade editions.
2. Bound rather than unbound.
3. If editions have different binding, apply the criteria in I.A.2-I.A.12, above.
4. With protective folders rather than without.

VII. MICROFORMS

A. *Related Materials:*
1. With indexes, study guides, or other printed matter rather than without.

B. *Permanence and Appearance:*
1. Silver halide rather than any other emulsion.
2. Positive rather than negative.
3. Color rather than black and white.

C. *Format (newspapers and newspaper-formatted serials):*
1. Reel microfilm rather than any other microfilm.

D. *Format (all other materials):*
1. Microfiche rather than reel microfilm.
2. Reel microfilm rather than microform cassettes.
3. Microfilm cassettes rather than micro-opaque prints.

E. *Size:*
1. 35 mm rather than 16 mm.

VIII. MACHINE-READABLE COPIES*

A. Computer Programs:
1. With documents and other accompanying material rather than without.

---

*This best edition requirement applies only to the deposit of copies for the Library of Congress under § 407 and does not apply to deposits submitted under § 408 for registration of claims to copyright.

2. Not copy-protected rather than copy-protected (if copy-protected then with a back up copy of the disk(s)).
3. *Format*:
    a. PC-DOS or MS-DOS (or other IBM compatible formats, such as XENIX):
        (i) 5 1/4" Diskette(s).
        (ii) 3 1/2" Diskette(s).
        (iii) Optical media, such as CD-ROM—best edition should adhere to prevailing NISO standards.
    b. Apple Macintosh:
        (i) 3 1/2" Diskette(s).
        (ii) Optical media such as CD-ROM—best edition should adhere to prevailing NISO standards.

B. Computerized Information Works, Including Statistical Compendia, Serials, or Reference Works:
1. With documentation and other accompanying material rather than without.
2. With best edition of accompanying program rather than without.
3. Not copy-protected rather than copy-protected (if copy-protected then with a backup copy of the disk(s)).
4. Format:
    a. PC-DOS or MS-DOS (or other IBM compatible formats, such as XENIX)
        (i) Optical media, such as CD-ROM—best edition should adhere to prevailing NISO standards.
        (ii) 5 1/4" Diskette(s).
        (iii) 3 1/2" Diskette(s).
    b. Apple Macintosh:
        (i) Optical media, such as CD-ROM—best edition should adhere to prevailing NISO standards.
        (ii) 3 1/2" Diskette(s).

IX. WORKS EXISTING IN MORE THAN ONE MEDIUM

Editions are listed below in descending order of preference.

A. Newspapers, dissertations and theses, newspaper-formatted serials:
1. Microform.
2. Printed matter.

B. All other materials:
1. Printed matter.
2. Microform.
3. Phonorecord.

(Effective November 3, 1997)

FOR FURTHER INFORMATION

The regulations governing registration are contained in Title 37, Subchapter A, Chapter II, *Code of Federal Regulations*, Part 202.

To request copyright application forms, circulars, and other publications, write to:
Library of Congress
Copyright Office
Publications Section, LM-455
101 Independence Avenue, S.E.
Washington, D.C. 20559-6000

Or call the Forms and Publications Hotline at (202) 707-9100 and leave a recorded request for application forms and circulars if you know which forms or circulars you want.

To speak with an information specialist, call (202) 707-3000, 8:30 a.m. to 5:00 p.m. Monday to Friday, eastern time, except federal holidays. Recorded information is available 24 hours a day. The TTY number is (202) 707-6737.

Selected circulars and announcements are available via fax. Call (202) 707-2600 from any touchtone telephone. Frequently requested Copyright Office circulars, announcements, regulations, and all copyright applications forms are available via the Internet at the following address: *http://www.loc.gov/copyright*.

DEPOSIT REQUIREMENTS FOR A WORK OF VISUAL ARTS

A deposit is sent with a copyright application and fee. For most works, a copy of the work is used as the deposit. For works of the visual arts, however, there are different requirements. This material, taken from Copyright Office publication, *Circular 40a*, explains the various deposit requirements for a work of the visual arts.

IN GENERAL

To register a claim to copyright in a work of the visual arts, submit a properly completed application Form VA, a nonrefundable filing fee of $30*, and an appropriate deposit, generally one complete copy of the work if unpublished, two complete copies of the best edition if the work was first published in the United States, or, for certain types of works, identifying material instead of actual copies.

This circular presents a simplified version of the deposit requirements for registration of claims to copyright in visual arts material. It should be viewed only as a basic guide. The items given on pages, 2,3, and 4 are only examples and are not meant to be restrictive. For more detailed information, write for a copy of Circular 96, Sections 202.19, 202.20, and 202.21, which contains the deposit regulations of the Copyright Office. (See "For More Information" on back page.)

BASIC DEFINITIONS

Complete Copy

A "complete copy" of an **unpublished** work is a copy that represents the complete copyrightable content of the work being registered. A complete copy of a **published** work is one that contains all elements of the unit of publication, including those which, if considered separately, would not be copyrightable subject matter. The copies deposited for registration should be physically undamaged.

Best Edition

The "best edition" is the edition published in the United States at any time before the date of deposit in the Copyright Office that the Library of Congress determines to be most suitable for its purposes. Generally, when more than one edition is available, the best edition is: larger rather than smaller; color rather than black and white; and printed on archival quality rather than less-permanent paper. Request Circular 7b, "Best Edition of Published Copyrighted Works for the Collections of the Library of Congress," for additional information.

Identifying Material (I.D. Material)

"Identifying material" or "I.D. material" generally consists of two-dimensional reproduction(s) or rendering(s) of a work in the form of photographic prints, transparencies, photocopies, or drawings that show the complete copyrightable content of the work being registered.

SPECIFICATIONS FOR VISUAL ARTS IDENTIFYING MATERIAL

Copyright Office regulations require the deposit of identifying material instead of copies for three-dimensional works and for works that have been

*NOTE: Registration filing fees are effective through June 30, 2002. For more information on the fee changes, please write the Copyright Office, check the Copyright Office Website at www.loc.gov/copyright, or call (202) 707-3000.

applied to three-dimensional objects. Examples of such works include sculpture, toys, jewelry, artwork on plates, and fabric or textile attached to or part of a three-dimensional object such as furniture. Identifying material must also be submitted for any pictorial, graphic, or sculptural work that exceeds 96" in any dimension.

In certain cases, identifying material is permitted; in other cases, it is required. (See chart.) Identifying material should meet the following specifications:

- **Type of identifying material:** The material should consist of photographic prints, transparencies, photocopies, drawings, or similar two-dimensional reproductions or renderings of the work, in a form visually perceivable without the aid of a machine or device.

- **Color or black and white:** If the work is a pictorial or graphic work, the material should reproduce the actual colors employed in the work. In all other cases, the material may be in black and white or may consist of a reproduction of the actual colors.

- **Completeness:** As many pieces of identifying material should be submitted as are necessary to show clearly the entire copyrightable content of the work for which registration is being sought.

- **Number of sets:** Only one set of complete identifying material is required. NOTE: With respect to three dimensional holograms, please write the Copyright Office for additional information.

- **Size:** Photographic transparencies must be at least 35 mm in size and, if 3 x 3 inches or less, must be fixed in cardboard, plastic, or similar mounts; transparencies larger than 3 x 3 inches should be mounted. All types of identifying material other than photographic transparencies must be not less than 3 x 3 inches and not more than 9 x 12 inches, but preferably 8 x 10 inches. The image of the work should show clearly the entire copyrightable content of the work.

- **Title and dimension:** At least one piece of identifying material must give the title of the work on its front, back, or mount, and should include an exact measurement of one or more dimensions of the work.

Copyright Notice

Before March 1, 1989, the use of copyright notice was mandatory on all published works, and any work first published before that date should have carried a notice. For works first published on and after March 1, 1989, use of the copyright notice is optional.

For a work published with notice of copyright, the notice and its position on the work must be clearly shown on at least one piece of identifying material. If necessary because of the size or position of the notice, a separate drawing or similar reproduction may be submitted. Such reproduction should be no smaller than 3 x 3 inches and no larger than 9 x 12 inches and should show the exact appearance and content of the notice and its specific position on the work. For more information about copyright notice, request Circular 3, "Copyright Notice."

FOR FURTHER INFORMATION

- **Information via the Internet:** Frequently requested circulars, announcements, regulations, other related materials, the Document Cover Sheet, and all copyright registration forms are available via the Internet. You may access these from the Copyright Office homepage at *www.loc.gov/copyright*, or the Library of Congress home page at *www.loc.gov.*

- **Information by fax:** Selected circulars and other information including the Document Cover Sheet (but not application forms) are available from **Fax-on-Demand** at **(202) 707-2600.**

- **Information by telephone:** For general information about copyright, call the Copyright Public Information Office at **(202) 707-3000.** The TTY number is **(202) 707-6737.** Information specialists are on duty from 8:30 a.m. to 5:00 p.m., eastern time, Monday through Friday, except federal holidays. Recorded information is available 24 hours a day. Or, if you know which forms and circulars you want, request them from the Forms and Publications Hotline at **(202) 707-9100** 24 hours a day. Leave a recorded message.

- **Information by regular mail:** To request Copyright Office publications including the Document Cover Sheet, application forms, and circulars, write to:

Library of Congress
Copyright Office
Publications Section, LM-455
101 Independence Avenue, S.E.
Washington, D.C. 20559-6000

TWO-DIMENSIONAL WORKS

Nature of Work	Required Deposit	
	Published	**Unpublished**
Advertisements (pictorial)	1 copy as published or pre-publication camera-ready copy	1 photocopy, proof, drawing, copy, or layout
Artwork for bed, bath, and table linens or for wearing apparel (For example: hat transfers or decals already applied to T-shirts)	I.D. material preferred in all cases; I.D. material required if copy cannot be folded to 4" thickness or less; 1 copy permitted if it can be folded to 4" thickness or less	same as published
Blueprints, architectural drawings, mechanical drawings, diagrams	1 complete copy	1 copy
Book jackets or record jackets	1 complete copy	1 copy
Commercial print published in newspaper or other periodical	1 copy of entire page or pages	
Commercial print or label (For example: flyers, labels, brochures, or catalogs used in connection with the sale of goods or services	1 complete copy	1 copy
Contributions to collective works (photographs, drawings, cartoons, etc., published as part of a periodical or anthology)	1 complete copy of the best edition of entire collective work complete section containing contribution if published in newspaper, entire page containing contribution, contribution cut from the newspaper, or photocopy of contribution as it was published	
Fabric, textile, wallpaper, carpeting, floor tile, wrapping paper, yard goods (if applied to a three-dimensional work, see below)	1 complete copy (or swatch) showing the design repeat and copyright notice, if any	1 complete copy (or I.D. material if the work has not been fixed in repeat)
Fabric emblems or patches, decals or heat transfers (not applied to clothing, bumper stickers, campaign buttons	1 complete copy	1 copy or I.D. material
Greeting cards, picture postcards, stationary, business cards, calendars	1 complete copy	1 copy or I.D. material
Holograms	1 actual copy if image is visible without the aid of a machine or device; otherwise 2 sets of display instructions and 2 sets of I.D. material showing the displayed image	1 copy or display instructions and I.D. material of image
Maps or cartographic material	1 copy of CD-ROM if work published in that format; otherwise, 2 complete copies	1 copy of CD-Rom if work fixed in that format; otherwise, 1 complete copy or I.D. material
Patterns, cross-stitch graphs, stitchery brochures, needlework and craft kits	1 complete copy	1 copy or I.D. material
Pictorial or graphic works fixed only in machine-readable form	I.D. material	1 copy or proof, photocopy, contact sheet
Posters, photographs, prints, brochures, exhibition catalogs	2 complete copies	
"Limited edition" posters, prints, or etchings (published in quantities of fewer than 5 copies, or 300 or fewer numbered copies if individual author is owner of copyright)	1 copy or I.D. material	
Oversize material (exceeding 96" in any dimension)	I.D. material	I.D. material

THREE DIMENSIONAL WORKS

Nature of Work	Published	Unpublished
Artwork or illustrations on 3-D objects (For example: artwork on plates, mugs)	I.D. material	I.D. material
Fabric or textile attached to or part of a 3-D object (such as furniture)	I.D. material	I.D. material
Games	1 complete copy if container is no larger than 12"x24"x6"; otherwise, I.D. material	1 copy if container is no larger than 12"x24"x6" or I.D. material
Globes, relief models, or relief maps	1 complete copy including the stand (I.D. material not acceptable)	1 complete copy or I.D. material*
Jewelry	I.D. material or 1 copy if fixed only in the form of jewelry cast in base metal not exceeding 4" in any dimension	same as published
Pictorial matter and/or text on a box or container that can be flattened (contents of container are not claimed)	1 copy of box or container if it can be flattened or 1 paper label	1 copy or I.D. material*
Prints or labels inseparable from a three-dimensional object (For example: silk screen label on a bottle)	I.D. material	I.D. material
Sculptures, toys, dolls, molds, relief plaques, statues	I.D. material	I.D. material
Sculpture (For example: doll) in a box with copyrightable pictorial and/or textual material claim in sculpture and artwork/text	I.D. material for sculpture plus 1 copy of box and any other printed material	I.D. material for sculpture plus copy of box or I.D. material*
Oversize material (exceeding 96" in any dimension)	I.D. material	I.D. material

ARCHITECTURAL WORKS

	Unconstructed Building	**Constructed Building**
To be eligible for copyright protection, an architectural work must have been created on or after December 1, 1990, or have been unconstructed and embodied only in unpublished drawings as of that date. (Request Circular 41, "Copyright Claims in Architectural Works," for more information.)	1 complete copy of an architectural drawing or blueprint showing the overall form of the building and any interior arrangement of spaces and/or design elements in which copyright is claimed	1 complete copy as described at left plus I.D. material in the form of photographs clearly identifying the architectural work being registered

*Because storage space is limited, the Copyright Office prefers I.D. material rather than a copy in these cases.

COPYRIGHT REGISTRATION FOR ONLINE WORKS

If your work is available over the Internet, it may be considered an online work. The following information provides requirements and guidelines for registering an online work. The information is from the Copyright Office's publication *Circular 66, Copyright Registration for Online Works*.

GENERAL INFORMATION

This circular gives information about copyright registration of online works made available over a communications network such as the Internet. This information applies also to works accessed via network (World Wide Web sites and homepages, FTP sites, Gopher sites) and files and documents transmitted and/or downloaded via network.

Copyright protects original authorship fixed in tangible form. 17 U.S.C. sec. 102(a). For works transmitted online, the copyrightable authorship may consist of text, artwork, music, audiovisual material (including any sounds), sound recordings, etc. Copyright does **NOT** protect ideas, procedures, systems, or methods of operation. 17 U.S.C. sec. 102(b).

Under U.S. law, copyright protection subsists from the time the work is fixed. Copyright registration is not mandatory, but it has important benefits. For general information about copyright, request Circular 1, "Copy-right Basics." See "For Further Information" on page 4 on how to obtain circulars and other information.

> This circular does NOT apply to electronic registration or electronic deposit of digital works through CORDS (the Copyright Office Electronic Registration, Recordation and Deposit System), which is currently under development. For more information about CORDS, please request SL-11, "CORDS—Copyright Office Electronic Registration, Recordation and Deposit System" or consult the Copyright Office Website at www.loc.gov/ copyright. Until CORDS is operational, online works must be registered under the current system using identifying material as the deposit. See the section that follows on "The Deposit."

What the registration of an online work covers

For all online works other than computer programs and databases, the registration will extend only to the copyrightable content of the work **as received in the** Copyright Office and identified as the subject of the claim. The application for registration should exclude any material that has been previously registered or published or that is in the public domain. For published works, the registration should be limited to **the content of the work asserted to be published on the date given on the application.**

> NOTE: For online computer programs and data-bases, the registration will extend to the entire copyrightable content of the work owned by the claimant, even though the entire content is not required in the identifying material deposited.

Revisions and updates

Many works transmitted online are revised or updated frequently. For individual works, however, there is no blanket registration available to cover revisions **published** on multiple dates. A revised version for each daily revision may be registered separately, provided the revisions constitute copyrightable authorship. A separate application and $30* filing fee would be required for each separately published update. See the filing fee information on page 4.

Databases

In some cases, a frequently updated online work may constitute an automated database. A group of updates, published or unpublished, to a database, covering up to a 3-month period within the same calendar year, may be combined in a single registration. For more information about registering databases, request Circular 65, "Copyright Registration for Automated Databases." All updates from a 3-month period may be registered with a single application and $30* filing fee. Serials and newsletters Group registration (a single registration covering multiple issues published on different dates) is available for serials (published **weekly or less often)** and daily newsletters (published **more often than weekly)**, including those published online.The requirements vary, depending on the type of work. For more information about registering serials, request Circular 62, "Copyright Registration for Serials on Form SE," for daily newsletters, request Circular 62a, "Group Registration of Daily News-papers and Newsletters." For group registration of serials and daily newspapers and newsletters, the filing fee is $10* per issue with a minimum fee of $30.

> **NOTE:** Group registration for serials is available only if the claim is in a "collective work." Thus, group registration is NOT available for electronic journals published one article at a time because such works are not collective works.

HOW TO REGISTER YOUR WORK

To register a work transmitted online, send the following three items together in the same envelope or package to:

> Library of Congress
> Copyright Office
> 101 Independence Avenue, S.E.
> Washington, D.C. 20559-6000

1. A properly completed and signed application form

2. Appropriate deposit material

3. A nonrefundable filing fee for each application in the form of a check or money order payable to *Register of Copyrights*

Detailed information on each of these is given below.

THE APPLICATION

What Form to Use

Use the form that corresponds to the type of authorship being registered, for example:

> Form TX—literary material, including computer programs and databases
>
> Form VA—pictorial and graphic works, including cartographic material
>
> Form PA—audiovisual material, including any sounds, music, or lyrics

(*See Filing Fee information on page 4.)

> Form SR—sound recording, excluding sounds accompanying an audiovisual work
>
> Form SE—a single issue of a serial
>
> Form SE/GROUP—a group of issues of a serial, including daily newsletters
>
> Form GR/CP—a group of contributions to a periodical. (This form must be used in conjunction with Form TX, PA, or VA.)

If the work contains more than one type of authorship, use the form that corresponds to the predominant material.

The various classes (TX, PA, VA, SR) are for administrative purposes only. A work may be registered

on any form. **Exceptions:** A sound recording (sounds that do not accompany a series of images) **must** be registered on Form SR. Form SE/GROUP may be used only for group registration of serials. For more information, see Circular 56, "Copyright for Sound Recordings."

How to complete the form

In general, complete the form as explained in the instructions and in applicable Copyright Office circulars. **Information specific to online works is given in more detail below.**

Space 2: How to describe the Nature of Authorship

In Space 2 of the application, give a brief statement describing the original authorship being registered. Use terms that clearly refer to copyrightable authorship. Examples are "text," "music," "artwork," "photographs," "audiovisual material" (including any sounds), "sound recording" (if the sounds do not accompany a series of images), and "computer program."

Do **NOT** give statements that refer to elements that may not be protected by copyright, that may be ambiguous, or that do not clearly reflect copyrightable author-ship. For example, do **NOT** use the terms "user interface," "format," "layout," "design," "lettering," "concept," or "game play."

Space 3: Determining if your work is published or unpublished

The definition of "publication" in the U.S. copyright law does not specifically address online transmission. As has been the long-standing practice, the Copyright Office asks the applicant, who knows the facts surrounding distribution of copies of a work, to determine whether the work is published or not.

In the current copyright law, "**publication**" is defined as "...the distribution of copies or phonorecords of a work to the public by sale or other transfer of ownership, or by rental, lease, or lending. The offering to distribute copies or phonorecords to a group of persons for purposes of further distribution, public performance, or public display, constitutes publication. A public performance or display of a work does not of itself constitute publication." 17 U.S.C. sec. 101.

Published works: If you determine that your work is published, give the complete date and nation of first publication in Space 3b of the application. For a revised version, the publication date should be the date the revised version was first published, not the date the original version first appeared online. For registration purposes, give a single nation of first publication, which may be the nation from which the work is uploaded.

Unpublished works: If you determine that your work is unpublished, leave Space 3b blank. Do **NOT** write "Internet," "homepage," or any other term in this space.

THE DEPOSIT

All works transmitted online excluding computer programs, databases, and works fixed in CD-ROM format:

The deposit regulations of the Copyright Office do not specifically address works transmitted online. Until the regulations are amended, and under the authority granted the Copyright Office by 37 C.F.R. 202.20(c)(2)(viii), the Office will require the deposit of one of the following:

> **NOTE:** If the same work is published both online and by the distribution of physical copies and these events occur on different dates, the publication date should refer to whichever occurred first. For what to deposit in this case, see the "Exception" below.

Option 1: a computer disk (clearly labeled with the title and author) containing the entire work **and** in addition, representative portions of the authorship being registered in a format that can be examined by the Office (printout, audio cassette, or videotape). If the work is short (e.g., five pages of text or artwork, or 3 minutes of music, sounds, or audiovisual material), deposit the entire work and confirm that it is complete. If the work is longer, deposit five representative pages or 3 representative minutes. This identifying material should include the title and author, and the copyright notice, if any.

OR

Option 2: a reproduction of the **entire work,** regardless of length. Send the format appropriate for the authorship being registered, for example, a printout, audio cassette, or videotape. No computer disk is required.

Exception: If a work is published **both** online and by the distribution of physical copies in any format, the requirement of the deposit regulations **for the copies** applies, not the options for online works given above. For example, if a work is published in the form of hardbound books and is also transmitted online, the deposit requirement is two copies of the hardbound book.

Computer programs, databases, and works fixed in CD-ROM format transmitted online:

For computer programs, databases, and works fixed in CD-ROM format, the specific provisions of Copyright Office deposit regulations apply to works transmitted online. 37 C.F.R. 202.20(c)(vii) and 202.20(c)(xix). For further information, request Circular 61, "Copyright Registration for Computer Programs," or Circular 65, "Copyright Registration for Automated Databases." For works fixed in CD-ROM format, a complete copy of the CD-ROM package, including any operating software or instruction manual, is required.

THE FILING FEE*

For a single work (Form TX, PA, VA, SR, or SE): **$30*** per application

For a group of serials or newsletters (Form SE/GROUP): **$10* per issue** (**$30*** minimum)

For a group of updates to a database, covering up to a 3-month period (Form TX): **$30*** per application

FOR FURTHER INFORMATION

Information via the Internet: Frequently requested circulars, announcements, regulations, other related materials, and all copyright application forms are available via the Internet. Access these from the Copyright Office homepage at **www.loc.gov/copyright.**

> ***NOTE:** Registration filing fees are effective through June 30, 2002. For information on fee changes, please write the Copyright Office, check the Copyright Office Website at www.loc.gov/copyright, or call (202) 707-3000 for the latest fee information.

Information by Fax: Circulars and other information (but not application forms) are available from Fax-on-Demand at (202) 707-2600.

Information by telephone: If you have specific questions about registering a work transmitted online and want to speak with a copyright examiner, please call the Literary Section of the Examining Division at **(202) 707-8250.** For general information about copyright, call the Public Information Office at **(202) 707-3000.** The TTY number is (202) 707-6737. Information specialists are on duty in the Public Information Office from 8:30 a.m. to 5:00 p.m., eastern time, Monday through Friday, except federal holidays. Recorded information is available 24 hours a day. Or, if you know which application forms and circulars you want, request them from the Forms and Publications Hotline at **(202) 707-9100** 24 hours a day.

Leave a recorded message.

Information by regular mail: Write to:

> Library of Congress
> Copyright Office
> Public Information Office, LM-401
> 101 Independence Avenue, S.E.
> Washington, D.C. 20559-6000

For more about how to obtain information online and via fax, request SL-10, **"Get It Quick Over the Net."**

Library of Congress • Copyright Office • 101 Independence Avenue, S.E. • Washington, D.C. 20559-6000
www.loc.gov/copyright

REV: June 1999—20,000
WEB REV: June 1999

☆U.S. GOVERNMENT PRINTING OFFICE: 1999-454-879/45

APPENDIX F
INTERNATIONAL COPYRIGHT
RELATIONS OF THE UNITED STATES

Generally, if your creative work is copyrighted in the United States, you are protected in most countries of the world. Your rights in other countries is determined by whether the country has passed one or more of the treaties listed below. The following information on International copyright relations of the United States is from Copyright Office *Circular 38A*.

GENERAL INFORMATION

This sets forth U.S. copyright relations of current interest with the other independent nations of the world. Each entry gives country name (and alternate name) and a statement of copyright relations. The following code is used:

Berne   Party to the Berne Convention for the Protection of Literary and Artistic Works as of the date given. Appearing within parentheses is the latest Act[1] of the Convention to which the country is party. The effective date for the United States is March 1, 1989. The latest Act of the Convention to which the United States is party, is the revision done at Paris on July 24, 1971.

Bilateral   Bilateral copyright relations with the United States by virtue of a proclamation or treaty, as of the date given. Where there is more than one proclamation or treaty, only the date of the first one is given.

BAC   Party to the Buenos Aires Convention of 1910, as of the date given. U.S. ratification deposited with the Government of Argentina, May 1, 1911; proclaimed by the President of the United States, July 13, 1914.

None   No copyright relations with the United States.

Phonogram   Party to the Convention for the Protection of Producers of Phonograms Against Unauthorized Duplication of Their Phonograms, Geneva, 1971, as of the date given. The effective date for the United States is March 10, 1974.

SAT   Party to the Convention Relating to the Distribution of Programme-Carrying Signals Transmitted by Satellite, Brussels, 1974, as of the date given. The effective date for the United States is March 7, 1985.

UCC Geneva   Party to the Universal Copyright Convention, Geneva, 1952, as of the date given. The effective date for the United States is September 16, 1955.

UCC Paris   Party to the Universal Copyright Convention as revised at Paris, 1971, as of the date given. The effective date for the United States is July 10, 1974.

Unclear   Became independent since 1943. Has not established copyright relations with the United States, but may be honoring obligations incurred under former political status.

WTO   (World Trade Organization) Member of the World Trade Organization, established pursuant to the Marrakesh Agreement of April 15, 1994, to implement the Uruguay Round Agreements. These Agreements affect, among other things, intangible property rights, including copyright and other intellectual property rights. The effective date of United States membership in the WTO is January 1, 1995. A country's membership in the World Trade Organization is effective as of the date indicated.

Explanations of footnotes appear on the last page.

RELATIONS AS OF MAY 1999

Afghanistan
None

Albania
Berne Mar. 6, 1994 (Paris)[1]

Algeria
UCC Geneva Aug. 28, 1973
UCC Paris July 10, 1974
Berne April 19, 1998 (Paris)

Andorra
UCC Geneva Sept. 16, 1955

Angola
WTO Nov. 23, 1996

Antigua and Barbudaa
WTO Jan. 1, 1995

Argentina
Bilateral Aug. 23, 1934
BAC Apr. 19, 1950
UCC Geneva Feb. 13, 1958
Berne June 10, 1967 (Brussels)[2]
Phonogram June 30, 1973[3]
WTO Jan. 1, 1995

Armenia
SAT Dec.13, 1993

Australia
Bilateral March 15, 1918
Berne Apr. 14, 1928 (Paris)[2]
UCC Geneva May 1, 1969
Phonogram June 22, 1974
UCC Paris Feb. 28, 1978

SAT Oct. 26,1990
WTO Jan. 1, 1995

Austria
Bilateral Sept. 20, 1907
Berne Oct. 1, 1920 (Paris)[2]
UCC Geneva July 2, 1957
SAT Aug. 6, 1982[4]
UCC Paris Aug. 14, 1982
Phonogram Aug. 21, 1982
WTO Jan. 1, 1995

Azerbaijan
UCC Geneva May 27, 1973

Bahamas, The
Berne July 10, 1973 (Brussels)
UCC Geneva Dec. 27, 1976
UCC Paris Dec. 27, 1976

Bahrain
WTO Jan. 1, 1995
Berne Mar. 2, 1997 (Paris)

Bangladesh
UCC Geneva Aug. 5, 1975
UCC Paris Aug. 5, 1975
WTO Jan. 1, 1995
Berne May 4, 1999 (Paris)

Barbados
UCC Geneva June 18, 1983
UCC Paris June 18, 1983
Berne July 30, 1983 (Paris)[2]
Phonogram July 29, 1983
WTO Jan. 1, 1995

Belarus
UCC Geneva May 27, 1973
Berne Dec. 12, 1997 (Paris)

Belau
(see Palau)

Belgium
Berne Dec. 5, 1887 (Brussels)[2]
Bilateral July 1, 1891
UCC Geneva Aug. 31, 1960
WTO Jan. 1, 1995

Belize
UCC Geneva Dec. 1, 1982
WTO Jan. 1, 1995

Benin (formerly Dahomey)
Berne Jan. 3, 1961 (Paris)[2]
WTO Feb. 22, 1996

Bhutan
None

Bolivia
BAC May 15, 1914
UCC Geneva Mar. 22, 1990
UCC Paris Mar. 22, 1990
Berne Nov. 4, 1993 (Paris)
WTO Sept. 13, 1995

Bosnia and Herzegovina
UCC Geneva May 11, 1966
UCC Paris July 10, 1974
Berne Mar. 6, 1992 (Paris)
SAT Mar. 6, 1992

Botswana
WTO May 31, 1995
Berne April 15, 1998 (Paris)

Brazil
BAC Aug. 31, 1915
Berne Feb. 9, 1922 (Paris)[2]
Dilateral Apr. 2, 1957
UCC Geneva Jan. 13, 1960
Phonogram Nov. 28, 1975
UCC Paris Dec. 11, 1975
WTO Jan. 1, 1995

Brunei Darussalam
WTO Jan. 1, 1995

Bulgaria
Berne Dec. 5, 1921 (Paris)[2]
UCC Geneva June 7, 1975
UCC Paris June 7, 1975
Phonogram Sept. 6, 1995
WTO Dec. 1, 1996

Burkina Faso (formerly Upper Volta)
Berne Aug. 19, 1963 (Paris)[2]
Phonogram Jan. 30, 1988
WTO June 3, 1995

Burma
(See Myanmar, Union of)

Burundi
WTO July 23, 1995

Cambodia
UCC Geneva Sept. 16, 1955

Cameroon
Berne Sept. 21, 1964 (Paris)[2]
UCC Geneva May 1, 1973
UCC Paris July 10, 1974
WTO Dec. 13, 1995

Canada
Bilateral Jan. 1, 1924
Berne Apr. 10, 1928 (Paris)[2]
UCC Geneva Aug. 10, 1962
WTO Jan. 1, 1995

Cape Verde
Berne July 7, 1997 (Paris)

Central African Republic
Berne Sept. 3, 1977 (Paris)[2]
WTO May 31, 1995

Chad
Berne Nov. 25, 1971 (Brussels)[2]
WTO Oct. 19, 1996

Chile
Bilateral May [2]5, 1896
BAC June 14, 1955
UCC Geneva Sept. 16, 1955
Berne June 5, 1970 (Paris)[2]
Phonogram Mar. 24, 1977
WTO Jan. 1, 1995

China
Bilateral Jan. 13, 1904[5]
Bilateral Mar. 17, 1992[9]
Berne Oct. 15, 1992 (Paris)
UCC Geneva Oct. 30, 1992
UCC Paris Oct. 30, 1992
Phonogram Apr. 30, 1993

Colombia
BAC Dec. 23, 1936
UCC Geneva June 18, 1976
UCC Paris June 18, 1976
Berne Mar. 7, 1988 (Paris)[2]
Phonogram May 16, 1994
WTO Apr. 30, 1995

Comoros
Unclear

Congo
Berne May 8, 1962 (Paris)[2]
WTO Mar. 27, 1997

Costa Rica 6
Bilateral Oct. 19, 1899
BAC Nov. 30, 1916
UCC Geneva Sept. 16, 1955
Berne June 10, 1978 (Paris)[2]
UCC Paris Mar. 7, 1980
Phonogram June 17, 1982
WTO Jan. 1, 1995

Cote d'Ivoire (Ivory Coast)
Berne Jan. 1, 1962 (Paris)[2]
WTO Jan. 1, 1995

Croatia
UCC Geneva May 11, 1966
UCC Paris July 10, 1974
Berne Oct. 8, 1991 (Paris)[2]
SAT Oct. 8, 1991

Cuba
Bilateral Nov. 17, 1903
UCC Geneva June 18, 1957
WTO Apr. 20, 1995
Berne Feb. 20, 1997 (Paris)

Cyprus
Berne Feb. 24, 1964 (Paris)[2]
UCC Geneva Dec. 19, 1990
UCC Paris Dec. 19,1990
Phonogram Sept. 30, 1993
WTO July 30, 1995

Czech Republic
UCC Geneva Jan. 6, 1960
UCC Paris Apr. 17, 1980
Berne Jan. 1, 1993 (Paris)
Phonogram Jan. 1, 1993
WTO Jan. 1, 1995

Czechoslovakia[11]
Bilateral Mar. 1, 1927

**Democratic Republic of Congo
(formerly Zaire)**
Berne Oct. 8, 1963 (Paris)[2]
Phonogram Nov. 29, 1977
WTO Jan. 1, 1997

Denmark
Bilateral May 8, 1893
Berne July 1, 1903 (Paris)[2]
UCC Geneva Feb. 9, 1962
Phonogram Mar. 24, 1977
UCC Paris July 11, 1979
WTO Jan. 1, 1995

Djibouti
WTO May 31, 1995

Dominica
WTO Jan. 1, 1995

Dominican Republic[6]
BAC Oct. 31, 1912
UCC Geneva May 8, 1983
UCC Paris May 8, 1983
WTO Mar. 9, 1995

Berne Dec. 24, 1997 (Paris)

Ecuador
BAC Aug. 31, 1914
UCC Geneva June 5, 1957
Phonogram Sept. 14, 1974
UCC Paris Sept. 6, 1991
Berne Oct. 9, 1991 (Paris)
WTO Jan. 21, 1996

Egypt
Berne June 7, 1977 (Paris)[2]
Phonogram Apr. 23, 1978
WTO June 30, 1995

El Salvador
Bilateral June 30, 1908 by virtue of
     Mexico City Convention, 1902
Phonogram Feb. 9, 1979
UCC Geneva Mar. 29, 1979
UCC Paris Mar. 29, 1979
Berne Feb. 19, 1994 (Paris)
WTO May 7, 1995

Equatorial Guinea
Berne Jun. 26, 1997 (Paris)

Estonia
Berne Oct. 26, 1994 (Paris)

Ethiopia
None

European Community
WTO Jan. 1, 1995

Fiji
Berne Dec.1, 1971 (Brussels) [2]
UCC Geneva Mar. 13, 1972
Phonogram Apr. 18, 1973 [3]
WTO Jan. 14, 1996

Finland
Berne Apr. 1, 1928 (Paris) [2]
Bilateral Jan. 1, 1929
UCC Geneva Apr. 16, 1963
Phonogram Apr. 18, 1973 [3]
UCC Paris Nov. 1, 1986
WTO Jan. 1, 1995

France
Berne Dec. 5, 1887 (Paris) [2]
Bilateral July 1, 1891
UCC Geneva Jan. 14, 1956
Phonogram Apr. 18, 1973 [3]
UCC Paris July 10, 1974
WTO Jan. 1, 1995

Gabon
Berne Mar. 26, 1962 (Paris) [2]
WTO Jan. 1, 1995

Gambia, The
Berne Mar. 7, 1993 (Paris)
WTO Oct. 23, 1996

Georgia
Berne May 16, 1995 (Paris)

Germany [10]
Berne Dec. 5, 1887 (Paris) [2,7]
Bilateral Apr. 15, 1892
UCC Geneva Sept. 16, 1955
Phonogram May 18, 1974
UCC Paris July 10, 1974
SAT Aug. 25, 1979 [4]
WTO Jan. 1, 1995

Ghana
UCC Geneva Aug. 22, 1962
Berne Oct. 11, 1991 (Paris)
WTO Jan. 1, 1995

Greece
Berne Nov. 9, 1920 (Paris) [2]
Bilateral Mar. 1, 1932
UCC Geneva Aug. 24, 1963
SAT Oct. 22, 1991
Phonogram Feb. 9, 1994
WTO Jan. 1, 1995

Grenada
WTO Feb. 22, 1996
Berne Sept. 22, 1998 (Paris)

Guatemala [6]
BAC Mar. 28, 1913
UCC Geneva Oct. 28, 1964
Phonogram Feb. 1, 1977
WTO July 21, 1995
Berne July 28, 1997 (Paris)

Guinea
Berne Nov. 20, 1980 (Paris) [2]
UCC Geneva Nov. 13, 1981
UCC Paris Nov. 13, 1981
WTO Oct. 25, 1995

Guinea-Bissau
Berne July 22, 1991 (Paris)
WTO May 31, 1995

Guyana
Berne Oct. 25, 1994 (Paris)
WTO Jan. 1, 1995

Haiti
BAC Nov. 27, 1919
UCC Geneva Sept. 16, 1955
Berne Jan. 11, 1996 (Paris)
WTO Jan. 30, 1996

Holy See
(See entry under Vatican City)

Honduras [6]
BAC Apr. 27, 1914
Berne Jan. 25,1990 (Paris)
Phonogram Mar. 6, 1990
WTO Jan. 1, 1995

Hong Kong
WTO Jan. 1, 1995

Hungary
Bilateral Oct. 16, 1912
Berne Feb. 14, 1922 (Paris) [2]
UCC Geneva Jan. 23, 1971
UCC Paris July 10, 1974
Phonogram May 28, 1975
WTO Jan. 1, 1995

Iceland
Berne Sept. 7, 1947 (Rome) [2]
UCC Geneva Dec. 18, 1956
WTO Jan. 1, 1995

India
Berne Apr. 1, 1928 (Paris) [7]
Bilateral Aug. 15, 1947
UCC Geneva Jan. 21, 1958
Phonogram Feb. 12, 1975
UCC Paris Apr. 7, 1988
WTO Jan. 1, 1995

Indonesia
Bilateral Aug. 1, 1989
WTO Jan. 1, 1995
Berne Sept. 5, 1997 (Paris)

Iran
None

Iraq
None

Ireland
Berne Oct. 5, 1927 (Brussels) [2]
Bilateral Oct. 1, 1929
UCC Geneva Jan. 20, 1959
WTO Jan. 1, 1995

Israel
Bilateral May 15, 1948

Berne Mar. 24, 1950 (Brussels) [2]
UCC Geneva Sept. 16, 1955
Phonogram May 1, 1978
WTO Apr. 21, 1995

Italy
Berne Dec. 5, 1887 (Paris) [2]
Bilateral Oct. 31, 1892
UCC Geneva Jan. 24, 1957
Phonogram Mar. 24, 1977
UCC Paris Jan. 25, 1980
SAT July 7, 1981 [4]
WTO Jan. 1, 1995

Ivory Coast
(See entry under Côte d'Ivoire)

Jamaica
Berne Jan. 1, 1994 (Paris)
Phonogram Jan. 11, 1994
WTO Mar. 9, 1995

Japan [8]
Berne July 15, 1899 (Paris) [2]
UCC Geneva Apr. 28, 1956
UCC Paris Oct. 21, 1977
Phonogram Oct. 14, 1978
WTO Jan. 1, 1995

Jordan
Unclear

Kazakhstan
UCC Geneva May 27, 1973
Berne April 12, 1999 (Paris)

Kenya
UCC Geneva Sept. 7, 1966
UCC Paris July 10, 1974
Phonogram Apr. 21, 1976
SAT Aug. 25, 1979 [4]
Berne June 11, 1993 (Paris)
WTO Jan. 1, 1995

Kiribati
Unclear

Korea
Democratic People's Republic of Korea
Unclear

Republic of Korea
UCC Geneva Oct. 1, 1987
UCC Paris Oct. 1, 1987
Phonogram Oct. 10, 1987
WTO Jan. 1, 1995
Berne Aug. 21, 1996 (Paris)

Kuwait
WTO Jan. 1, 1995

Kyrzyg Republic
WTO Dec. 20, 1998

Laos
UCC Geneva Sept. 16, 1955

Latvia
Berne Aug. 11, 1995 (Paris)
Phonogram Aug 23, 1997
WTO Feb. 10, 1999

Lebanon
Berne Sept. 30, 1947 (Rome) [2]
UCC Geneva Oct. 17, 1959

Lesotho
Berne Sept. 28, 1989 (Paris)
WTO May 31, 1995

Liberia
UCC Geneva July 27, 1956
Berne Mar. 8, 1989 (Paris)

Libya
Berne Sept. 28, 1976 (Paris) [2]

Liechtenstein
Berne July 30, 1931 (Brussels) [2]
UCC Geneva Jan. 22, 1959
WTO Sept. 1, 1995

Lithuania
Berne Dec. 14, 1994 (Paris)

Luxembourg
Berne June 20, 1888 (Paris) [2]
Bilateral June 29, 1910
UCC Geneva Oct. 15, 1955
Phonogram Mar. 8, 1976
WTO Jan. 1, 1995

Macau
WTO Jan. 1, 1995

Macedonia (former Yugoslav Republic of)
Berne Sept. 8, 1991 (Paris)
SAT Nov. 17, 1991
UCC Geneva July 30, 1997
UCC Paris July 30, 1997
Phonogram Mar. 2, 1998

Madagascar (Malagasy Republic)
Berne Jan. 1, 1966 (Brussels) [2]
WTO Nov. 17, 1995

Malawi
UCC Geneva Oct. 26, 1965
Berne Oct. 12, 1991 (Paris)
WTO May 31, 1995

Malaysia
Berne Oct. 1, 1990 (Paris)
WTO Jan. 1, 1995

Maldives
WTO May 31, 1995

Mali
Berne Mar. 19, 1962 (Paris) [2]
WTO May 31, 1995

Malta
Berne Sept. 21, 1964 (Rome) [2]
UCC Geneva Nov. 19, 1968
WTO Jan. 1, 1995

Mauritania
Berne Feb. 6, 1973 (Paris) [2]
WTO May 31, 1995

Mauritius
UCC Geneva Mar. 12, 1968
Berne May 10, 1989 (Paris)
WTO Jan. 1, 1995

Mexico
Bilateral Feb. 27, 1896
UCC Geneva May 12, 1957
BAC Apr. 24, 1964
Berne June 11, 1967 (Paris) [2]
Phonogram Dec. 21, 1973 [3]
UCC Paris Oct. 31, 1975
SAT Aug. 25, 1979 [4]
WTO Jan. 1, 1995

Moldova
Berne Nov. 2, 1995 (Paris)
UCC Geneva July 18, 1997

Monaco
Berne May 30, 1889 (Paris) [2]
Bilateral Oct. 15, 1952
UCC Geneva Sept. 16, 1955
Phonogram Dec. 2, 1974
UCC Paris Dec. 13, 1974

Mongolia
WTO Jan. 29, 1997
Berne Mar. 12, 1998 (Paris)

Morocco
Berne June 16, 1917 (Paris) [2]
UCC Geneva May 8, 1972
UCC Paris Jan. 28, 1976

SAT June 30, 1983 [4]
WTO Jan. 1, 1995

Mozambique
WTO Aug. 26, 1995

Myanmar, Union of (formerly Burma)
WTO Jan. 1, 1995

Namibia
Berne Mar. 21, 1990 (Paris)
WTO Jan. 1, 1995

Nauru
Unclear

Nepal
None

Netherlands
Bilateral Nov. 20, 1899
Berne Nov. 1, 1912 (Paris) [2]
UCC Geneva June 22, 1967
UCC Paris Nov. 30, 1985
Phonogram Oct. 12, 1993
WTO Jan. 1, 1995

New Zealand
Bilateral Dec. 1, 1916
Berne Apr. 24, 1928 (Rome) [2]
UCC Geneva Sept. 11, 1964
Phonogram Aug. 13, 1976
WTO Jan. 1, 1995

Nicaragua [6]
BAC Dec. 15, 1913
UCC Geneva Aug. 16, 1961
SAT Aug. 25, 1979 [4]
WTO Sept. 3, 1995

Niger
Berne May 2, 1962 (Paris) [2]
UCC Geneva May 15, 1989
UCC Paris May 15, 1989
WTO Dec. 13, 1996

Nigeria
UCC Geneva Feb. 14, 1962
Berne Sept. 14, 1993 (Paris)
WTO Jan. 1, 1995

Norway
Berne Apr. 13, 1896 (Paris) [2]
Bilateral July 1, 1905
UCC Geneva Jan. 23, 1963
UCC Paris Aug. 7, 1974
Phonogram Aug. 1, 1978
WTO Jan. 1, 1995

103

Oman
None

Pakistan
Berne July 5, 1948 (Rome) [2]
UCC Geneva Sept. 16, 1955
WTO Jan. 1, 1995

Palau
Unclear

Panama
BAC Nov. 25, 1913
UCC Geneva Oct. 17, 1962
Phonogram June 29, 1974
UCC Paris Sept. 3, 1980
SAT Sept. 25, 1985
Berne Jun. 8, 1996 (Paris)

Papua New Guinea
WTO Jun. 9, 1996

Paraguay
BAC Sept. 20, 1917
UCC Geneva Mar. 11, 1962
Phonogram Feb. 13, 1979
Berne Jan. 2, 1992 (Paris)
WTO Jan. 1, 1995

Peru
BAC Apr. 30, 1920
UCC Geneva Oct. 16, 1963
UCC Paris July 22, 1985
SAT Aug. 7, 1985
Phonogram Aug. 24, 1985
Berne Aug. 20, 1988 (Paris) [2]
WTO Jan. 1, 1995

Philippines
Bilateral Oct. 21, 1948
Berne Aug. 1, 1951 (Brussels) [2]
UCC status undetermined by UNESCO
    (Copyright Office considers that UCC relations
    do not exist.)
WTO Jan. 1, 1995

Poland
Berne Jan. 28, 1920 (Paris) [2]
Bilateral Feb. 16, 1927
UCC Geneva Mar. 9, 1977
UCC Paris Mar. 9, 1977
WTO July 1, 1995

Portugal
Bilateral July 20, 1893
Berne Mar. 29, 1911 (Paris) [2]
UCC Geneva Dec. 25, 1956
UCC Paris July 30, 1981
WTO Jan. 1, 1995

SAT Mar. 11, 1996

Qatar
WTO Jan. 13, 1996

Romania
Berne Jan. 1, 1927 (Rome) [2]
Bilateral May 14, 1928
WTO Jan. 1, 1995
Phonogram Oct. 1, 1998

Russian Federation
UCC Geneva May 27, 1973
SAT Dec. 25, 1991
UCC Paris Mar. 9, 1995
Berne Mar. 13, 1995 (Paris)
Phonogram Mar. 13, 1995

Rwanda
Berne Mar. 1, 1984 (Paris) [2]
UCC Geneva Nov. 10, 1989
UCC Paris Nov. 10, 1989
WTO May 22, 1996

St. Christopher (St. Kitts) and Nevis
Berne Apr. 9, 1995 (Paris) [2]
WTO Feb. 21, 1996

Saint Lucia
Berne Aug. 24, 1993 (Paris) [2]
WTO Jan. 1, 1995

Saint Vincent and the Grenadines
UCC Geneva Apr. 22, 1985
UCC Paris Apr. 22, 1985
WTO Jan. 1, 1995
Berne Aug. 29, 1995 (Paris)

San Marino
None

São Tomé and Príncipe
Unclear

Saudi Arabia
UCC Geneva July 13, 1994
UCC Paris July 13, 1994

Senegal
Berne Aug. 25, 1962 (Paris) [2]
UCC Geneva July 9, 1974
UCC Paris July 10, 1974
WTO Jan. 1, 1995

Seychelles
Unclear

Sierra Leone
WTO July 23, 1995

Singapore
Bilateral May 18, 1987
WTO Jan. 1, 1995
Berne Dec. 21, 1998 (Paris)

Slovakia
UCC Geneva Jan. 6, 1960
UCC Paris Apr. 17, 1980
Berne Jan. 1, 1993 (Paris) [2]
Phonogram Jan. 1, 1993
WTO Jan. 1, 1995

Slovenia
UCC Geneva May 11, 1966
UCC Paris July 10, 1974
Berne June 25, 1991 (Paris) [2]
SAT June 25, 1991
WTO July 30, 1995
Phonogram Oct. 15, 1996

Solomon Islands
WTO July 26, 1996

Somalia
Unclear

South Africa
Bilateral July 1, 1924
Berne Oct. 3, 1928 (Brussels) [2]
WTO Jan. 1, 1995

Soviet Union
(See entry under Russian Federation)

Spain
Berne Dec. 5, 1887 (Paris) [2]
Bilateral July 10, 1895
UCC Geneva Sept. 16, 1955
UCC Paris July 10, 1974
Phonogram Aug. 24, 1974
WTO Jan. 1, 1995

Sri Lanka (formerly Ceylon)
Berne July 20, 1959 (Rome) [2]
UCC Geneva Jan. 25, 1984
UCC Paris Jan. 25, 1984
WTO Jan. 1, 1995

Sudan
Unclear

Suriname
Berne Feb. 23, 1977 (Paris) [2]
WTO Jan. 1, 1995

Swaziland
WTO Jan. 1, 1995
Berne Dec. 14, 1998 (Paris)

Sweden
Berne Aug. 1, 1904 (Paris) [2]
Bilateral June 1, 1911
UCC Geneva July 1, 1961
Phonogram Apr. 18, 1973 [3]
UCC Paris July 10, 1974
WTO Jan. 1, 1995

Switzerland
Berne Dec. 5, 1887 (Paris) [2]
Bilateral July 1, 1891
UCC Geneva Mar. 30, 1956
UCC Paris Sept. 21, 1993
SAT Sept. 24, 1993
Phonogram Sept. 30, 1993
WTO July 1, 1995

Syria
Unclear

Tajikistan
UCC Geneva May 27, 1973

Tanzania
Berne July 25, 1994 (Paris)
WTO Jan. 1, 1995

Thailand
Bilateral Sept. 1, 1921
Berne July 17, 1931 (Paris) [2]
WTO Jan. 1, 1995

Togo
Berne Apr. 30, 1975 (Paris) [2]
WTO May 31, 1995

Tonga
None

Trinidad and Tobago
Berne Aug. 16, 1988 (Paris) [2]
UCC Geneva Aug. 19, 1988
UCC Paris Aug. 19, 1988
Phonogram Oct. 1, 1988
WTO Mar. 1, 1995
SAT Nov. 1, 1996

Tunisia
Berne Dec. 5, 1887 (Paris) [2]
UCC Geneva June 19, 1969
UCC Paris June 10, 1975
WTO Mar. 29, 1995

Turkey
Berne Jan. 1, 1952 (Paris) [2]
WTO Mar. 26, 1995

Tuvalu
Unclear

Uganda
WTO Jan. 1, 1995

Ukraine
UCC Geneva May 27, 1973
Berne Oct. 25, 1995 (Paris)

United Arab Emirates
WTO Apr. 10, 1996

United Kingdom
Berne Dec. 5, 1887 (Paris) [2]
Bilateral July 1, 1891
UCC Geneva Sept. 27, 1957
Phonogram Apr. 18, 1973 [3]
UCC Paris July 10, 1974
WTO Jan. 1, 1995

Upper Volta
(See entry under Burkina Faso)

Uruguay
BAC Dec. 17, 1919
Berne July 10, 1967 (Paris) [2]
Phonogram Jan. 18, 1983
UCC Geneva Apr. 12, 1993
UCC Paris Apr. 12, 1993
WTO Jan. 1, 1995

Vanuatu
Unclear

Vatican City (Holy See)
Berne Sept. 12, 1935 (Paris) [2]
UCC Geneva Oct. 5, 1955
Phonogram July 18, 1977
UCC Paris May 6, 1980

Venezuela
UCC Geneva Sept. 30, 1966
Phonogram Nov. 18, 1982
Berne Dec. 30, 1982 (Paris) [2]
WTO Jan. 1, 1995
UCC Paris Feb 11, 1997

Vietnam
Bilateral Dec. 23, 1998 [13]

Western Samoa
Unclear

Yemen (Aden)
Unclear

Yemen (San'a)
None

Yugoslavia
Berne June 17, 1930 (Paris) [2]
UCC Geneva May 11, 1966
UCC Paris July 10, 1974
SAT Aug. 25, 1979 [4]

Zaire
(See entry under Democratic
Republic of Congo)

Zambia
UCC Geneva June 1, 1965
Berne Jan. 2, 1992 (Paris) [2]
WTO Jan. 1, 1995

Zimbabwe
Berne Apr. 18, 1980 (Rome) [2]
WTO Mar. 3, 1995

STATUTORY PROVISIONS

The copyright law embodied in title 17 of the United States Code was completely revised by the Act of October 19, 1976 (Public Law 94-553, 90 Stat. 2541) which became fully effective on January 1, 1978. Reprinted below is section 104 of that Act, as amended by the Act of October 31, 1988 (Public Law 100-568, 102 Stat. 2853, 2855).

§ 104. Subject matter of copyright: National origin

(a) UNPUBLISHED WORKS.—The works specified by sections 102 and 108, while unpublished, are subject to protection under this title without regard to the nationality or domicile of the author.

(b) PUBLISHED WORKS.—The works specified by sections 102 and 103, when published, are subject to protection under this title if—

(1) on the date of first publication, one or more of the authors is a national or domiciliary of the United States, or is a national, domiciliary, or sovereign authority of a foreign nation that is a party to a copyright treaty to which the United States is also a party, or is a stateless person, wherever that person may be domiciled; or

(2) the work is first published in the United States or in a foreign nation that, on the date of first publication, is a party to the Universal Copyright Convention; or

(3) the work is first published by the United Nations or any of its specialized agencies, or by the Organization of American States; or

(4) the work is a Berne Convention work; or

(5) the work comes within the scope of a Presidential proclamation. Whenever the President finds that a particular foreign nation extends, to works by authors

who are nationals or domiciliaries of the United States or to works that are first published in the United States, copyright protection on substantially the same basis as that on which the foreign nation extends protection to works of its own nationals and domiciliaries and works first published in that nation, the President may by proclamation extend protection under this title to works of which one or more of the authors is, on the date of first publication, a national, domiciliary, or sovereign authority of that nation, or which was first published in that nation. The President may revise, suspend, or revoke any such proclamation or impose any conditions or limitations on protection under a proclamation.

(c) EFFECT OF BERNE CONVENTION.—No right or interest in a work eligible for protection under this title may be claimed by virtue of, or in reliance upon, the provisions of the Berne Convention, or the adherence of the United States thereto. Any rights in a work eligible for protection under this title that derive from this title, other Federal or State statutes, or the common law, shall not be expanded or reduced by virtue of, or in reliance upon, the provisions of the Berne Convention, or the adherence of the United States thereto.

NOTE: Subsequent amendments to the Copyright Act of October 19, 1976, included the North American Free Trade Agreement Implementation Act of December 8, 1993, Pub. L. 103-182, 107 Stat. 2057, and the Uruguay Round Agreements Act of December 8, 1994, Pub. L. 103-465, 108 Stat. 4809. The latter Act amended section 104A of the Copyright Act in its entirety so as to provide for the automatic restoration of copyright in certain foreign works that are in the public domain in the United States but are protected by copyright or neighboring rights in their country of origin. The effective date for restoration of copyright in such foreign works is January 1, 1996.

SOME POINTS TO REMEMBER REGARDING THE INTERNATIONAL PROTECTION OF LITERARY AND ARTISTIC WORKS

There is no such thing as an "international copyright" that will automatically protect an author's writings throughout the world. Protection against unauthorized use in a particular country basically depends on the national laws of that country. However, most countries offer protection to foreign works under certain conditions which have been greatly simplified by international copyright treaties and conventions. There are two principal international copyright conventions, the Berne Union for the Protection of Literary and Artistic Property (Berne Convention) and the Universal Copyright Convention (UCC).

An author who wishes copyright protection for his or her work in a particular country should first determine the extent of the protection available to works of foreign authors in that country. If possible, this should be done before the work is published anywhere, because protection may depend on the facts existing at the time of first publication.

If the country in which protection is sought is a party to one of the international copyright conventions, the work generally may be protected by complying with the conditions of that convention. Even if the work cannot be brought under an international convention, protection under the specific provisions of the country's national laws may still be possible. There are, however, some countries that offer little or no copyright protection to any foreign works. For current information on the requirements and protection provided by other countries, it may be advisable to consult an expert familiar with foreign copyright laws. The U.S. Copyright Office is not permitted to recommend agents or attorneys or to give legal advice on foreign laws.

Footnotes

[1] "Paris" means the Berne Convention for the Protection of Literary and Artistic Works as revised at Paris on July 24, 1971 (Paris Act); "Stockholm" means the said Convention as revised at Stockholm on July 14, 1967 (Stockholm Act); "Brussels" means the said Convention as revised at Brussels on June 26, 1948 (Brussels Act); "Rome" means the said Convention as revised at Rome on June 2, 1928 (Rome Act); "Berlin" means the said Convention as revised at Berlin on November 13, 1908 (Berlin Act). NOTE: In each case the reference to Act signifies adherence to the substantive provisions of such Act only, e.g., Articles 1 to 21 and the Appendix of the Paris Act. Articles 22 to 38 deal with administration and structure.

[2] The Berne Convention for the Protection of Literary and Artistic Works of September 9, 1886, as revised at Paris on July 24, 1971, did not enter into force with respect to the United States until March 1, 1989.

[3] The Convention for the Protection of Producers of Phonograms Against Unauthorized Duplication of Their Phonograms done at Geneva on October 29, 1971, did not enter into force with respect to the United States until March 10, 1974.

[4] The Convention Relating to the Distribution of Programme-Carrying Signals Transmitted by Satellite done at Brussels on May 21, 1974, did not enter into force with respect to the United States until March 7, 1985.

[5] The government of the People's Republic of China views this treaty as not binding on the PRC. In the

territory administered by the authorities on Taiwan the treaty is considered to be in force.

[6] This country became a party to the Mexico City Convention, 1902, effective June 30, 1908, to which the United States also became a party, effective on the same date. As regards copyright relations with the United States, this Convention is considered to have been superseded by adherence of this country and the United States to the Buenos Aires Convention of 1910.

[7] Date on which the accession by the German Empire became effective.

[8] Bilateral copyright relations between Japan and the United States, which were formulated effective May 10, 1906, are considered to have been abrogated and superseded by the adherence of Japan to the UCC Geneva, effective April 28, 1956.

[9] Bilateral copyright relations between the People's Republic of China and the United States of America were established, effective March 17, 1992, by a Presidential Proclamation of the same date, under the authority of section 104 of title 17 of the United States Code, as amended by the Act of October 31, 1988 (Public Law 100-568, 102 Stat. 2853, 2855).

[10] The dates of adherence by Germany to multilateral treaties include adherence by the Federal Republic of Germany when that country was divided into the Federal Republic of Germany and the German Democratic Republic. However, through the accession, effective October 3, 1990, of the German Democratic Republic to the Federal Republic of Germany, in accordance with the German Unification Treaty of August 31, 1990, the German Democratic Republic ceased, on the said date, to be a sovereign state. Previously, the German Democratic Republic had become party to the Paris Act of the Berne Convention for the Protection of Literary and Artistic Works on February 18, 1978, but ceased to be a party to the said Convention on October 3, 1990. The German Democratic Republic had also been a member of the Universal Copyright Convention, having become party to the Geneva text of the said Convention on October 5, 1973, and party to the revised Paris text of the same Convention on December 10, 1980.

[11] See also Czech Republic and Slovakia.

[12] Prior to the return of Hong Kong to China, bilateral copyright relations existed with Hong Kong through the United Kingdom (from August 1, 1973), and Phonogram Convention Membership existed through the United Kingdom (from March 4, 1975.)

[13] Bilateral copyright relations between the Socialist Republic of Vietnam and the United States were established effective   December 23, 1998, by Presidential Proclamation No. 7161 of that same state, at 63 Fed. Reg. 71571 (1998), under the authority of sections 104(b)(5) and 104A(g) of title 17 of the United States Code, as amended.

Library of Congress *U.S. Copyright Office *101 Independence Ave., S.E.• Washington D.C. 20559-6000

http://ww,loc.gov/copyright

May 1999-5,000   U.S. Government Printing Office 1999-454-879/80.075

APPENDIX G
SAMPLE FILLED-IN FORMS

The following pages contain selected filled-in copyright forms mentioned throughout this book. Use these samples when filling in the blanks in Appendix H. The form number of each form corresponds with the form numbers in Appendix H.

The instructions provided with each form are in Appendix H and are very easy to understand. Be sure to read them thoroughly to avoid having your application rejected.

FORM TX
For a Nondramatic Literary Work
UNITED STATES COPYRIGHT OFFICE

REGISTRATION NUMBER

	TX	TXU

EFFECTIVE DATE OF REGISTRATION

Month	Day	Year

DO NOT WRITE ABOVE THIS LINE. IF YOU NEED MORE SPACE, USE A SEPARATE CONTINUATION SHEET.

1

TITLE OF THIS WORK ▼

THE JOY OF SLEEPING

PREVIOUS OR ALTERNATIVE TITLES ▼

PUBLICATION AS A CONTRIBUTION If this work was published as a contribution to a periodical, serial, or collection, give information about the collective work in which the contribution appeared.   **Title of Collective Work ▼**

If published in a periodical or serial give: **Volume ▼**   **Number ▼**   **Issue Date ▼**   **On Pages ▼**

2

a

NAME OF AUTHOR ▼

RIP VAN WINKLE

DATES OF BIRTH AND DEATH
Year Born ▼   Year Died ▼
1899

Was this contribution to the work a "work made for hire"?
☐ Yes
☒ No

AUTHOR'S NATIONALITY OR DOMICILE
Name of Country
OR { Citizen of ▶ U.S.A.
{ Domiciled in ▶

WAS THIS AUTHOR'S CONTRIBUTION TO THE WORK
Anonymous? ☐ Yes ☒ No
Pseudonymous? ☐ Yes ☒ No
If the answer to either of these questions is "Yes," see detailed instructions.

NATURE OF AUTHORSHIP Briefly describe nature of material created by this author in which copyright is claimed. ▼ entire work

NOTE

Under the law, the "author" of a "work made for hire" is generally the employer, not the employee (see instructions). For any part of this work that was "made for hire" check "Yes" in the space provided, give the employer (or other person for whom the work was prepared) as "Author" of that part, and leave the space for dates of birth and death blank.

b

NAME OF AUTHOR ▼

DATES OF BIRTH AND DEATH
Year Born ▼   Year Died ▼

Was this contribution to the work a "work made for hire"?
☐ Yes
☐ No

AUTHOR'S NATIONALITY OR DOMICILE
Name of Country
OR { Citizen of ▶
{ Domiciled in ▶

WAS THIS AUTHOR'S CONTRIBUTION TO THE WORK
Anonymous? ☐ Yes ☐ No
Pseudonymous? ☐ Yes ☐ No
If the answer to either of these questions is "Yes," see detailed instructions.

NATURE OF AUTHORSHIP Briefly describe nature of material created by this author in which copyright is claimed. ▼

c

NAME OF AUTHOR ▼

DATES OF BIRTH AND DEATH
Year Born ▼   Year Died ▼

Was this contribution to the work a "work made for hire"?
☐ Yes
☐ No

AUTHOR'S NATIONALITY OR DOMICILE
Name of Country
OR { Citizen of ▶
{ Domiciled in ▶

WAS THIS AUTHOR'S CONTRIBUTION TO THE WORK
Anonymous? ☐ Yes ☐ No
Pseudonymous? ☐ Yes ☐ No
If the answer to either of these questions is "Yes," see detailed instructions.

NATURE OF AUTHORSHIP Briefly describe nature of material created by this author in which copyright is claimed. ▼

3

a

YEAR IN WHICH CREATION OF THIS WORK WAS COMPLETED This information must be given in all cases.
1999 ◀ Year

b

DATE AND NATION OF FIRST PUBLICATION OF THIS PARTICULAR WORK
Complete this information ONLY if this work has been published.
Month ▶ JUNE Day ▶ 20 Year ▶ 1999
U.S.A. ◀ Nation

4

See instructions before completing this space.

COPYRIGHT CLAIMANT(S) Name and address must be given even if the claimant is the same as the author given in space 2. ▼

RIP VAN WINKLE
P.O. BOX 25
CLEARWATER, FL 33757

TRANSFER If the claimant(s) named here in space 4 is (are) different from the author(s) named in space 2, give a brief statement of how the claimant(s) obtained ownership of the copyright. ▼

DO NOT WRITE HERE — OFFICE USE ONLY

APPLICATION RECEIVED

ONE DEPOSIT RECEIVED

TWO DEPOSITS RECEIVED

FUNDS RECEIVED

MORE ON BACK ▶ • Complete all applicable spaces (numbers 5-9) on the reverse side of this page.
• See detailed instructions.   • Sign the form at line 8.

DO NOT WRITE HERE
Page 1 of _____ pages

EXAMINED BY _____

CHECKED BY _____

☐ CORRESPONDENCE
   Yes

DO NOT WRITE ABOVE THIS LINE. IF YOU NEED MORE SPACE, USE A SEPARATE CONTINUATION SHEET.

PREVIOUS REGISTRATION Has registration for this work, or for an earlier version of this work, already been made in the Copyright Office?

☐ **Yes** ☐ **No** If your answer is "Yes," why is another registration being sought? (Check appropriate box.) ▼

a. ☐ This is the first published edition of a work previously registered in unpublished form.

b. ☐ This is the first application submitted by this author as copyright claimant.

c. ☐ This is a changed version of the work, as shown by space 6 on this application.

If your answer is "Yes," give: **Previous Registration Number** ▶   **Year of Registration** ▶

5

DERIVATIVE WORK OR COMPILATION

Preexisting Material Identify any preexisting work or works that this work is based on or incorporates. ▼

a

6

Material Added to This Work Give a brief, general statement of the material that has been added to this work and in which copyright is claimed. ▼

b

See instructions before completing this space.

DEPOSIT ACCOUNT If the registration fee is to be charged to a Deposit Account established in the Copyright Office, give name and number of Account.

Name ▼   **Account Number** ▼

a

7

CORRESPONDENCE Give name and address to which correspondence about this application should be sent. Name/Address/Apt/City/State/ZIP ▼

RIP VAN WINKLE
P.O. BOX 25
CLEARWATER, FL 33757

b

Area code and daytime telephone number ▶ 727-581-0909   Fax number ▶ 727-587-4567

Email ▶ ripvan@earthlink.net

CERTIFICATION* I, the undersigned, hereby certify that I am the

Check only one ▶

☒ author
☐ other copyright claimant
☐ owner of exclusive right(s)
☐ authorized agent of _____

Name of author or other copyright claimant, or owner of exclusive right(s) ▲

of the work identified in this application and that the statements made by me in this application are correct to the best of my knowledge.

8

Typed or printed name and date ▼ If this application gives a date of publication in space 3, do not sign and submit it before that date.

Rip Van Winkle   Date ▶ June 23, 1999

Handwritten signature (X) ▼

X _____ *Rip Van Winkle* _____

Certificate will be mailed in window envelope to this address:

Name ▼
RIP VAN WINKLE

Number/Street/Apt ▼
P.O. BOX 25

City/State/ZIP ▼
CLEARWATER, FL 33757

YOU MUST:
• Complete all necessary spaces
• Sign your application in space 8

SEND ALL 3 ELEMENTS IN THE SAME PACKAGE:
1. Application form
2. Nonrefundable filing fee in check or money order payable to *Register of Copyrights*
3. Deposit material

MAIL TO:
Library of Congress
Copyright Office
101 Independence Avenue, S.E.
Washington, D.C. 20559-6000

As of July 1, 1999, the filing fee for Form TX is $30.

9

June 1999—200,000   ♻ PRINTED ON RECYCLED PAPER   ☆U.S. GOVERNMENT PRINTING OFFICE: 1999-454-879/49
WEB REV: June 1999

FORM SE

For a Serial
UNITED STATES COPYRIGHT OFFICE

REGISTRATION NUMBER

_____ U

EFFECTIVE DATE OF REGISTRATION

_____

Month   Day   Year

DO NOT WRITE ABOVE THIS LINE. IF YOU NEED MORE SPACE, USE A SEPARATE CONTINUATION SHEET.

1 TITLE OF THIS SERIAL ▼

Manics Weekly

Volume ▼	Number ▼	Date on Copies ▼	Frequency of Publication ▼

PREVIOUS OR ALTERNATIVE TITLES ▼

2

a

NAME OF AUTHOR ▼

Manics, Inc.

DATES OF BIRTH AND DEATH
Year Born ▼   Year Died ▼

Was this contribution to the work a "work made for hire"?
[X] Yes
[ ] No

AUTHOR'S NATIONALITY OR DOMICILE
Name of Country
OR { Citizen of ▶ _____ U.S.A
{ Domiciled in ▶ _____

WAS THIS AUTHOR'S CONTRIBUTION TO THE WORK
Anonymous?   [ ] Yes [X] No
Pseudonymous? [ ] Yes [X] No

If the answer to either of these questions is "Yes," see detailed instructions.

NATURE OF AUTHORSHIP Briefly describe nature of material created by this author in which copyright is claimed. ▼
[X] Collective Work   Other:

NOTE

Under the law, the "author" of a "work made for hire" is generally the employer, not the employee (see instructions). For any part of this work that was "made for hire" check "Yes" in the space provided, give the employer (or other person for whom the work was prepared) as "Author" of that part, and leave the space for dates of birth and death blank.

b

NAME OF AUTHOR ▼

DATES OF BIRTH AND DEATH
Year Born ▼   Year Died ▼

Was this contribution to the work a "work made for hire"?
[ ] Yes
[ ] No

AUTHOR'S NATIONALITY OR DOMICILE
Name of Country
OR { Citizen of ▶ _____
{ Domiciled in ▶ _____

WAS THIS AUTHOR'S CONTRIBUTION TO THE WORK
Anonymous?   [ ] Yes [ ] No
Pseudonymous? [ ] Yes [ ] No

If the answer to either of these questions is "Yes," see detailed instructions.

NATURE OF AUTHORSHIP Briefly describe nature of material created by this author in which copyright is claimed. ▼
[ ] Collective Work   Other:

c

NAME OF AUTHOR ▼

DATES OF BIRTH AND DEATH
Year Born ▼   Year Died ▼

Was this contribution to the work a "work made for hire"?
[ ] Yes
[ ] No

AUTHOR'S NATIONALITY OR DOMICILE
Name of Country
OR { Citizen of ▶ _____
{ Domiciled in ▶ _____

WAS THIS AUTHOR'S CONTRIBUTION TO THE WORK
Anonymous?   [ ] Yes [ ] No
Pseudonymous? [ ] Yes [ ] No

If the answer to either of these questions is "Yes," see detailed instructions.

NATURE OF AUTHORSHIP Briefly describe nature of material created by this author in which copyright is claimed. ▼
[ ] Collective Work   Other:

3

a YEAR IN WHICH CREATION OF THIS ISSUE WAS COMPLETED This information must be given in all cases.
2003 ◀ Year

b DATE AND NATION OF FIRST PUBLICATION OF THIS PARTICULAR ISSUE Complete this information ONLY if this work has been published.
Month ▶ April   Day ▶ 1   Year ▶ 2003
U.S.A.   ◀ Nation

4

COPYRIGHT CLAIMANT(S) Name and address must be given even if the claimant is the same as the author given in space 2. ▼

Manics, Inc.
1432 Bananas Lane
Paris, TX 21005

See instructions before completing this space.

TRANSFER If the claimant(s) named here in space 4 is (are) different from the author(s) named in space 2, give a brief statement of how the claimant(s) obtained ownership of the copyright. ▼

DO NOT WRITE HERE OFFICE USE ONLY

APPLICATION RECEIVED
_____
ONE DEPOSIT RECEIVED
_____
TWO DEPOSITS RECEIVED
_____
FUNDS RECEIVED
_____

MORE ON BACK ▶ • Complete all applicable spaces (numbers 5-9) on the reverse side of this page.
• See detailed instructions.   • Sign the form at line 8.

DO NOT WRITE HERE

Page 1 of _____ pages

DO NOT WRITE ABOVE THIS LINE. IF YOU NEED MORE SPACE, USE A SEPARATE CONTINUATION SHEET.

PREVIOUS REGISTRATION Has registration for this work, or for an earlier version of this work, already been made in the Copyright Office?

☐ **Yes** ☐ **No** If your answer is "Yes," why is another registration being sought? (Check appropriate box.) ▼

a. ☐ This is the first published edition of a work previously registered in unpublished form.

b. ☐ This is the first application submitted by this author as copyright claimant.

c. ☐ This is a changed version of the work, as shown by space 6 on this application.

If your answer is "Yes," give: **Previous Registration Number** ▼   **Year of Registration** ▼

5

DERIVATIVE WORK OR COMPILATION   Complete both space 6a and 6b for a derivative work; complete only 6b for a compilation.
Preexisting Material Identify any preexisting work or works that this work is based on or incorporates. ▼

a

6

Material Added to This Work Give a brief, general statement of the material that has been added to this work and in which copyright is claimed. ▼

b

See instructions
before completing
this space.

DEPOSIT ACCOUNT If the registration fee is to be charged to a Deposit Account established in the Copyright Office, give name and number of Account.
Name ▼   **Account Number** ▼

a

7

CORRESPONDENCE Give name and address to which correspondence about this application should be sent.   Name/Address/Apt/City/State/ZIP ▼

Manics, Inc.
1432 Bananas Lane
Paris, TX 21005

Area code and telephone number ▶ 815-000-4321

Fax number ▶ 815-001-3456

Email ▶ manics.weekly@aol.com

b

CERTIFICATION* I, the undersigned, hereby certify that I am the

Check only one ▶ {
☒ author
☐ other copyright claimant
☐ owner of exclusive right(s)
☐ authorized agent of _____

of the work identified in this application and that the statements made
by me in this application are correct to the best of my knowledge.

Name of author or other copyright claimant, or owner of exclusive right(s) ▲

8

Typed or printed name and date ▼ If this application gives a date of publication in space 3, do not sign and submit it before that date.

George Benuts, president   Date ▶ April 8, 2003

☞ Handwritten signature (X) ▼

X _____ *George Benuts, president* _____

**Certificate
will be
mailed in
window
envelope
to this
address:**

Name ▼

Manics, Inc.

Number/Street/Apt ▼

1432 Bananas Lane

City/State/ZIP ▼

Paris, TX 21005

9

*17 U.S.C. § 506(e): Any person who knowingly makes a false representation of a material fact in the application for copyright registration provided for by section 409, or in any written statement filed in connection
with the application, shall be fined not more than $2,500.

June 1999—50,000
WEB REV: June 1999

♻ PRINTED ON RECYCLED PAPER

☆U.S. GOVERNMENT PRINTING OFFICE: 1999-454-879/59

FORM PA
For a Work of the Performing Arts
UNITED STATES COPYRIGHT OFFICE

REGISTRATION NUMBER

PA	PAU

EFFECTIVE DATE OF REGISTRATION

Month	Day	Year

DO NOT WRITE ABOVE THIS LINE. IF YOU NEED MORE SPACE, USE A SEPARATE CONTINUATION SHEET.

1

TITLE OF THIS WORK ▼

Amblin' Stephen

PREVIOUS OR ALTERNATIVE TITLES ▼

NATURE OF THIS WORK ▼ See instructions

motion picture

2

a

NAME OF AUTHOR ▼

Maddie Ford

DATES OF BIRTH AND DEATH
Year Born ▼ 1969   Year Died ▼

Was this contribution to the work a "work made for hire"?
☒ Yes
☐ No

AUTHOR'S NATIONALITY OR DOMICILE
Name of Country
OR { Citizen of ▶ U.S.A.
{ Domiciled in ▶

WAS THIS AUTHOR'S CONTRIBUTION TO THE WORK
Anonymous? ☐ Yes ☒ No
Pseudonymous? ☐ Yes ☒ No
If the answer to either of these questions is "Yes," see detailed instructions.

NATURE OF AUTHORSHIP Briefly describe nature of material created by this author in which copyright is claimed. ▼   Screenplay

b

NAME OF AUTHOR ▼

Belinda Fisher

DATES OF BIRTH AND DEATH
Year Born ▼ 1969   Year Died ▼

Was this contribution to the work a "work made for hire"?
☒ Yes
☐ No

AUTHOR'S NATIONALITY OR DOMICILE
Name of Country
OR { Citizen of ▶ U.S.A.
{ Domiciled in ▶

WAS THIS AUTHOR'S CONTRIBUTION TO THE WORK
Anonymous? ☐ Yes ☒ No
Pseudonymous? ☐ Yes ☒ No
If the answer to either of these questions is "Yes," see detailed instructions.

NATURE OF AUTHORSHIP Briefly describe nature of material created by this author in which copyright is claimed. ▼   Author of Music

c

NAME OF AUTHOR ▼

DATES OF BIRTH AND DEATH
Year Born ▼   Year Died ▼

Was this contribution to the work a "work made for hire"?
☐ Yes
☐ No

AUTHOR'S NATIONALITY OR DOMICILE
Name of Country
OR { Citizen of ▶
{ Domiciled in ▶

WAS THIS AUTHOR'S CONTRIBUTION TO THE WORK
Anonymous? ☐ Yes ☐ No
Pseudonymous? ☐ Yes ☐ No
If the answer to either of these questions is "Yes," see detailed instructions.

NATURE OF AUTHORSHIP Briefly describe nature of material created by this author in which copyright is claimed. ▼

NOTE

Under the law, the "author" of a "work made for hire" is generally the employer, not the employee (see instructions). For any part of this work that was "made for hire" check "Yes" in the space provided, give the employer (or other person for whom the work was prepared) as "Author" of that part, and leave the space for dates of birth and death blank.

3

a

YEAR IN WHICH CREATION OF THIS WORK WAS COMPLETED This information must be given in all cases.
2002 ◀ Year

b

DATE AND NATION OF FIRST PUBLICATION OF THIS PARTICULAR WORK
Complete this information ONLY if this work has been published.
Month ▶ August   Day ▶ 14   Year ▶ 2002
U.S.A. ◀ Nation

4

COPYRIGHT CLAIMANT(S) Name and address must be given even if the claimant is the same as the author given in space 2. ▼

Maddie Ford
1138 Hamill Ave.
San Diego, CA 95214

Belinda Fisher
408 Lukas Dr.
San Diego, CA 95214

See instructions before completing this space.

TRANSFER If the claimant(s) named here in space 4 is (are) different from the author(s) named in space 2, give a brief statement of how the claimant(s) obtained ownership of the copyright. ▼

APPLICATION RECEIVED
ONE DEPOSIT RECEIVED
TWO DEPOSITS RECEIVED
FUNDS RECEIVED

DO NOT WRITE HERE
OFFICE USE ONLY

MORE ON BACK ▶
• Complete all applicable spaces (numbers 5-9) on the reverse side of this page.
• See detailed instructions.   • Sign the form at line 8.

DO NOT WRITE HERE
Page 1 of _____ pages

DO NOT WRITE ABOVE THIS LINE. IF YOU NEED MORE SPACE, USE A SEPARATE CONTINUATION SHEET.

PREVIOUS REGISTRATION Has registration for this work, or for an earlier version of this work, already been made in the Copyright Office?

☐ **Yes** ☐ **No** If your answer is "Yes," why is another registration being sought? (Check appropriate box.) ▼ If your answer is "no," go to space 7.

a. ☐ This is the first published edition of a work previously registered in unpublished form.

b. ☐ This is the first application submitted by this author as copyright claimant.

c. ☐ This is a changed version of the work, as shown by space 6 on this application.

If your answer is "Yes," give: **Previous Registration Number** ▼   **Year of Registration** ▼

5

DERIVATIVE WORK OR COMPILATION Complete both space 6a and 6b for a derivative work; complete only 6b for a compilation.

Preexisting Material Identify any preexisting work or works that this work is based on or incorporates. ▼

Material Added to This Work Give a brief, general statement of the material that has been added to this work and in which copyright is claimed. ▼

a
b

6

See instructions before completing this space.

DEPOSIT ACCOUNT If the registration fee is to be charged to a Deposit Account established in the Copyright Office, give name and number of Account.

Name ▼   **Account Number** ▼

CORRESPONDENCE Give name and address to which correspondence about this application should be sent.   Name/Address/Apt/City/State/ZIP ▼

Maddie Ford
1138 Hamill Ave.
San Diego, CA 95214

Area code and daytime telephone number ▶ (214)567-8900   Fax number ▶ (214)568-7690

Email ▶ 2raiders@sandiego.rr.com

a
b

7

CERTIFICATION* I, the undersigned, hereby certify that I am the

Check only one ▶
{
☒ author
☐ other copyright claimant
☐ owner of exclusive right(s)
☐ authorized agent of _____
Name of author or other copyright claimant, or owner of exclusive right(s) ▲
}

of the work identified in this application and that the statements made by me in this application are correct to the best of my knowledge.

8

Typed or printed name and date ▼ If this application gives a date of publication in space 3, do not sign and submit it before that date.

Maddie Ford   Date ▶ 8/16/02

Handwritten signature (X) ▼

☞   x _____ *Maddie Ford* _____

Certificate will be mailed in window envelope to this address:

Name ▼
Maddie Ford

Number/Street/Apt ▼
1138 Hamill Ave.

City/State/ZIP ▼
San Diego, CA 95214

YOU MUST:
• Complete all necessary spaces
• Sign your application in space 8

SEND ALL 3 ELEMENTS IN THE SAME PACKAGE:
1. Application form
2. Nonrefundable filing fee in check or money order payable to *Register of Copyrights*
3. Deposit material

MAIL TO:
Library of Congress
Copyright Office
101 Independence Avenue, S.E.
Washington, D.C. 20559-6000

As of July 1, 1999, the filing fee for Form PA is $30.

9

FORM VA

For a Work of the Visual Arts
UNITED STATES COPYRIGHT OFFICE

REGISTRATION NUMBER

_____

VA   VAU

EFFECTIVE DATE OF REGISTRATION

_____

| Month | Day | Year |

DO NOT WRITE ABOVE THIS LINE. IF YOU NEED MORE SPACE, USE A SEPARATE CONTINUATION SHEET.

1

TITLE OF THIS WORK ▼

Warhole with Toast

NATURE OF THIS WORK ▼ See instructions

mixed media

PREVIOUS OR ALTERNATIVE TITLES ▼

Publication as a Contribution If this work was published as a contribution to a periodical, serial, or collection, give information about the collective work in which the contribution appeared.　**Title of Collective Work ▼**

If published in a periodical or serial give:　**Volume ▼**　　**Number ▼**　　**Issue Date ▼**　　**On Pages ▼**

2

NOTE

Under the law, the "author" of a "work made for hire" is generally the employer, not the employee (see instructions). For any part of this work that was "made for hire" check "Yes" in the space provided, give the employer (or other person for whom the work was prepared) as "Author" of that part, and leave the space for dates of birth and death blank.

a **NAME OF AUTHOR ▼**

Thomas Fiennes

DATES OF BIRTH AND DEATH
Year Born ▼　　Year Died ▼
1970

Was this contribution to the work a "work made for hire"?
☐ Yes
☒ No

Author's Nationality or Domicile
Name of Country
OR { Citizen of ▶ U.S.A
Domiciled in ▶ U.S.A

Was This Author's Contribution to the Work
Anonymous?　☐ Yes　☒ No
Pseudonymous?　☐ Yes　☒ No

If the answer to either of these questions is "Yes," see detailed instructions.

NATURE OF AUTHORSHIP Check appropriate box(es). **See instructions**
☐ 3-Dimensional sculpture　☐ Map　☐ Technical drawing
☒ 2-Dimensional artwork　☐ Photograph　☐ Text
☐ Reproduction of work of art　☐ Jewelry design　☐ Architectural work

b **NAME OF AUTHOR ▼**

DATES OF BIRTH AND DEATH
Year Born ▼　　Year Died ▼

Was this contribution to the work a "work made for hire"?
☐ Yes
☐ No

Author's Nationality or Domicile
Name of Country
OR { Citizen of ▶
Domiciled in ▶

Was This Author's Contribution to the Work
Anonymous?　☐ Yes　☐ No
Pseudonymous?　☐ Yes　☐ No

If the answer to either of these questions is "Yes," see detailed instructions.

NATURE OF AUTHORSHIP Check appropriate box(es). **See instructions**
☐ 3-Dimensional sculpture　☐ Map　☐ Technical drawing
☐ 2-Dimensional artwork　☐ Photograph　☐ Text
☐ Reproduction of work of art　☐ Jewelry design　☐ Architectural work

3

a **Year in Which Creation of This Work Was Completed**
2002 ◀ Year
This information must be given in all cases.

b **Date and Nation of First Publication of This Particular Work**
Complete this information ONLY if this work has been published.
Month ▶ September Day ▶ 17 Year ▶ 2002
U.S.A. ◀ Nation

4

See instructions before completing this space.

COPYRIGHT CLAIMANT(S) Name and address must be given even if the claimant is the same as the author given in space 2. ▼

Thomas Fiennes
1234 Jones St.
Raphael, NM 00000

Transfer If the claimant(s) named here in space 4 is (are) different from the author(s) named in space 2, give a brief statement of how the claimant(s) obtained ownership of the copyright. ▼

APPLICATION RECEIVED

ONE DEPOSIT RECEIVED

TWO DEPOSITS RECEIVED

FUNDS RECEIVED

MORE ON BACK ▶　• Complete all applicable spaces (numbers 5-9) on the reverse side of this page.
• See detailed instructions.　　• Sign the form at line 8.

DO NOT WRITE HERE
Page 1 of _____ pages

EXAMINED BY

CHECKED BY

☐ CORRESPONDENCE
Yes

FORM VA

FOR
COPYRIGHT
OFFICE
USE
ONLY

DO NOT WRITE ABOVE THIS LINE. IF YOU NEED MORE SPACE, USE A SEPARATE CONTINUATION SHEET.

PREVIOUS REGISTRATION Has registration for this work, or for an earlier version of this work, already been made in the Copyright Office?

☐ **Yes** ☐ **No** If your answer is "Yes," why is another registration being sought? (Check appropriate box.) ▼

a. ☐ This is the first published edition of a work previously registered in unpublished form.

b. ☐ This is the first application submitted by this author as copyright claimant.

c. ☐ This is a changed version of the work, as shown by space 6 on this application.

If your answer is "Yes," give: **Previous Registration Number** ▼   **Year of Registration** ▼

5

DERIVATIVE WORK OR COMPILATION Complete both space 6a and 6b for a derivative work; complete only 6b for a compilation.
a. Preexisting Material Identify any preexisting work or works that this work is based on or incorporates. ▼

b. Material Added to This Work Give a brief, general statement of the material that has been added to this work and in which copyright is claimed. ▼

6

a
See instructions
before completing
this space.

b

DEPOSIT ACCOUNT If the registration fee is to be charged to a Deposit Account established in the Copyright Office, give name and number of Account.
Name ▼   **Account Number** ▼

7

a

CORRESPONDENCE Give name and address to which correspondence about this application should be sent.   Name/Address/Apt/City/State/ZIP ▼

Thomas Fiennes
1234 Jones St.
Raphael, NM 00000

b

Area code and daytime telephone number ▶ (985) 709-0976   Fax number ▶ (985) 710-9696

Email ▶ warhole2pollek@gte.net

CERTIFICATION* I, the undersigned, hereby certify that I am the

check only one ▶ {
☒ author
☐ other copyright claimant
☐ owner of exclusive right(s)
☐ authorized agent of _____
                        Name of author or other copyright claimant, or owner of exclusive right(s) ▲

8

of the work identified in this application and that the statements made by me in this application are correct to the best of my knowledge.

Typed or printed name and date ▼ If this application gives a date of publication in space 3, do not sign and submit it before that date.

Thomas Fiennes   Date ▶ 9/17/02

Handwritten signature (X) ▼

☞ X _____ *Thomas Fiennes*

Certificate will be mailed in window envelope to this address:	Name ▼ Thomas Fiennes Number/Street/Apt ▼ 1234 Jones St. City/State/ZIP ▼ Raphael, NM 00000

YOU MUST:
• Complete all necessary spaces
• Sign your application in space 8

SEND ALL 3 ELEMENTS IN THE SAME PACKAGE:
1. Application form
2. Nonrefundable filing fee in check or money order payable to *Register of Copyrights*
3. Deposit material

As of July 1, 1999, the filing fee for Form VA is $30.

MAIL TO:
Library of Congress
Copyright Office
101 Independence Avenue, S.E.
Washington, D.C. 20559-6000

9

FORM SR

For a Sound Recording
UNITED STATES COPYRIGHT OFFICE

REGISTRATION NUMBER

_____

SR   SRU

EFFECTIVE DATE OF REGISTRATION

Month   Day   Year

DO NOT WRITE ABOVE THIS LINE. IF YOU NEED MORE SPACE, USE A SEPARATE CONTINUATION SHEET.

1 **TITLE OF THIS WORK ▼**

Stormy Blues

PREVIOUS, ALTERNATIVE, OR CONTENTS TITLES (CIRCLE ONE) ▼

2

a **NAME OF AUTHOR ▼**

Edwin Hammitup

DATES OF BIRTH AND DEATH
Year Born ▼   Year Died ▼
1953

Was this contribution to the work a "work made for hire"?
☒ Yes
☐ No

AUTHOR'S NATIONALITY OR DOMICILE
Name of Country
OR { Citizen of ▶ U.S.A.
Domiciled in ▶ U.S.A.

WAS THIS AUTHOR'S CONTRIBUTION TO THE WORK
Anonymous? ☐ Yes ☒ No
Pseudonymous? ☐ Yes ☒ No
If the answer to either of these questions is "Yes," see detailed instructions.

NATURE OF AUTHORSHIP Briefly describe nature of material created by this author in which copyright is claimed. ▼

words & music

NOTE

Under the law, the "author" of a "work made for hire" is generally the employer, not the employee (see instructions). For any part of this work that was "made for hire," check "Yes" in the space provided, give the employer (or other person for whom the work was prepared) as "Author" of that part, and leave the space for dates of birth and death blank.

b **NAME OF AUTHOR ▼**

DATES OF BIRTH AND DEATH
Year Born ▼   Year Died ▼

Was this contribution to the work a "work made for hire"?
☐ Yes
☐ No

AUTHOR'S NATIONALITY OR DOMICILE
Name of Country
OR { Citizen of ▶ _____
Domiciled in ▶ _____

WAS THIS AUTHOR'S CONTRIBUTION TO THE WORK
Anonymous? ☐ Yes ☐ No
Pseudonymous? ☐ Yes ☐ No
If the answer to either of these questions is "Yes," see detailed instructions.

NATURE OF AUTHORSHIP Briefly describe nature of material created by this author in which copyright is claimed. ▼

c **NAME OF AUTHOR ▼**

DATES OF BIRTH AND DEATH
Year Born ▼   Year Died ▼

Was this contribution to the work a "work made for hire"?
☐ Yes
☐ No

AUTHOR'S NATIONALITY OR DOMICILE
Name of Country
OR { Citizen of ▶ _____
Domiciled in ▶ _____

WAS THIS AUTHOR'S CONTRIBUTION TO THE WORK
Anonymous? ☐ Yes ☐ No
Pseudonymous? ☐ Yes ☐ No
If the answer to either of these questions is "Yes," see detailed instructions.

NATURE OF AUTHORSHIP Briefly describe nature of material created by this author in which copyright is claimed. ▼

3

a **YEAR IN WHICH CREATION OF THIS WORK WAS COMPLETED**
2000 ◀ Year
This information must be given in all cases.

b **DATE AND NATION OF FIRST PUBLICATION OF THIS PARTICULAR WORK**
Complete this information ONLY if this work has been published.
Month ▶ June Day ▶ 4 Year ▶ 2000
U.S.A. ◀ Nation

4

a **COPYRIGHT CLAIMANT(S)** Name and address must be given even if the claimant is the same as the author given in space 2. ▼

Edwin Hammitup
1402 Rocky Rd.
Jonesborough, NY 31500

See instructions before completing this space.

TRANSFER If the claimant(s) named here in space 4 is (are) different from the author(s) named in space 2, give a brief statement of how the claimant(s) obtained ownership of the copyright. ▼

b

**DO NOT WRITE HERE
OFFICE USE ONLY**

APPLICATION RECEIVED

ONE DEPOSIT RECEIVED

TWO DEPOSITS RECEIVED

FUNDS RECEIVED

MORE ON BACK ▶ • Complete all applicable spaces (numbers 5-9) on the reverse side of this page.
• See detailed instructions.   • Sign the form at line 8.

DO NOT WRITE HERE
Page 1 of _____ pages

DO NOT WRITE ABOVE THIS LINE. IF YOU NEED MORE SPACE, USE A SEPARATE CONTINUATION SHEET.

PREVIOUS REGISTRATION Has registration for this work, or for an earlier version of this work, already been made in the Copyright Office?

☐ Yes ☐ No If your answer is "Yes," why is another registration being sought? (Check appropriate box) ▼

a. ☐ This work was previously registered in unpublished form and now has been published for the first time.

b. ☐ This is the first application submitted by this author as copyright claimant.

c. ☐ This is a changed version of the work, as shown by space 6 on this application.

If your answer is "Yes," give: **Previous Registration Number** ▼   **Year of Registration** ▼

5

DERIVATIVE WORK OR COMPILATION

Preexisting Material Identify any preexisting work or works that this work is based on or incorporates. ▼

a

Material Added to This Work Give a brief, general statement of the material that has been added to this work and in which copyright is claimed. ▼

b

6

See instructions
before completing
this space.

DEPOSIT ACCOUNT If the registration fee is to be charged to a Deposit Account established in the Copyright Office, give name and number of Account.

Name ▼   Account Number ▼

a

7

CORRESPONDENCE Give name and address to which correspondence about this application should be sent.   Name/Address/Apt/City/State/ZIP ▼

b
    Edwin Hammitup
    1402 Rocky Rd.
    Jonesborough, NY 31500

Area code and daytime telephone number ▶ 212 987-6543   Fax number ▶ 212 986-4321

Email ▶ eddyed@hammitup.com

CERTIFICATION* I, the undersigned, hereby certify that I am the

Check only one ▼

☒ author

☐ other copyright claimant

☐ owner of exclusive right(s)

☐ authorized agent of _____

Name of author or other copyright claimant, or owner of exclusive right(s) ▲

of the work identified in this application and that the statements made by me in this application are correct to the best of my knowledge.

Typed or printed name and date ▼ If this application gives a date of publication in space 3, do not sign and submit it before that date.

    Edwin Hammitup

Date ▶ 6/15/00

Handwritten signature (x) ▼

☞ X _____ *Edwin Hammitup* _____

8

9

FORM CA
For Supplementary Registration
UNITED STATES COPYRIGHT OFFICE

REGISTRATION NUMBER

TX	TXU	PA	PAU	VA	VAU	SR	SRU	RE

EFFECTIVE DATE OF SUPPLEMENTARY REGISTRATION

_____ _____ _____
Month   Day   Year

DO NOT WRITE ABOVE THIS LINE. IF YOU NEED MORE SPACE, USE A SEPARATE CONTINUATION SHEET.

A

Title of Work ▼

Mooning over Miami

Registration Number of the Basic Registration ▼

TX 506812938

Year of Basic Registration ▼

1999

Name(s) of Author(s) ▼

Carole Center
Allen Fortene

Name(s) of Copyright Claimant(s) ▼

Carole Center
Allen Fortene

B

Location and Nature of Incorrect Information in Basic Registration ▼

Line Number _____1_____ Line Heading or Description _title of this work_

Incorrect Information as It Appears in Basic Registration ▼

Mooningover miami

Corrected Information ▼

Mooning over Miami

Explanation of Correction ▼

typo

C

Location and Nature of Information in Basic Registration to be Amplified ▼

Line Number _____ Line Heading or Description _____

Amplified Information and Explanation of Information ▼

MORE ON BACK ▶
• Complete all applicable spaces (D-G) on the reverse side of this page.
• See detailed instructions.   • Sign the form at Space F.

DO NOT WRITE HERE

Page 1 of _____ pages

DO NOT WRITE ABOVE THIS LINE. IF YOU NEED MORE SPACE, USE A SEPARATE CONTINUATION SHEET.

Continuation of: ❏ Part B *or* ❏ Part C

D

Correspondence: Give name and address to which correspondence about this application should be sent.

Carole Center
6126 Joyjoy Lane
Florida City, Florida 30732

Phone (305) 456-7890   Fax (305) 455-6789   Email moonovermi@center.net

E

Deposit Account: If the registration fee is to be charged to a Deposit Account established in the Copyright Office, give name and number of Account.

Name _____

Account Number _____

Certification* I, the undersigned, hereby certify that I am the: (Check only one)

☒ author   ❏ owner of exclusive right(s)
❏ other copyright claimant   ❏ duly authorized agent of _____
                 Name of author or other copyright claimant, or owner of exclusive right(s) ▲

of the work identified in this application and that the statements made by me in this application are correct to the best of my knowledge.

F

Typed or printed name ▼   Carole Center   Date ▼   7/30/01

Handwritten signature (X) ▼   *Carole Center*   ☞

Certificate will be mailed in window envelope to this address:

Name ▼
  Carole Center

Number/Street/Apt ▼
  6126 Joyjoy Lane

City/State/ZIP ▼
  Florida City, Florida 30732

YOU MUST:
• Complete all necessary spaces
• Sign your application in Space F

SEND ALL ELEMENTS IN THE SAME PACKAGE:
1. Application form
2. Nonrefundable filing fee in check or money order payable to *Register of Copyrights*

MAIL TO:
Library of Congress
Copyright Office
101 Independence Avenue, S.E.
Washington, D.C. 20559-6000

As of July 1, 1999, the fee for filing Form CA is $65.

G

CONTINUATION SHEET
FOR APPLICATION FORMS

*Ⓔ***FORM** ___TX___ **/CON**

UNITED STATES COPYRIGHT OFFICE

REGISTRATION NUMBER

PA	PAU	SE	SEG	SEU	SR	SRU	TX	TXU	VA	VAU

EFFECTIVE DATE OF REGISTRATION

(Month)   (Day)   (Year)

CONTINUATION SHEET RECEIVED

Page _____ of _____ pages

- This Continuation Sheet is used in conjunction with Forms CA, PA, SE, SR, TX, and VA, **only**. Indicate which basic form you are continuing in the space in the upper right-hand corner.
- If at all possible, try to fit the information called for into the spaces provided on the basic form.
- If you do not have enough space for all the information you need to give on the basic form, use this Continuation Sheet and submit it with the basic form.
- If you submit this Continuation Sheet, clip (do not tape or staple) it to the basic form and fold the two together before submitting them.
- **Space A of this sheet is intended to identify the basic application.**
   Space B is a continuation of Space 2 on the basic application. Space B is not applicable to Short forms.
   Space C (on the reverse side of this sheet) is for the continuation of Spaces 1, 4, or 6 on the basic application or for the continuation of Space 1 on any of the three Short Forms PA, TX, or VA.

DO NOT WRITE ABOVE THIS LINE. FOR COPYRIGHT OFFICE USE ONLY

A
Identification of Application

IDENTIFICATION OF CONTINUATION SHEET: This sheet is a continuation of the application for copyright registration on the basic form submitted for the following work:
- TITLE: (Give the title as given under the heading "Title of this Work" in Space 1 of the basic form.)

..Squirrel-zone..

- NAME(S) AND ADDRESS(ES) OF COPYRIGHT CLAIMANT(S) : (Give the name and address of at least one copyright claimant as given in Space 4 of the basic form or Space 2 of any of the Short Forms PA, TX, or VA.)

Martha Rocks 1935 Socoul Ave., Anywhere, LA 21900

B
Continuation of Space 2

d

NAME OF AUTHOR ▼

Martha Rocks

DATES OF BIRTH AND DEATH
Year Born▼   Year Died▼

1975

Was this contribution to the work a"work made for hire"?
☒ Yes
☐ No

AUTHOR'S NATIONALITY OR DOMICILE
Name of Country
OR { Citizen of ▶ _U.S.A._____
      { Domiciled in ▶ __U.S.A._____

WAS THIS AUTHOR'S CONTRIBUTION TO THE WORK
Anonymous? ☐ Yes ☒ No
Pseudonymous? ☐ Yes ☒ No

If the answer to either of these questions is "Yes," see detailed instructions.

NATURE OF AUTHORSHIP Briefly describe nature of the material created by the author in which copyright is claimed. ▼

Chapters 6 & 7

e

NAME OF AUTHOR ▼

DATES OF BIRTH AND DEATH
Year Born▼   Year Died▼

Was this contribution to the work a"work made for hire"?
☐ Yes
☐ No

AUTHOR'S NATIONALITY OR DOMICILE
Name of Country
OR { Citizen of ▶ _____
      { Domiciled in ▶ _____

WAS THIS AUTHOR'S CONTRIBUTION TO THE WORK
Anonymous? ☐ Yes ☐ No
Pseudonymous? ☐ Yes ☐ No

If the answer to either of these questions is "Yes," see detailed instructions.

NATURE OF AUTHORSHIP Briefly describe nature of the material created by the author in which copyright is claimed. ▼

f

NAME OF AUTHOR ▼

DATES OF BIRTH AND DEATH
Year Born▼   Year Died▼

Was this contribution to the work a"work made for hire"?
☐ Yes
☐ No

AUTHOR'S NATIONALITY OR DOMICILE
Name of Country
OR { Citizen of ▶ _____
      { Domiciled in ▶ _____

WAS THIS AUTHOR'S CONTRIBUTION TO THE WORK
Anonymous? ☐ Yes ☐ No
Pseudonymous? ☐ Yes ☐ No

If the answer to either of these questions is "Yes," see detailed instructions.

NATURE OF AUTHORSHIP Briefly describe nature of the material created by the author in which copyright is claimed. ▼

Use the reverse side of this sheet if you need more space for continuation of Spaces 1, 4, or 6 of the basic form or for the continuation of Space 1 on any of the Short Forms PA, TX, or VA.

CONTINUATION OF (Check which): ☐ Space 1   ☐ Space 4   ☒ Space 6

"Squirrel-zone" also copyrighted in animated format using form VA

C

Continuation
of other
Spaces

Certificate will be mailed in window envelope to this address:

Name ▼
Martha Rocks

Number/Street/Apt ▼
1935 Socoul Ave.

City/State/ZIP ▼
Anywhere, LA 21900

YOU MUST:
• Complete all necessary spaces
• Sign your application

SEND ALL 3 ELEMENTS IN THE SAME PACKAGE:
1. Application form
2. Nonrefundable fee in check or money order payable to *Register of Copyrights*
3. Deposit Material

MAIL TO:
Library of Congress, Copyright Office
101 Independence Avenue, S.E.
Washington, D.C. 20559-6000

D

Fees are effective through June 30, 2002. After that date, check the Copyright office Website at www.loc.gov/copyright or call (202) 707-3000 for current fee information.

November 1999–30,000
WEB REV: June 1999   ✪ PRINTED ON RECYCLED PAPER   ☆U.S.GOVERNMENT PRINTING OFFICE: 2000-461-113/78

DOCUMENT COVER SHEET
For Recordation of Documents
UNITED STATES COPYRIGHT OFFICE

DATE OF RECORDATION
(Assigned by Copyright Office)

Month   Day   Year

Volume _____   Page _____

Volume _____   Page _____

FUNDS RECEIVED _____

Do not write above this line.

To the Register of Copyrights:

Please record the accompanying original document or copy thereof.

FOR OFFICE USE ONLY

1 Name of the party or parties to the document spelled as they appear in the document (List up to the first three)

Greta Tiste

Dan Buyenall

2 Date of execution and/or effective date of the accompanying document   05 (month)   20 (day)   02 (year)

3 Completeness of document
☒ Document is complete by its own terms.
☐ Document is not complete. Record "as is."

4 Description of document
☒ Transfer of Copyright
☐ Security Interest
☐ Change of Name of Owner
☐ Termination of Transfer(s) [Section 304]
☐ Shareware
☐ Life, Identity, Death Statement [Section 302]
☐ Transfer of Mask Works
☐ Other _____

5 Title of first work as given in the document   the sunset

6 Total number of titles in document   1

7 Amount of fee calculated $ 30

8 Fee enclosed
☒ Check
☐ Money Order

☐ Fee authorized to be charged to :
Copyright Office
Deposit Account number _____

Account name _____

9 Affirmation:* I hereby affirm to the Copyright Office that the information given on this form is a true and correct representation of the accompanying document. This affirmation will not suffice as a certification of a photocopy signature on the document.
(Affirmation *must* be signed even if you are also signing Space 10.)

Dan Buyenall
Signature
May 20, 2002
Date
101-222-3456   101-222-4567
Phone Number   Fax Number

10 Certification:* Complete this certification in addition to the Affirmation if a photocopy of the original signed document is substituted for a document bearing the actual signature.
NOTE: This space *may not* be used for an official certification.
I certify under penalty of perjury under the laws of the United States of America that the accompanying document is a true copy of the original document.

Signature _____

Duly Authorized Agent of: _____

Date _____

Recordation will be mailed in window envelope to this address:

Name▼
Dan Buyenall

Number/Street/Apt▼
P.O. Box 3846

City/State/ZIP▼
Sioux City, IA 01010

YOU MUST:
• Complete all necessary spaces
• Sign your Cover Sheet in Space 9
SEND ALL 3 ELEMENTS TOGETHER:
1. Two copies of the Document Cover Sheet
2. Check/money order payable to *Register of Copyrights*
3. Document
MAIL TO:
Library of Congress, Copyright Office
Documents Recordation Section, LM-462
101 Independence Avenue, S.E.
Washington, D.C. 20559-6000

The recordation fee for the Document Cover Sheet is $50 and $15 for each group of 10 additional titles as of July 1, 1999.

*Knowingly and willfully falsifying material facts on this form may result in criminal liability. 18 U.S.C.§1001.
June 1999—20,000
WEB REV: June 1999   ♲ PRINTED ON RECYCLED PAPER   ☆U.S. GOVERNMENT PRINTING OFFICE: 1999-454-879/

Work Made-for-Hire Agreement

This Agreement is made the <u>8th</u> day of <u>August</u>, 20<u>02</u>, between <u>Daniel Llama</u> as Owner and <u>Fred Ferngold</u> as Author/Artist.

Whereas <u>Daniel Llama</u> wishes to commission a Work called<u>Index</u> which shall consist of <u>a four page index to owner's book *Twenty-five Years in Tibet*</u>

_____

_____ and

Whereas <u>Fred Ferngold</u> has represented that he/she can create said work according to the specifications provided by Owner,

It is agreed between the parties hereto that in consideration of the sum of $<u>100.00</u>, to be paid by Owner to Author/Artist within thirty days of satisfactory completion of the work, Author/Artist shall create the Work as specified. Upon payment, Owner shall acquire all rights to the commissioned Work including copyright.

Author/Artist warrants that the Work will be original and will not infringe or plagiarize any other work; will not libel any person or invade any person's right to privacy; and will not contain any unlawful materials. Author/Artist shall indemnify and save Owner harmless from any loss or liability due to any breach of these warranties, including reasonable attorney fees.

Author/Artist shall be responsible for all costs in creation of the Work unless otherwise agreed in writing by the Owner.

This Agreement shall not be modified or terminated except in writing signed by the parties hereto.

In witness whereof, the Owner and Author/Artist have executed this Agreement the date above written.

Daniel Llama
_____
Owner

Fred Ferngold
_____
Author/Artist

Work Made-for-Hire Employment Agreement

This Agreement is made the <u>29th</u> day of <u>February</u>, 20<u>04</u>, between <u>Figueras Enterprises</u> as Employer and <u>Pablo Dali</u> as Employee.

Whereas Employer wishes to have a Work created which shall consist of <u>_____</u> <u>a mural depicting six cows climbing Mount Olympus</u> <u>_____</u> <u>_____</u> <u>_____</u> and

Whereas Employee has represented that he/she can create said work according to the specifications previously provided by Employer,

It is agreed between the parties hereto that in consideration of the sum of $<u>5,000.00</u>, to be paid by Employer to Employee at a rate of $<u>500.00</u> per <u>week</u>, Employee shall create the Work as specified. In consideration of this payment, Employer shall be entitled to all rights to said work, including the copyright.

The parties agree that Employer shall have the right to control the manner and means by which the Work is created and

Employee warrants that the Work will be original and will not infringe or plagiarize any other work; will not libel any person or invade any person's right to privacy; and will not contain any unlawful materials. Employee shall indemnify and save Employer harmless from any loss or liability due to any breach of these warranties, including reasonable attorney fees.

Employee will not disclose to any parties outside of Employer's business any trade secrets or confidential information of Employer.

This Agreement shall not be modified or terminated except in writing signed by the parties hereto.

In witness whereof, the Employer and Employee have executed this Agreement the date above written.

Figueras Enterprises —
Bobbi Figueras, pres.
Employer

Pablo Dali
Employee

Independent Contractor Agreement

This Agreement is made the _6th_ day of _June_, 20_04_, between _BIGCO, Inc._ as Purchaser and _Joe Effstopp_ as Author/Artist.

Whereas Purchaser wishes to purchase a Work called _Washington's Cherries_ which shall consist of _Twenty-two photographs of cherry trees in Washington, D.C._ and and shall be used for _illustration in our 2005 Annual Report_ and

Whereas Author/Artist has represented that he/she can create said work according to the specifications provided by Owner.

It is agreed between the parties hereto that in consideration of the sum of $_220.00_, to be paid by Purchaser to Author/Artist upon completion of the work, Author/Artist shall create the Work according to the specifications agreed to between Purchaser and Author/Artist. It is understood that while Purchaser shall own the work itself, Author/Artist retains the copyright to the Work, including the right to reproduce the work and license the Work to others.

Author/Artist warrants that the Work will be original and will not infringe or plagiarize any other work; will not libel any person or invade any person's right to privacy; and will not contain any unlawful materials. Author/Artist shall indemnify and save Purchaser harmless from any loss or liability due to any breach of these warranties, including reasonable attorney fees.

Author/Artist shall be responsible for all costs in creation of the Work unless otherwise agreed in writing by the Purchaser.

This Agreement shall not be modified or terminated except in writing signed by the parties hereto.

In witness whereof, the Purchaser and Author/Artist have executed this Agreement the date above written.

BIGCO, Inc. — Bill Biggs, pres.
Purchaser

Joe Effstopp
Author/Artist

Collaboration Agreement

This Agreement is made the __25__ day of __MAY_____, 20__02__, between and among the following Collaborators:

JOHN SMITH_____   _____

BILL JONES_____   _____

Whereas the parties hereto wish to collaborate on a Work to be known as ____STUMP OF INEQUITY_____ which shall consist of ___A 20 FOOT HIGH CONCRETE STRUCTURE IN THE SHAPE OF A TREE STUMP_____ _____ and

Whereas the parties have agreed that they will contribute to the work as follows:

Party: Contribution:

JOHN SMITH_____   ORIGINAL STUMP DESIGN AND PLASTER MODEL_____

BILL JONES_____   LABOR AND MATERIALS FOR CONSTRUCTION_____

_____   _____

_____   _____

Their names shall appear on any attribution of the work in the order appearing next to their contribution.

It is agreed between the parties hereto that in consideration of their mutual agreements they shall each contribute as stated in this agreement and shall own the resulting work in the following percentages:

Party: Ownership:

JOHN SMITH_____   __50__ %

BILL JONES_____   __50__ %

_____   _____ %

_____   _____ %

The parties agree that they shall each complete their share of the work as follows:

Party: Date:

JOHN SMITH_____   AUGUST 1, 2002_____

BILL JONES_____   JUNE 1, 2003_____

_____   _____

_____   _____

Each party warrants that their contribution to the Work will be original and will not infringe or plagiarize any other work; will not libel any person or invade any person's right to privacy; and will not contain any unlawful materials. Each party shall indemnify and save other parties harmless from any loss or liability due to his or her breach of these warranties, including reasonable attorney fees.

The parties to this agreement are independent of each other and do not intend to create a partnership or joint venture. Each shall be responsible for his or her own debts and expenses.

No party shall transfer his or her interest in this agreement without the consent of the other collaborators.

This Agreement shall not be modified or terminated except in writing signed by the parties hereto.

In witness whereof, the parties have executed this Agreement the date above written.

John Smith _____

Bill Jones _____

_____

_____

Assignment of Copyright

This Assignment is made the __20th__ day of ___May___, 20__02__, between ___Greta Tiste___ as Owner of the copyright on the Work known as ___the sunset, an oil on canvas 24" x 36"___ _____, and ___Dan Byenall___ Purchaser.

Whereas Owner is sole owner of all rights in the Work and whereas Purchaser is desirous of purchasing all such rights,

It is agreed between the parties hereto that in consideration of the sum of $__1,200.00__, the receipt of which is hereby acknowledged, the Owner hereby assigns to Purchaser all of his/her interest in the Work and the copyright thereon, which interest shall be held for the full term of said copyright.

In witness whereof, the Owner has executed this Assignment the date above written.

_____ *Greta Tiste* _____

State of __Hawaii__)

County of __Maui__)

Acknowledgment

Before me, a Notary Public in and for the said state and county, personally appeared ___Greta Tiste___ who acknowledged that he/she did sign the foregoing Assignment as his/her free act and deed.

In testimony whereof, I have hereunto affixed my name and official seal this __1st__ day of ___February___, 20__02__.

_____ *C.U. Sine* _____
Notary Public

My commission expires: **March 15, 2010**

Note: In some states the notary paragraph must be worded according to the local law to be valid.

Copyright License

This License is made the <u>19th</u> day of <u>June</u>, 20<u>02</u>, between <u>Fotopeepl, Inc.</u> as Owner of the copyright on the Work known as <u>Stock photo #3056JH, South View of the White House</u>

<u>   </u>,

and <u>Bookers Press</u> as Licensee.

Whereas <u>Fotopeepl, Inc.</u> is sole owner of all rights in the Work and whereas <u>Bookers Press</u> is desirous of purchasing rights in said Work,

It is agreed between the parties hereto that in consideration of the sum of $<u>200.00</u>, the receipt of which is hereby acknowledged, the Owner hereby licenses the Licensee to use the copyrighted Work as follows:

<u>On the cover of the book *White House Scandals of the 20th Century*, on all</u>
<u>editions, and any number of printings. Also to use the book cover in ads,</u>
<u>brochures, television commercials, and on the Internet. This is an exclusive</u>
<u>license to use the photo for a book cover.</u>

<u>   </u>

<u>   </u>

It is understood between the parties that this License covers only those uses listed above for the time period stated. All other rights in and to the copyrighted work shall remain the property of the Owner.

In witness whereof, the Owner has executed this Copyright License the date above written.

<u>Fotopeepl, Inc. by *Pete Peepl, pres.*</u>
Owner

<u>Booker Press by *Joe Booker, owner*</u>
Licensee

APPENDIX H
BLANK FORMS

The following pages contain the forms of the copyright office mentioned throughout this book. You can remove the forms from this book, or you can photocopy them. If you do photocopy them, be sure to use good grade paper, copy both sides of the page and photocopy them head-to-head. In either case, blank out the form number designated in the outside corner of the first page of each form. These numbers (1-28) were assigned for easy reference in this book only, and are not a part of the official form.

The instructions provided with each form are very easy to understand. Be sure to read them thoroughly to avoid having your application rejected.

There are also agreements in this appendix that spell out the basic positions of the parties, and this may help to avoid disagreements and litigation. However, in some cases a longer agreement may be beneficial. Often there are numerous other legal issues to consider and a lawyer should be consulted. This should be considered in relation to the financial value of the work and the cost of having a longer agreement prepared.

For guidance in filling out the forms, samples of many of the forms are included in Appendix G

⊘ Application Form TX ⊘

Detach and read these instructions before completing this form.
Make sure all applicable spaces have been filled in before you return this form.

BASIC INFORMATION

When to Use This Form: Use Form TX for registration of published or unpublished nondramatic literary works, excluding periodicals or serial issues. This class includes a wide variety of works: fiction, nonfiction, poetry, textbooks, reference works, directories, catalogs, advertising copy, compilations of information, and computer programs. For periodicals and serials, use Form SE.

Deposit to Accompany Application: An application for copyright registration must be accompanied by a deposit consisting of copies or phonorecords representing the entire work for which registration is to be made. The following are the general deposit requirements as set forth in the statute:

Unpublished Work: Deposit one complete copy (or phonorecord)

Published Work: Deposit two complete copies (or one phonorecord) of the best edition.

Work First Published Outside the United States: Deposit one complete copy (or phonorecord) of the first foreign edition.

Contribution to a Collective Work: Deposit one complete copy (or phonorecord) of the best edition of the collective work.

The Copyright Notice: Before March 1, 1989, the use of copyright notice was mandatory on all published works, and any work first published before that date should have carried a notice. For works first published on and after March 1, 1989, use of the copyright notice is optional. For more information about copyright notice, see Circular 3, "Copyright Notices."

For Further Information: To speak to an information specialist, call (202) 707-3000 (TTY: (202) 707-6737). Recorded information is available 24 hours a day. Order forms and other publications from the address in space 9 or call the Forms and Publications Hotline at (202) 707-9100. Most circulars (but not forms) are available via fax. Call (202) 707-2600 from a touchtone phone. Access and download circulars, forms, and other information from the Copyright Office Website at www.loc.gov/copyright.

LINE BY LINE INSTRUCTIONS

Please type or print using black ink. The form is used to produce the certificate.

1 SPACE 1: Title

Title of This Work: Every work submitted for copyright registration must be given a title to identify that particular work. If the copies or phonorecords of the work bear a title or an identifying phrase that could serve as a title, transcribe that wording *completely* and *exactly* on the application. Indexing of the registration and future identification of the work will depend on the information you give here.

Previous or Alternative Titles: Complete this space if there are any additional titles for the work under which someone searching for the registration might be likely to look or under which a document pertaining to the work might be recorded.

Publication as a Contribution: If the work being registered is a contribution to a periodical, serial, or collection, give the title of the contribution in the "Title of This Work" space. Then, in the line headed "Publication as a Contribution," give information about the collective work in which the contribution appeared.

2 SPACE 2: Author(s)

General Instructions: After reading these instructions, decide who are the "authors" of this work for copyright purposes. Then, unless the work is a "collective work," give the requested information about every "author" who contributed any appreciable amount of copyrightable matter to this version of the work. If you need further space, request Continuation Sheets. In the case of a collective work, such as an anthology, collection of essays, or encyclopedia, give information about the author of the collective work as a whole.

Name of Author: The fullest form of the author's name should be given. Unless the work was "made for hire," the individual who actually created the work is its "author." In the case of a work made for hire, the statute provides that "the employer or other person for whom the work was prepared is considered the author."

What is a "Work Made for Hire"? A "work made for hire" is defined as (1) "a work prepared by an employee within the scope of his or her employment"; or (2) "a work specially ordered or commissioned for use as a contribution to a collective work, as a part of a motion picture or other audiovisual work, as a translation, as a supplementary work, as a compilation, as an instructional text, as a test, as answer material for a test, or as an atlas, if the parties expressly agree in a written instrument signed by them that the works shall be considered a work made for hire." If you have checked "Yes" to indicate that the work was "made for hire," you must give the full legal name of the employer (or other person for whom the work was prepared). You may also include the name of the employee along with the name of the employer (for example: "Elster Publishing Co., employer for hire of John Ferguson").

"Anonymous" or "Pseudonymous" Work: An author's contribution to a work is "anonymous" if that author is not identified on the copies or phonorecords of the work. An author's contribution to a work is "pseudonymous" if that author is identified on the copies or phonorecords under a fictitious name. If the work is "anonymous" you may: (1) leave the line blank; or (2) state "anonymous" on the line; or (3) reveal the author's identity. If the work is "pseudonymous" you may: (1) leave the line blank; or (2) give the pseudonym and identify it as such (for example: "Huntley Haverstock, pseudonym"); or (3) reveal the author's name, making clear which is the real name and which is the pseudonym (for example, "Judith Barton, whose pseudonym is Madeline Elster"). However, the citizenship or domicile of the author **must** be given in all cases.

Dates of Birth and Death: If the author is dead, the statute requires that the year of death be included in the application unless the work is anonymous or pseudonymous. The author's birth date is optional but is useful as a form of identification. Leave this space blank if the author's contribution was a "work made for hire."

Author's Nationality or Domicile: Give the country of which the author is a citizen or the country in which the author is domiciled. Nationality or domicile **must** be given in all cases.

Nature of Authorship: After the words "Nature of Authorship," give a brief general statement of the nature of this particular author's contribution to the work. Examples: "Entire text"; "Coauthor of entire text"; "Computer program"; "Editorial revisions"; "Compilation and English translation"; "New text."

3 SPACE 3: Creation and Publication

General Instructions: Do not confuse "creation" with "publication." Every application for copyright registration must state "the year in which creation of the work was completed." Give the date and nation of first publication only if the work has been published.

Creation: Under the statute, a work is "created" when it is fixed in a copy or phonorecord for the first time. Where a work has been prepared over a period of time, the part of the work existing in fixed form on a particular date constitutes the created work on that date. The date you give here should be the year in which the author completed the particular version for which registration is now being sought, even if other versions exist or if further changes or additions are planned.

Publication: The statute defines "publication" as "the distribution of copies or phonorecords of a work to the public by sale or other transfer of ownership, or by rental, lease, or lending." A work is also "published" if there has been an "offering to distribute copies or phonorecords to a group of persons for purposes of further distribution, public performance, or public display." Give the full date (month, day, year) when, and the country where, publication first occurred. If first publication took place simultaneously in the United States and other countries, it is sufficient to state "U.S.A."

4 SPACE 4: Claimant(s)

Name(s) and Address(es) of Copyright Claimant(s): Give the name(s) and address(es) of the copyright claimant(s) in this work even if the claimant is the same as the author. Copyright in a work belongs initially to the author of the work (including, in the case of a work made for hire, the employer or other person for whom the work was prepared). The copyright claimant is either the author of the work or a person or organization to whom the copyright initially belonging to the author has been transferred.

Transfer: The statute provides that, if the copyright claimant is not the author, the application for registration must contain "a brief statement of how the claimant obtained ownership of the copyright." If any copyright claimant named in space 4 is not an author named in space 2, give a brief statement explaining how the claimant(s) obtained ownership of the copyright. Examples: "By written contract"; "Transfer of all rights by author"; "Assignment"; "By will." Do not attach transfer documents or other attachments or riders.

5 SPACE 5: Previous Registration

General Instructions: The questions in space 5 are intended to show whether an earlier registration has been made for this work and, if so, whether there is any basis for a new registration. As a general rule, only one basic copyright registration can be made for the same version of a particular work.

Same Version: If this version is substantially the same as the work covered by a previous registration, a second registration is not generally possible unless: (1) the work has been registered in unpublished form and a second registration is now being sought to cover this first published edition; or (2) someone other than the author is identified as copyright claimant in the earlier registration, and the author is now seeking registration in his or her own name. If either of these two exceptions applies, check the appropriate box and give the earlier registration number and date. Otherwise, do not submit Form TX. Instead, write the Copyright Office for information about supplementary registration or recordation of transfers of copyright ownership.

Changed Version: If the work has been changed and you are now seeking registration to cover the additions or revisions, check the last box in space 5, give the earlier registration number and date, and complete both parts of space 6 in accordance with the instructions below.

Previous Registration Number and Date: If more than one previous registration has been made for the work, give the number and date of the latest registration.

6 SPACE 6: Derivative Work or Compilation

General Instructions: Complete space 6 if this work is a "changed version," "compilation," or "derivative work" and if it incorporates one or more earlier works that have already been published or registered for copyright or that have fallen into the public domain. A "compilation" is defined as "a work formed by the collection and assembling of preexisting materials or of data that are selected, coordinated, or arranged in such a way that the resulting work as a whole constitutes an original work of authorship." A "derivative work" is "a work based on one or more preexisting works." Examples of derivative works include translations, fictionalizations, abridgments, condensations, or "any other form in which a work may be recast, transformed, or adapted." Derivative works also include works "consisting of editorial revisions, annotations, or other modifications" if these changes, as a whole, represent an original work of authorship.

Preexisting Material (space 6a): For derivative works, complete this space **and** space 6b. In space 6a identify the preexisting work that has been recast, transformed, or adapted. The preexisting work may be material that has been previously published, previously registered, or that is in the public domain. An example of preexisting material might be: "Russian version of Goncharov's 'Oblomov.'"

Material Added to This Work (space 6b): Give a brief, general statement of the new material covered by the copyright claim for which registration is sought. **Derivative work** examples include: "Foreword, editing, critical annotations"; "Translation"; "Chapters 11-17." If the work is a **compilation**, describe both the compilation itself and the material that has been compiled. Example: "Compilation of certain 1917 Speeches by Woodrow Wilson." A work may be both a derivative work and compilation, in which case a sample statement might be: "Compilation and additional new material."

7,8,9 SPACE 7,8,9: Fee, Correspondence, Certification, Return Address

Deposit Account: If you maintain a Deposit Account in the Copyright Office, identify it in space 7a. Otherwise leave the space blank and send the fee of $30 (effective through June 30, 2002) with your application and deposit.

Correspondence (space 7b): This space should contain the name, address, area code, telephone number, fax number, and email address (if available) of the person to be consulted if correspondence about this application becomes necessary.

Certification (space 8): The application cannot be accepted unless it bears the date and the **handwritten signature** of the author or other copyright claimant, or of the owner of exclusive right(s), or of the duly authorized agent of author, claimant, or owner of exclusive right(s).

Address for Return of Certificate (space 9): The address box must be completed legibly since the certificate will be returned in a window envelope.

FORM TX

For a Nondramatic Literary Work
UNITED STATES COPYRIGHT OFFICE

REGISTRATION NUMBER

TX   TXU

EFFECTIVE DATE OF REGISTRATION

Month   Day   Year

DO NOT WRITE ABOVE THIS LINE. IF YOU NEED MORE SPACE, USE A SEPARATE CONTINUATION SHEET.

1

TITLE OF THIS WORK ▼

PREVIOUS OR ALTERNATIVE TITLES ▼

PUBLICATION AS A CONTRIBUTION If this work was published as a contribution to a periodical, serial, or collection, give information about the collective work in which the contribution appeared.   **Title of Collective Work ▼**

If published in a periodical or serial give: **Volume ▼**   **Number ▼**   **Issue Date ▼**   **On Pages ▼**

2

a

NAME OF AUTHOR ▼

DATES OF BIRTH AND DEATH
Year Born ▼   Year Died ▼

Was this contribution to the work a "work made for hire"?
☐ Yes
☐ No

AUTHOR'S NATIONALITY OR DOMICILE
Name of Country
OR { Citizen of ▶
Domiciled in ▶

WAS THIS AUTHOR'S CONTRIBUTION TO THE WORK
Anonymous? ☐ Yes ☐ No
Pseudonymous? ☐ Yes ☐ No
If the answer to either of these questions is "Yes," see detailed instructions.

NATURE OF AUTHORSHIP Briefly describe nature of material created by this author in which copyright is claimed. ▼

NOTE

Under the law, the "author" of a "work made for hire" is generally the employer, not the employee (see instructions). For any part of this work that was "made for hire" check "Yes" in the space provided, give the employer (or other person for whom the work was prepared) as "Author" of that part, and leave the space for dates of birth and death blank.

b

NAME OF AUTHOR ▼

DATES OF BIRTH AND DEATH
Year Born ▼   Year Died ▼

Was this contribution to the work a "work made for hire"?
☐ Yes
☐ No

AUTHOR'S NATIONALITY OR DOMICILE
Name of Country
OR { Citizen of ▶
Domiciled in ▶

WAS THIS AUTHOR'S CONTRIBUTION TO THE WORK
Anonymous? ☐ Yes ☐ No
Pseudonymous? ☐ Yes ☐ No
If the answer to either of these questions is "Yes," see detailed instructions

NATURE OF AUTHORSHIP Briefly describe nature of material created by this author in which copyright is claimed. ▼

c

NAME OF AUTHOR ▼

DATES OF BIRTH AND DEATH
Year Born ▼   Year Died ▼

Was this contribution to the work a "work made for hire"?
☐ Yes
☐ No

AUTHOR'S NATIONALITY OR DOMICILE
Name of Country
OR { Citizen of ▶
Domiciled in ▶

WAS THIS AUTHOR'S CONTRIBUTION TO THE WORK
Anonymous? ☐ Yes ☐ No
Pseudonymous? ☐ Yes ☐ No
If the answer to either of these questions is "Yes," see detailed instructions.

NATURE OF AUTHORSHIP Briefly describe nature of material created by this author in which copyright is claimed. ▼

3

a
YEAR IN WHICH CREATION OF THIS WORK WAS COMPLETED This information must be given ◀Year in all cases.

b
DATE AND NATION OF FIRST PUBLICATION OF THIS PARTICULAR WORK
Complete this information ONLY if this work has been published.   Month ▶ _____ Day ▶ _____ Year ▶ _____ ◀ Nation

4

See instructions before completing this space.

COPYRIGHT CLAIMANT(S) Name and address must be given even if the claimant is the same as the author given in space 2. ▼

TRANSFER If the claimant(s) named here in space 4 is (are) different from the author(s) named in space 2, give a brief statement of how the claimant(s) obtained ownership of the copyright. ▼

DO NOT WRITE HERE OFFICE USE ONLY

APPLICATION RECEIVED

ONE DEPOSIT RECEIVED

TWO DEPOSITS RECEIVED

FUNDS RECEIVED

MORE ON BACK ▶ • Complete all applicable spaces (numbers 5-9) on the reverse side of this page.
• See detailed instructions.   • Sign the form at line 8.

DO NOT WRITE HERE

DO NOT WRITE ABOVE THIS LINE. IF YOU NEED MORE SPACE, USE A SEPARATE CONTINUATION SHEET.

PREVIOUS REGISTRATION Has registration for this work, or for an earlier version of this work, already been made in the Copyright Office?

□ **Yes** □ **No** If your answer is "Yes," why is another registration being sought? (Check appropriate box.) ▼

a. □ This is the first published edition of a work previously registered in unpublished form.

b. □ This is the first application submitted by this author as copyright claimant.

c. □ This is a changed version of the work, as shown by space 6 on this application.

If your answer is "Yes," give: **Previous Registration Number** ▶   **Year of Registration** ▶

5

DERIVATIVE WORK OR COMPILATION

Preexisting Material Identify any preexisting work or works that this work is based on or incorporates. ▼

a

6

Material Added to This Work Give a brief, general statement of the material that has been added to this work and in which copyright is claimed. ▼

b

See instructions before completing this space.

DEPOSIT ACCOUNT If the registration fee is to be charged to a Deposit Account established in the Copyright Office, give name and number of Account.

Name ▼   **Account Number** ▼

a

7

CORRESPONDENCE Give name and address to which correspondence about this application should be sent.   Name/Address/Apt/City/State/ZIP ▼

b

Area code and daytime telephone number ▶   Fax number ▶

Email ▶

CERTIFICATION* I, the undersigned, hereby certify that I am the

Check only one ▶ {
□ author
□ other copyright claimant
□ owner of exclusive right(s)
□ authorized agent of _____

8

of the work identified in this application and that the statements made by me in this application are correct to the best of my knowledge.

Name of author or other copyright claimant, or owner of exclusive right(s) ▲

Typed or printed name and date ▼ If this application gives a date of publication in space 3, do not sign and submit it before that date.

Date ▶ _____

Handwritten signature (X) ▼

X _____

*For nondramatic literary works, including fiction and nonfiction, books, short stories, poems,
collections of poetry, essays, articles in serials, and computer programs*

USE THIS FORM IF—

1. You are the **only** author and copyright owner of this work, *and*
2. The work was **not** made for hire, *and*
3. The work is completely new (does not contain a substantial amount of material that has been previously published or registered or is in the public domain).

If any of the above does not apply, you must use standard Form TX.
NOTE: *Short Form TX is not appropriate for an anonymous author who does not wish to reveal his or her identity.*

HOW TO COMPLETE SHORT FORM TX

- Type or print in black ink.
- Be clear and legible. (Your certificate of registration will be copied from your form.)
- Give only the information requested.

NOTE: You may use a continuation sheet (Form __/CON) to list individual titles in a collection. Complete Space A and list the individual titles under Space C on the back page. Space B is not applicable to short forms.

1 Title of This Work

You must give a title. If there is no title, state "UNTITLED." If you are registering an unpublished collection, give the collection title you want to appear in our records (for example: "Joan's Poems, Volume 1"). Alternative title: If the work is known by two titles, you also may give the second title. If the work has been published as part of a larger work (including a periodical), give the title of that larger work in addition to the title of the contribution.

2 Name and Address of Author and Owner of the Copyright

Give your name and mailing address. You may include your pseudonym followed by "pseud." Also, give the nation of which you are a citizen or where you have your domicile (i.e., permanent residence).
Please give daytime phone and fax numbers and email address, if available.

3 Year of Creation

Give the latest year in which you completed the work you are registering at this time. A work is "created" when it is written down, stored in a computer, or otherwise "fixed" in a tangible form.

4 Publication

If the work has been published (i.e., if copies have been distributed to the public), give the complete date of publication (month, day, and year) and the nation where the publication first took place.

5 Type of Authorship in This Work

Check the box or boxes that describe your authorship in the copy you are sending with the application. For example, if you are registering a story and are planning to add illustrations later, check only the box for "text."

A "compilation" of terms or of data is a selection, coordination, or arrangement of such information into a chart, directory, or other form. A compilation of previously published or public domain material must be registered using a standard Form TX.

6 Signature of Author

Sign the application in black ink and check the appropriate box. The person signing the application should be the author or his/her authorized agent.

7 Person to Contact for Rights and Permissions

This space is optional. You may give the name and address of the person or organization to contact for permission to use the work. You may also provide phone, fax, or email information.

8 Certificate Will Be Mailed

This space must be completed. Your certificate of registration will be mailed in a window envelope to this address. Also, if the Copyright Office needs to contact you, we will write to this address.

9 Deposit Account

Complete this space only if you currently maintain a deposit account in the Copyright Office.

MAIL WITH THE FORM

- A $30 (effective through June 30, 2002) filing fee in the form of a check or money order *(no cash)* payable to "Register of Copyrights," **and**
- One or two copies of the work. If the work is unpublished, send one copy. If published, send two copies of the best published edition. (If first published outside the U.S., send one copy either as first published or of the best edition.) **Note:** Inquire about special requirements for works first published before 1978. Copies submitted become the property of the U.S. Government.

Mail everything **(application form, copy or copies, and fee)** *in one package* to:

> Library of Congress
> Copyright Office
> 101 Independence Avenue, S.E.
> Washington, D.C. 20559-6000

QUESTIONS? Call (202) 707-3000 [TTY: (202) 707-6737] between 8:30 a.m. and 5:00 p.m. eastern time, Monday through Friday. For forms and informational circulars, call (202) 707-9100 24 hours a day, 7 days a week, or download them from the Internet at www.loc.gov/copyright. Selected informational circulars but not forms are available from Fax-on-Demand at (202) 707-2600.

Registration Number

TX _____ TXU _____

Effective Date of Registration

Application Received

Deposit Received
One _____ | Two _____

Examined By _____

Correspondence ☐

Fee Received

TYPE OR PRINT IN BLACK INK. DO NOT WRITE ABOVE THIS LINE.

1 **Title of This Work:**

Alternative title or title of larger work in which this work was published:

2 **Name and Address of Author and Owner of the Copyright:**

Nationality or domicile:
Phone, fax, and email:

Phone ( )   Fax ( )

Email

3 **Year of Creation:**

4 **If work has been published, Date and Nation of Publication:**

a. Date _____ _____ _____
                Month   Day   Year   (Month, day, and year all required)

b. Nation

5 **Type of Authorship in This Work:**

Check all that this author created.

☐ Text (includes fiction, nonfiction, poetry, computer programs, etc.)
☐ Illustrations
☐ Photographs
☐ Compilation of terms or data

6 **Signature:**

Registration cannot be completed without a signature.

I certify that the statements made by me in this application are correct to the best of my knowledge. Check one:

☐ Author   ☐ Authorized agent

X _

OPTIONAL

7 **Name and Address of Person to Contact for Rights and Permissions:**
Phone, fax, and email:

☐ Check here if same as #2 above.

Phone ( )   Fax ( )

Email

8 **Certificate will be mailed in window envelope to this address:**

Name ▼

Number/Street/Apt ▼

City/State/ZIP ▼

Complete this space only if you currently hold a Deposit Account in the Copyright Office.

9 Deposit Account # _____

Name _____

DO NOT WRITE HERE   Page 1 of _____ pages

*17 U.S.C. § 506(e): Any person who knowingly makes a false representation of a material fact in the application for copyright registration provided for by section 409, or in any written statement filed in connection with the application, shall be fined not more than $2,500.

June 1999—100,000
WEB REV: June 1999

♻ PRINTED ON RECYCLED PAPER

☆U.S. GOVERNMENT PRINTING OFFICE: 1999-454-879/53

⌬ Application Form SE ⌬

Detach and read these instructions before completing this form.
Make sure all applicable spaces have been filled in before you return this form.

BASIC INFORMATION

When To Use This Form: Use a separate Form SE for registration of each individual issue of a serial, Class SE. A serial is defined as a work issued or intended to be issued in successive parts bearing numerical or chronological designations and intended to be continued indefinitely. This class includes a variety of works: periodicals; newspapers; annuals; the journals, proceedings, transactions, etc., of societies. Do not use Form SE to register an individual contribution to a serial. Request Form TX for such contributions.

Deposit to Accompany Application: An application for copyright registration must be accompanied by a deposit consisting of copies or phonorecords representing the entire work for which registration is to be made. The following are the general deposit requirements as set forth in the statute:
Unpublished Work: Deposit one complete copy (or phonorecord).
Published Work: Deposit two complete copies (or one phonorecord) of the best edition.
Work First Published Outside the United States: Deposit one complete copy (or phonorecord) of the first foreign edition.

Mailing Requirements: It is important that you send the application, the deposit copy or copies, and the $30 registration fee (effective through June 30, 2002) together in the same envelope or package. The Copyright Office cannot process them unless they are received together.

Send to: *Library of Congress, Copyright Office, 101 Independence Avenue, S.E., Washington, D. C. 20559-6000.*

The Copyright Notice: Before March 1, 1989, the use of copyright notice was mandatory on all published works, and any work first published before that date should have carried a notice. For works first published on and after March 1, 1989, use of the copyright notice is optional. For more information about copyright notice, see Circular 3, "Copyright Notices."

For Further Information: To speak to an information specialist, call (202) 707-3000 (TTY: (202) 707-6737). Recorded information is available 24 hours a day. Order forms and other publications from the address in space 9 or call the Forms and Publications Hotline at (202) 707-9100. Most circulars (but not forms) are available via fax. Call (202) 707-2600 from a touchtone phone. Access and download circulars, forms, and other information from the Copyright Office Website at www.loc.gov/copyright.

LINE-BY-LINE INSTRUCTIONS

Please type or print using black ink.

SPACE 1: Title
Title of This Serial: Every work submitted for copyright registration must be given a title to identify that particular work. If the copies or phonorecords of the work bear a title (or an identifying phrase that could serve as a title), copy that wording *completely* and *exactly* on the application. Give the volume and number of the periodical issue for which you are seeking registration. The "Date on Copies" in space 1 should be the date appearing on the actual copies (for example: "June 1981," " Winter 1981"). Indexing of the registration and future identification of the work will depend on the information you give here.

Previous or Alternative Titles: Complete this space only if there are any additional titles for the serial under which someone searching for the registration might be likely to look or under which a document pertaining to the work might be recorded.

SPACE 2: Author(s)
General Instructions: After reading these instructions, decide who are the "authors" of this work for copyright purposes. In the case of a serial issue, the organization that directs the creation of the serial issue as a whole is generally considered the author of the "collective work" (see "Nature of Authorship") whether it employs a staff or uses the efforts of volunteers. Where, however, an individual is independently responsible for the serial issue, name that person as author of the "collective work."

Name of Author: The fullest form of the author's name should be given. In the case of a "work made for hire," the statute provides that "the employer or other person for whom the work was prepared is considered the author." If this issue is a "work made for hire," the author's name will be the full legal name of the hiring organization, corporation, or individual. The title of the periodical should not ordinarily be listed as "author" because the title itself does not usually correspond to a legal entity capable of authorship. When an individual creates an issue of a serial independently and not as an "employee" of an organization or corporation, that individual should be listed as the "author."

Author's Nationality or Domicile: Give the country of which the author is a citizen, or the country in which the author is domiciled. Nationality or domicile **must** be given in all cases. The citizenship of an organization formed under U. S. federal or state law should be stated as "U.S.A."

What is a "Work Made for Hire"? A "work made for hire" is defined as (1) "a work prepared by an employee within the scope of his or her employment"; or (2) "a work specially ordered or commissioned for use as a contribution to a collective work, as a part of a motion picture or other audiovisual work, as a translation, as a supplementary work, as a compilation, as an instructional text, as a test, as answer material for a test, or as an atlas, if the parties expressly agree in a written instrument signed by them that the work shall be considered a work made for hire." An organization that uses the efforts of volunteers in the creation of a "collective work" (see "Nature of Authorship") may also be considered the author of a "work made for hire" even though those volunteers were not specifically paid by the organization. In the case of a "work made for hire," give the full legal name of the employer and check "Yes" to indicate that the work was made for hire. You may also include the name of the employee along with the name of the employer (for example: "Elster Publishing Co., employer for hire of John Ferguson").

"Anonymous" or "Pseudonymous" Work: Leave this space **blank** if the serial is a "work made for hire." An author's contribution to a work is "anonymous" if that author is not identified on the copies or phonorecords of the work. An author's contribution to a work is "pseudonymous" if that author is identified on the copies or phonorecords under a fictitious name. If the work is "anonymous" you may: (1) leave the line blank; or (2) state "anonymous" on the line; or (3) reveal the author's identify. If the work is "pseudonymous" you may: (1) leave the line blank; or (2) give the pseudonym and identify it as such (for example: "Huntley Haverstock, pseudonym"); or (3) reveal the author's name, making clear which is the real name and which is the pseudonym (for example: "Judith Barton, whose pseudonym is Madeline Elster"). However, the citizenship or domicile of the author **must** be given in all cases.

Dates of Birth and Death: Leave this space blank if the author's contribution was a "work made for hire." If the author is dead, the statute requires that the year of death be included in the application unless the work is anonymous or pseudonymous. The author's birth date is optional but is useful as a form of identification.

Nature of Authorship: Give a brief statement of the nature of the particular author's contribution to the work. If an organization directed, controlled, and supervised the creation of the serial issue as a whole, check the box "collective work." The term "collective work" means that the author is responsible for compilation and editorial revision and may also be responsible for certain individual contributions to the serial issue. Further examples of "Authorship" which may apply both to organizational and to individual authors are "Entire text"; "Entire text and/or illustrations"; "Editorial revision, compilation, plus additional new material."

SPACE 3: Creation and Publication

General Instructions: Do not confuse "creation" with "publication." Every application for copyright registration must state "the year in which creation of the work was completed." Give the date and nation of first publication only if the work has been published.

Creation: Under the statute, a work is "created" when it is fixed in a copy or phonorecord for the first time. Where a work has been prepared over a period of time, the part of the work existing in fixed form on a particular date constitutes the created work on that date. The date you give here should be the year in which this particular issue was completed.

Publication: The statute defines "publication" as "the distribution of copies or phonorecords of a work to the public by sale or other transfer of ownership or by rental, lease, or lending"; a work is also "published" if there has been an "offering to distribute copies or phonorecords to a group of persons for purposes of further distribution, public performance, or public display." Give the full date (month, day, year) when, and the country where, publication of this particular issue first occurred. If first publication took place simultaneously in the United States and other countries, it is sufficient to state "U.S.A."

SPACE 4: Claimant(s)

Name(s) and Address(es) of Copyright Claimant(s): This space must be completed. Give the name(s) and address(es) of the copyright claimant(s) of this work even if the claimant is the same as the author named in space 2. Copyright in a work belongs initially to the author of the work (including, in the case of a work made for hire, the employer or other person for whom the work was prepared). The copyright claimant is either the author of the work or a person or organization to whom the copyright initially belonging to the author has been transferred.

Transfer: The statute provides that, if the copyright claimant is not the author, the application for registration must contain "a brief statement of how the claimant obtained ownership of the copyright." If any copyright claimant named in space 4 is not an author named in space 2, give a brief statement explaining how the claimant(s) obtained ownership of the copyright. Examples: "By written contract"; "Transfer of all rights by author"; "Assignment"; "By will." Do not attach transfer documents or other attachments or riders.

SPACE 5: Previous Registration

General Instructions: This space rarely applies to serials. Complete space 5 if this particular issue has been registered earlier or if it contains a substantial amount of material that has been previously registered. Do not complete this space if the previous registrations are simply those made for earlier issues.

Previous Registration:

a. Check this box if this issue has been registered in unpublished form and a second registration is now sought to cover the first published edition.

b. Check this box if someone other than the author is identified as copyright claimant in the earlier registration and the author is now seeking registration

in his or her own name. If the work in question is a contribution to a collective work as opposed to the issue as a whole, file Form TX, not Form SE.

c. Check this box (and complete space 6) if this particular issue or a substantial portion of the material in it has been previously registered and you are now seeking registration for the additions and revisions which appear in this issue for the first time.

Previous Registration Number and Date: Complete this line if you checked one of the boxes above. If more than one previous registration has been made for the issue or for material in it, give only the number and year date for the latest registration.

SPACE 6: Derivative Work or Compilation

General Instructions: Complete space 6 if this issue is a "changed version," "compilation," or "derivative work" that incorporates one or more earlier works that have already been published or registered for copyright or that have fallen into the public domain. Do not complete space 6 for an issue consisting of entirely new material appearing for the first time such as a new issue of a continuing serial. A "compilation" is defined as "a work formed by the collection and assembling of preexisting materials or of data that are selected, coordinated, or arranged in such a way that the resulting work as a whole constitutes an original work of authorship." A "derivative work" is "a work based on one or more preexisting works." Examples of derivative works include translations, fictionalizations, abridgments, condensations, or "any other form in which a work may be recast, transformed, or adapted." Derivative works also include works "consisting of editorial revisions, annotations, or other modifications" if these changes, as a whole, represent an original work of authorship.

Preexisting Material (space 6a): For derivative works, complete this space **and** space 6b. In space 6a identify the preexisting work that has been recast, transformed, adapted, or updated. Example: "1978 Morgan Co. Sales Catalog." Do not complete space 6a for compilations.

Material Added to This Work (space 6b): Give a brief, general statement of the new material covered by the copyright claim for which registration is sought. **Derivative work** examples include: "Editorial revisions and additions to the Catalog"; "Translation"; "Additional material." If a periodical issue is a **compilation**, describe both the compilation itself and the material that has been compiled. Examples: "Compilation of previously published journal articles"; "Compilation of previously published data." An issue may be both a derivative work and a compilation, in which case a sample statement might be: "Compilation of [describe] and additional new material."

SPACE 7,8,9: Fee, Correspondence, Certification, Return Address

Deposit Account (Space 7a): If you maintain a Deposit Account in the Copyright Office, identify it in space 7a. Otherwise leave the space blank and send the fee of $30 (effective through June 30, 2002) with your application and deposit.

Correspondence (space 7b): This space should contain the name, address, area code, and telephone and fax number and email address of the person to be consulted if correspondence about this application becomes necessary.

Certification (space 8): The application cannot be accepted unless it bears the date and the **handwritten signature** of the author or other copyright claimant, or of the owner of exclusive right(s), or of the duly authorized agent of the author, claimant, or owner of exclusive right(s).

Address for Return of Certificate (space 9): The address box must be completed legibly since the certificate will be returned in a window envelope.

FORM SE
For a Serial
UNITED STATES COPYRIGHT OFFICE

REGISTRATION NUMBER

U

EFFECTIVE DATE OF REGISTRATION

_____
Month   Day   Year

DO NOT WRITE ABOVE THIS LINE. IF YOU NEED MORE SPACE, USE A SEPARATE CONTINUATION SHEET.

1

TITLE OF THIS SERIAL ▼

Volume ▼	Number ▼	Date on Copies ▼	Frequency of Publication ▼

PREVIOUS OR ALTERNATIVE TITLES ▼

2 a

NAME OF AUTHOR ▼

DATES OF BIRTH AND DEATH
Year Born ▼   Year Died ▼

Was this contribution to the work a "work made for hire"?
☐ Yes
☐ No

AUTHOR'S NATIONALITY OR DOMICILE
Name of Country
OR { Citizen of ▶ _____
Domiciled in ▶ _____

WAS THIS AUTHOR'S CONTRIBUTION TO THE WORK
Anonymous?   ☐ Yes ☐ No
Pseudonymous? ☐ Yes ☐ No

If the answer to either of these questions is "Yes," see detailed instructions.

NATURE OF AUTHORSHIP Briefly describe nature of material created by this author in which copyright is claimed. ▼
☐ Collective Work   Other:

NOTE

Under the law, the "author" of a "work made for hire" is generally the employer, not the employee (see instructions). For any part of this work that was "made for hire" check "Yes" in the space provided, give the employer (or other person for whom the work was prepared) as "Author" of that part, and leave the space for dates of birth and death blank.

b

NAME OF AUTHOR ▼

DATES OF BIRTH AND DEATH
Year Born ▼   Year Died ▼

Was this contribution to the work a "work made for hire"?
☐ Yes
☐ No

AUTHOR'S NATIONALITY OR DOMICILE
Name of Country
OR { Citizen of ▶ _____
Domiciled in ▶ _____

WAS THIS AUTHOR'S CONTRIBUTION TO THE WORK
Anonymous?   ☐ Yes ☐ No
Pseudonymous? ☐ Yes ☐ No

If the answer to either of these questions is "Yes," see detailed instructions.

NATURE OF AUTHORSHIP Briefly describe nature of material created by this author in which copyright is claimed. ▼
☐ Collective Work   Other:

c

NAME OF AUTHOR ▼

DATES OF BIRTH AND DEATH
Year Born ▼   Year Died ▼

Was this contribution to the work a "work made for hire"?
☐ Yes
☐ No

AUTHOR'S NATIONALITY OR DOMICILE
Name of Country
OR { Citizen of ▶ _____
Domiciled in ▶ _____

WAS THIS AUTHOR'S CONTRIBUTION TO THE WORK
Anonymous?   ☐ Yes ☐ No
Pseudonymous? ☐ Yes ☐ No

If the answer to either of these questions is "Yes," see detailed instructions.

NATURE OF AUTHORSHIP Briefly describe nature of material created by this author in which copyright is claimed. ▼
☐ Collective Work   Other:

3 a

YEAR IN WHICH CREATION OF THIS ISSUE WAS COMPLETED
This information must be given in all cases.
◀ Year

b **DATE AND NATION OF FIRST PUBLICATION OF THIS PARTICULAR ISSUE**
Complete this information ONLY if this work has been published.
Month ▶ _____ Day ▶ _____ Year ▶ _____
◀ Nation

4

See instructions before completing this space.

COPYRIGHT CLAIMANT(S) Name and address must be given even if the claimant is the same as the author given in space 2. ▼

TRANSFER If the claimant(s) named here in space 4 is (are) different from the author(s) named in space 2, give a brief statement of how the claimant(s) obtained ownership of the copyright. ▼

DO NOT WRITE HERE OFFICE USE ONLY

APPLICATION RECEIVED

ONE DEPOSIT RECEIVED

TWO DEPOSITS RECEIVED

FUNDS RECEIVED

MORE ON BACK ▶
• Complete all applicable spaces (numbers 5-9) on the reverse side of this page.
• See detailed instructions.   • Sign the form at line 8.

DO NOT WRITE HERE

Page 1 of _____ pages

DO NOT WRITE ABOVE THIS LINE. IF YOU NEED MORE SPACE, USE A SEPARATE CONTINUATION SHEET.

PREVIOUS REGISTRATION Has registration for this work, or for an earlier version of this work, already been made in the Copyright Office?

☐ **Yes** ☐ **No** If your answer is "Yes," why is another registration being sought? (Check appropriate box.) ▼

a. ☐ This is the first published edition of a work previously registered in unpublished form.

b. ☐ This is the first application submitted by this author as copyright claimant.

c. ☐ This is a changed version of the work, as shown by space 6 on this application.

If your answer is "Yes," give: **Previous Registration Number** ▼   **Year of Registration** ▼

5

DERIVATIVE WORK OR COMPILATION Complete both space 6a and 6b for a derivative work; complete only 6b for a compilation.

Preexisting Material Identify any preexisting work or works that this work is based on or incorporates. ▼

a

6

Material Added to This Work Give a brief, general statement of the material that has been added to this work and in which copyright is claimed. ▼

b

See instructions before completing this space.

DEPOSIT ACCOUNT If the registration fee is to be charged to a Deposit Account established in the Copyright Office, give name and number of Account.

Name ▼   **Account Number** ▼

a

7

CORRESPONDENCE Give name and address to which correspondence about this application should be sent.   Name/Address/Apt/City/State/ZIP ▼

b

Area code and telephone number ▶   Fax number ▶

Email ▶

CERTIFICATION* I, the undersigned, hereby certify that I am the

Check only one ▶ {
☐ author
☐ other copyright claimant
☐ owner of exclusive right(s)
☐ authorized agent of _____

of the work identified in this application and that the statements made by me in this application are correct to the best of my knowledge.

Name of author or other copyright claimant, or owner of exclusive right(s) ▲

8

Typed or printed name and date ▼ If this application gives a date of publication in space 3, do not sign and submit it before that date.

_____   Date ▶ _____

👉 **Handwritten signature (X)** ▼

X _____

Certificate will be mailed in window envelope to this address:

Name ▼

Number/Street/Apt ▼

City/State/ZIP ▼

YOU MUST:
• Complete all necessary spaces
• Sign your application in space 8

SEND ALL 3 ELEMENTS IN THE SAME PACKAGE:
1. Application form
2. Nonrefundable filing fee in check or money order payable to *Register of Copyrights*
3. Deposit material

MAIL TO:
Library of Congress
Copyright Office
101 Independence Avenue, S.E.
Washington, D.C. 20559-6000

As of July 1, 1999, the filing fee for Form SE is $30.

9

Instructions for Short Form SE

Read these instructions before completing this form. Make sure all applicable spaces have been filled in before you return this form.

When to Use This Form: All the following conditions must be met in order to use this form. If any one of the conditions does not apply, you must use Form SE. Incorrect use of this form will result in a delay in your registration.

1. The claim must be in a collective work.

2. The work must be essentially an all-new collective work or issue.

3. The author must be a citizen or domiciliary of the United States.

4. The work must be a work made for hire.

5. The author(s) and claimant(s) must be the same person(s) or organization(s).

6. The work must be first published in the United States.

Deposit to Accompany Application: An application for registration of a copyright claim in a serial issue first published in the United States must be accompanied by a deposit consisting of two copies (or phonorecords) of the best edition.

Fee: The filing fee of $30 (effective through June 30, 2002) must be sent for each issue to be registered. Do not send cash or currency.

Mailing Requirements: Mail everything (application form, copy or copies, and fee) in one package to Library of Congress, Copyright Office, 101 Independence Avenue, S.E., Washington D.C. 20559-6000.

Collective Work: The term "collective work" refers to a work, such as a serial issue, in which a number of contributions are assembled into a collective whole. A claim in the "collective work" extends to all copyrightable authorship created by employees of the author, as well as any independent contributions in which the claimant has acquired ownership of the copyright.

Publication: The statute defines "publication" as "the distribution of copies or phonorecords of a work to the public by sale or other transfer of ownership, or by rental, lease, or lending"; a work is also "published" if there has been an "offering to distribute copies or phonorecords to a group of persons for purposes of further distribution, public performance, or public display."

Creation: A work is "created" when it is fixed in a copy (or phonorecord) for the first time.

Work Made for Hire: A "work made for hire" is defined as: (1) a work prepared by an employee within the scope of his or her employment; or (2) a work specially ordered or commissioned for certain uses (including use as a contribution to a collective work), if the parties expressly agree in a written instrument signed by them that the work shall be considered a work made for hire. The employer is the author of a work made for hire.

The Copyright Notice: Before March 1, 1989, the use of copyright notice was mandatory on all published works, and any work first published before that date should have carried a notice. For works first published on and after March 1, 1989, use of the copyright notice is optional. For more information about copyright notice, see Circular 3, "Copyright Notices."

For Further Information: To speak to an information specialist, call (202) 707-3000 (TTY: (202) 707-6737). Recorded information is available 24 hours a day. Order forms and other publications from the address at the bottom of page 2 or call the Forms and Publications Hotline at (202) 707-9100. Most circulars (but not forms) are available via fax. Call (202) 707-2600 from a touchtone phone. Access and download circulars, forms, and other information from the Copyright Office Website at www.loc.gov/copyright.

SPACE-BY-SPACE INSTRUCTIONS

SPACE 1: Title

Every work submitted for copyright registration must be given a title to identify that particular work. Give the complete title of the periodical, including the volume, number, issue date, or other indicia printed on the copies. If possible, give the International Standard Serial Number (ISSN).

SPACE 2: Author and Copyright Claimant

Give the fullest form of the author and claimant's name. If there are joint authors and owners, give the names of all the author/owners. It is assumed that the authors and claimants are the same, that the work is made for hire, and that the claim is in the collective work.

SPACE 3: Date of Publication of This Particular Work

Give the exact date on which publication of this issue first took place. The full date, including month, day, and year must be given.

Year in Which Creation of This Issue Was Completed: Give the year in which this serial issue was first fixed in a copy or phonorecord. If no year is given, it is assumed that the issue was created in the same year in which it was published. The date must be the same as or no later than the publication date.

Certification: The application cannot be accepted unless it bears the handwritten signature of the copyright claimant or the duly authorized agent of the copyright claimant.

Person to Contact for Correspondence About This Claim: Give the name, daytime phone and fax numbers, and email address (if available) of the person to whom any correspondence concerning this claim should be addressed. Give the address only if it is different from the address for mailing of the certificate.

Deposit Account: Complete this space only if you currently maintain a deposit account in the Copyright Office. Otherwise, leave the space blank and forward the filing fee with your application and deposit.

Mailing Address of Certificate: This address must be complete and legible since the certificate will be mailed in a window envelope.

SHORT FORM SE ©

For a Serial
UNITED STATES COPYRIGHT OFFICE

Registration Number

_____

Effective Date of Registration

_____

Examined By

Application Received

Correspondence ❏

Deposit Received
One | Two

Fee Received

DO NOT WRITE ABOVE THIS LINE.

1   TITLE OF THIS SERIAL AS IT APPEARS ON THE COPY

Volume▼   Number▼   Date on copies▼   ISSN▼

2   NAME AND ADDRESS OF THE AUTHOR AND COPYRIGHT CLAIMANT IN THIS COLLECTIVE WORK MADE FOR HIRE

3   DATE OF PUBLICATION OF THIS PARTICULAR ISSUE

Month ▼   Day ▼   Year ▼

YEAR IN WHICH CREATION OF THIS ISSUE WAS COMPLETED (IF EARLIER THAN THE YEAR OF PUBLICATION):

Year ▶

CERTIFICATION*:   I, the undersigned, hereby certify that I am the copyright claimant or the authorized agent of the copyright claimant of the work identified in this application, that all the conditions specified in the instructions on the back of this form are met, that the statements made by me in this application are correct to the best of my knowledge.

Handwritten signature (X) _____

Typed or printed name of signer _____

PERSON TO CONTACT FOR CORRESPONDENCE ABOUT THIS CLAIM

Name ▶ _____
Address (if other than given below) ▶ _____
Daytime phone ▶ (____) _____
Fax ▶ (____)   Email ▶ _____

DEPOSIT ACCOUNT

Account number ▶ _____
Name of account ▶ _____

Certificate will be mailed in window envelope to this address:

Name▼

Number/Street/Apt ▼

City/State/ZIP▼

YOU MUST:
• Complete all necessary spaces
• Sign your application

SEND ALL 3 ELEMENTS IN THE SAME PACKAGE:
1. Application form
2. Nonrefundable $30 filing fee in check or money order payable to *Register of Copyrights*
3. Deposit material

MAIL TO:
Library of Congress
Copyright Office
101 Independence Avenue, S.E.
Washington, D.C. 20559-6000

As of July 1, 1999, the filing fee for Short Form SE is $30.

Form SE/GROUP

BASIC INFORMATION

Read these instructions before completing this form.
Make sure all applicable spaces have been filled in before you return this form.

When to Use This Form: All the following conditions must be met in order to use this form. If any one of the conditions does not apply, you must register the issues separately using Form SE or Short Form SE.

1. You must have given a complimentary subscription for two copies of the serial to the Library of Congress, confirmed by letter to:

> Library of Congress
> Group Periodicals Registration
> Washington, D.C. 20540-4161

Subscription copies must be mailed separately to the same address.

2. The claim must be in the collective works.
3. The works must be essentially all new collective works or issues.
4. Each issue must be a work made for hire.
5. The author(s) and claimant(s) must be the same person(s) or organization(s) for all the issues.
6. Each issue must have been created no more than 1 year prior to publication.
7. All issues in the group must have been published within the same calendar year.

For copyright purposes, serials are defined as works issued or intended to be issued in successive parts bearing numerical or chronological designations and intended to be continued indefinitely. The classification "serial" includes periodicals, newspapers, magazines, bulletins, newsletters, annuals, journals, proceedings of societies, and other similar works.

Which Issues May Be Included in a Group Registration: You may register two or more issues of a serial published at intervals of 1 week or longer under the same continuing title, provided that the issues were published within a 90-day period during the same calendar year.

Deposit to Accompany Application: Send one copy of each issue included in the group registration with the application and fee.

Fee: A nonrefundable filing fee of $10 (minimum fee: $30) FOR EACH ISSUE LISTED ON FORM SE/GROUP must be sent with the application or charged to an active deposit account in the Copyright Office. **Fees are effective through June 30, 2002.** Make checks payable to **Register of Copyrights.**

Special handling is not available for Form SE/Group.

Mailing Instructions: Send the application, deposit copies, and fee together in the same package to: *Library of Congress, Copyright Office, 101 Independence Ave., S.E., Washington, D.C. 20559-6000.*

International Standard Serial Number (ISSN): ISSN is an internationally accepted code for the identification of serial publications. If a published serial has not been assigned an ISSN, application forms and additional information my be obtained from Library of Congress, National Serials Data Program, Serial Record Division, Washington, D.C. 20540-

4160. Call (202) 707-6452. Or obtain information via the Internet at www.loc.gov/issn/.Do not contact the Copyright Office for ISSNs.

Collective Work: The term "collective work" refers to a work, such as a serial issue, in which a number of contributions are assembled into a collective whole. A claim in the "collective work" extends to all copyrightable authorship created by employees of the author, as well as any independent contributions in which the claimant has acquired ownership of the copyright.

Publication: The statute defines "publication" as "the distribution of copies or phonorecords of a work to the public by sale or other transfer of ownership, or by rental, lease, or lending." A work is also "published" if there has been an "offering to distribute copies or phonorecords to a group of persons for purposes of further distribution, public performance, or public display."

Creation: A work is "created" when it is fixed in a copy (or phonorecord) for the first time. For a serial, the year in which the collective work was completed is the creation date.

Work Made for Hire: A "work made for hire" is defined as: (1) a work prepared by an employee within the scope of his or her employment; or (2) a work specially ordered or commissioned for certain uses (including use as a contribution to a collective work), if the parties expressly agree in a written instrument signed by them that the work shall be considered a work made for hire. The employer is the author of a work made for hire.

The Copyright Notice: Before March 1, 1989, the use of copyright notice was mandatory on all published works, and any work first published before that date should have carried a notice. For works first published on and after March 1, 1989, use of the copyright notice is optional. For more information about copyright notice, see Circular 3, "Copyright Notices."

For Further Information: To speak to an information specialist, call (202) 707-3000 (TTY: (202) 707-6737). Recorded information is available 24 hours a day. Order forms and other publications from the address at the bottom of page 2, or call the Forms and Publications Hotline at (202) 707-9100. Most circulars (but not forms) are available via fax. Call (202) 707-2600 from a touchtone phone. Access and download circulars, forms, and other information from the Copyright Office Website at www.loc.gov/copyright.

LINE-BY-LINE INSTRUCTIONS

SPACE 1: Title and Date of Publication

Give the complete title of the serial, followed by the International Standard Serial Number (ISSN), if available. List the issues in the order of publication. For each issue, give the volume, number, and issue date appearing on the copies, followed by the complete date of publication, including month, day, and year. If you have not previously registered this identical title under Section 408 of the Copyright Act, please indicate by checking the box.

SPACE 2: Author and Copyright Claimant

Give the fullest form of the author and claimant's name and mailing address. If there are joint authors and claimants, give the names and addresses of all the author/claimants. If the work is not of U.S. origin, add the citizenship or domicile of the author/claimant, or the nation of publication.

Certification: The application cannot be accepted unless it bears the handwritten signature of the copyright claimant or the duly authorized agent of the copyright claimant.

Person to Contact for Correspondence About This Claim: Give the name, address, telephone number, area code, fax number, and email address (if available) of the person to whom any correspondence concerning this claim should be addressed. Give the address only if it is different from the address for mailing of the certificate.

Deposit Account: If the filing fee is to be charged against a deposit account in the Copyright Office, give the name and number of the account in this space. Otherwise, leave the space blank and forward the filing fee with your application and deposit.

Mailing Address of Certificate: This address must be complete and legible since the certificate will be mailed in a window envelope.

(Information continues on reverse ▶)

FORM SE/GROUP

UNITED STATES COPYRIGHT OFFICE

REGISTRATION NUMBER

_____

EFFECTIVE DATE OF REGISTRATION

_____

APPLICATION RECEIVED

_____

ONE DEPOSIT RECEIVED

_____

EXAMINED BY _____ CORRESPONDENCE ☐

DO NOT WRITE ABOVE THIS LINE.

1

List in order of publication

No previous registration under identical title ☐

TITLE ▼   **ISSN▼**

	Volume▼	Number▼	Issue date on copies▼	Month, day, and year of publication ▼
1.				
2.				
3.				
4.				
5.				
6.				
7.				
8.				
9.				
10.				
11.				
12.				
13.				
14.				

2

NAME AND ADDRESS OF THE AUTHOR/COPYRIGHT CLAIMANT IN THESE COLLECTIVE WORKS MADE FOR HIRE ▼

FOR NON-U.S. WORKS: Author's citizenship ▼   Domicile ▼   Nation of publication ▼

CERTIFICATION*: I, the undersigned, hereby certify that I am the copyright claimant or the authorized agent of the copyright claimant of the works identified in this application, that all the conditions specified in the instructions on the back of this form are met, that I have deposited two complimentary subscription copies with the Library of Congress, and that the statements made by me in this application are correct to the best of my knowledge.

☞ Handwritten signature (X) _____

Typed or printed name _____

PERSON TO CONTACT FOR CORRESPONDENCE ABOUT THIS CLAIM

Name ▶ _____   Daytime telephone ▶ _____

Address (if other than given below) ▶ _____

Fax ▶ _____   Email ▶ _____

Certificate will be mailed in window envelope to this address:

Name▼

Number/Street/Apt ▼

City/State/ZIP▼

DEPOSIT ACCOUNT

Account number ▶ _____

Name of account ▶ _____

MAIL TO:
Library of Congress
Copyright Office
101 Independence Avenue, S.E.
Washington, D.C. 20559-6000

June 1999—20,000
WEB REV: June 1999

♻ PRINTED ON RECYCLED PAPER

☆ U.S. GOVERNMENT PRINTING OFFICE: 1999-454-879/61

Form Group/Daily Newspapers and Newsletters

Read these instructions before completing this form. Make sure all applicable spaces have been filled in before you return this form.

▌ BASIC INFORMATION ▐

NEWSPAPERS

When to use this form for newspapers:

All the following conditions must be met to use this form. If any one of the conditions does not apply, you must use Form SE.

1. The work must be a daily **newspaper**. See definition below.
2. The work must be a "work made for hire," and the author and copyright claimant must be the same person or organization.
3. Each issue must be an essentially all new collective work or an essentially all new issue that has not been published before.
4. The claims must include **all issue dates** within 1 calendar month within the same year.
5. The application must be filed within 3 months of the last publication date included in the group.
6. The required deposit must be submitted. See below.

What to deposit for newspapers:

A deposit of positive 35mm silver-halide microfilm that includes all issues within the calendar month must accompany the application. Final editions are required when two or more daily editions are published.

In some cases, the publisher may be exempted from sending microfilm. The Copyright Acquisitions Division of the Copyright Office will notify the publisher if a newspaper is exempted. For an exempted newspaper, an optional deposit may accompany the application. This deposit should consist of (1) complete print copies of the first and last issues of the month, **or** (2) print copies of the first section of the first and last issues of the month, **or** (3) print copies of the first page of the first and last issues of the month.

NEWSLETTERS

When to use this form for newsletters:

All the following conditions must be met to use this form. If any one of the conditions does not apply, you must use Form SE.

1. The work must be a daily **newsletter**. See definition below.
2. The work must be a "work made for hire," and the author and copyright claimant must be the same person or organization.
3. Each issue must be an essentially all new collective work or an essentially all new issue that has not been published before.
4. The claims must include **two or more issue dates** within 1 calendar month within the same year.
5. The application must be filed within 3 months of the last publication date included in the group.
6. **All issues in the group must have been first published on or after July 1, 1999.** For information about newsletters published before July 1, 1999, please call the Examining Division at (202) 707-8250.
7. The required deposit must be submitted. See below.

What to deposit for newsletters:

In all cases, one complete copy of each issue included in the group must accompany the Form G/DN. If the newsletter is published only online, one complete print-out of each issue or a computer disk (or CD-ROM) containing all the issues **and** a print-out of the first and last issues included in the group must be sent.

Additional material must be sent **only if specifically requested by the Copyright Acquisitions Division.** The request will specify the nature of the additional material, which will be either (1) one microfilm copy meeting the specifications given above for newspapers, or (2) one or two complimentary subscriptions for the Library of Congress.

> **IMPORTANT:** The microfilm or subscriptions should be sent to a separate address specified in the request from the Copyright Acquisitions Division. This material should **not** be sent with Form G/DN. Unless expressly requested, no microfilm or subscription copies are required.

▌ INSTRUCTIONS ▐

HOW TO REGISTER

Send the following three items together in the same envelope or package:

1. completed and signed Form G/DN
2. deposit (see above)
3. $55 filing fee

Send this material to:
Library of Congress
Copyright Office
101 Independence Avenue, S.E.
Washington, D.C. 20559-6000

> **IMPORTANT:** Fees are effective through June 30, 2002. After that date, check the Copyright Office Website at www.loc.gov/copyright or call (202) 707-3000 for current fee information.

DEFINITIONS

Newspaper: As defined by the Newspaper Section of the Serials and Government Publications Division of the Library of Congress, works classified as newspapers are serials mainly designed to be a primary source of written information on current events, either local, national, or international in scope. Newspapers contain a broad range of news on all subjects and activities and are not limited to any specific subject matter. Newspapers are intended either for the general public or for a particular group.

Newsletter: For registration purposes, a daily newsletter is defined as a serial published and distributed by mail or electronic media (online, telefacsimile, cassette tape, diskette, or CD-ROM). Publication must occur at least 2 days per week, and the newsletter must contain news or information of interest chiefly to a special group (for example, trade and professional associations, corporations, schools, colleges, and churches). Daily newsletters are customarily available by subscription and are not sold on newsstands.

Collective Work: A "collective work" is a work, such as a periodical issue, in which a number of contributions, constituting separate and independent works in themselves, are assembled into a collective whole.

Work Made for Hire: A "work made for hire" is defined as: (1) a work prepared by an employee within the scope of his or her employment; or (2) a work specially ordered or commissioned for certain uses (including use as a contribution to a collective work), if the parties expressly agree in a written instrument signed by them that the work shall be considered a work made for hire. The employer is the author of a work made for hire. For more information, request Circular 9, "Works Made for Hire Under the 1976 Copyright Act."

FORM G/DN
For Group/Daily Newspapers and Newsletters
UNITED STATES COPYRIGHT OFFICE

REGISTRATION NUMBER

EFFECTIVE DATE OF REGISTRATION
(Assigned by Copyright Office)

Month	Day	Year

APPLICATION RECEIVED

EXAMINED BY

ONE DEPOSIT RECEIVED

CORRESPONDENCE ☐

FEE RECEIVED

DO NOT WRITE ABOVE THIS LINE.

1

TITLE OF THIS ☐ NEWSPAPER AS IT APPEARS ON THE COPIES ▼ City/State ▼
☐ NEWSLETTER

If no previous registration under identical title, check here ☐

Month and year date on copies ▼   Number of issues in this group ▼   ISSN ▼   Edition ▼

2

NAME AND ADDRESS OF THE AUTHOR/COPYRIGHT CLAIMANT IN THESE WORKS MADE FOR HIRE

AUTHOR'S CONTRIBUTION (check all that apply)

☐ Editing   ☐ Compilation   ☐ Text   ☐ Other _____

3

DATE OF PUBLICATION OF THE FIRST AND LAST ISSUES IN THIS GROUP Important: Give month, day, and year

(First) _____   (Last) _____
Month ▲   Day ▲   Year ▲   Month ▲   Day ▲   Year ▲

CERTIFICATION*:   I, the undersigned, hereby certify that I am the copyright claimant or the authorized agent of the copyright claimant of the works identified in this application, that all the conditions specified in the instructions on the back of this form are met, and that the statements made by me in this application are correct to the best of my knowledge.

Handwritten signature (X) _____

Typed or printed name of signer _____

PERSON TO CONTACT FOR CORRESPONDENCE ABOUT THIS CLAIM

Name ▶ _____
Daytime telephone number ▶ ( ) _____
Address (if other than given below) ▶ _____
_____

Fax ▶ _____   Email ▶ _____

DEPOSIT ACCOUNT

Account number ▶ _____
Name of account ▶ _____

Certificate will be mailed in window envelope to this address

Name ▼ _____
Number/Street/Apt ▼ _____
City/State/ZIP ▼ _____

YOU MUST:
• Complete all necessary spaces
• Sign your application

SEND ALL 3 ELEMENTS IN THE SAME PACKAGE:
1. Application form
2. Nonrefundable filing fee in check or money order payable to *Register of Copyrights*
3. Deposit material

MAIL TO:
Library of Congress, Copyright Office
101 Independence Avenue, S.E.
Washington, D.C. 20559-6000

As of July 1, 1999, the filing fee for Form G/DN is $55.

February 2000—30,000
WEB REV: February 2000

PRINTED ON RECYCLED PAPER

☆ U.S. GOVERNMENT PRINTING OFFICE: 2000-461-113/98

Detach and read these instructions before completing this form.
Make sure all applicable spaces have been filled in before you return this form.

BASIC INFORMATION

When to Use This Form: Use Form PA for registration of published or unpublished works of the performing arts. This class includes works prepared for the purpose of being "performed" directly before an audience or indirectly "by means of any device or process." Works of the performing arts include: (1) musical works, including any accompanying words; (2) dramatic works, including any accompanying music; (3) pantomimes and choreographic works; and (4) motion pictures and other audiovisual works.

Deposit to Accompany Application: An application for copyright registration must be accompanied by a deposit consisting of copies or phonorecords representing the entire work for which registration is made. The following are the general deposit requirements as set forth in the statute:

Unpublished Work: Deposit one complete copy (or phonorecord).
Published Work: Deposit two complete copies (or one phonorecord) of the best edition.
Work First Published Outside the United States: Deposit one complete copy (or phonorecord) of the first foreign edition.
Contribution to a Collective Work: Deposit one complete copy (or phonorecord) of the best edition of the collective work.
Motion Pictures: Deposit *both* of the following: (1) a separate written description of the contents of the motion picture; and (2) for a published work, one complete copy of the best edition of the motion picture; or, for an unpublished work, one complete copy of the motion picture or identifying material. Identifying material may be either an audiorecording of the entire soundtrack or one frame enlargement or similar visual print from each 10-minute segment.

The Copyright Notice: Before March 1, 1989, the use of copyright notice was mandatory on all published works, and any work first published before that date should have carried a notice. For works first published on and after March 1, 1989, use of the copyright notice is optional. For more information about copyright notice, see Circular 3, "Copyright Notice."

For Further Information: To speak to an information specialist, call (202) 707-3000 (TTY: (202) 707-6737). Recorded information is available 24 hours a day. Order forms and other publications from the address in space 9 or call the Forms and Publications Hotline at (202) 707-9100. Most circulars (but not forms) are available via fax. Call (202) 707-2600 from a touchtone phone. Access and download circulars, forms, and other information from the Copyright Office Website at www.loc.gov/copyright.

LINE-BY-LINE INSTRUCTIONS

Please type or print using black ink. The form is used to produce the certificate.

SPACE 1: Title

Title of This Work: Every work submitted for copyright registration must be given a title to identify that particular work. If the copies or phonorecords of the work bear a title (or an identifying phrase that could serve as a title), transcribe that wording *completely* and *exactly* on the application. Indexing of the registration and future identification of the work will depend on the information you give here. If the work you are registering is an entire "collective work" (such as a collection of plays or songs), give the overall title of the collection. If you are registering one or more individual contributions to a collective work, give the title of each contribution, followed by the title of the collection. For an unpublished collection, you may give the titles of the individual works after the collection title.

Previous or Alternative Titles: Complete this space if there are any additional titles for the work under which someone searching for the registration might be likely to look, or under which a document pertaining to the work might be recorded.

Nature of This Work: Briefly describe the general nature or character of the work being registered for copyright. Examples: "Music"; "Song Lyrics"; "Words and Music"; "Drama"; "Musical Play"; "Choreography"; "Pantomime"; "Motion Picture"; "Audiovisual Work."

SPACE 2: Author(s)

General Instructions: After reading these instructions, decide who are the "authors" of this work for copyright purposes. Then, unless the work is a "collective work," give the requested information about every "author" who contributed any appreciable amount of copyrightable matter to this version of the work. If you need further space, request additional Continuation Sheets. In the case of a collective work such as a songbook or a collection of plays, give information about the author of the collective work as a whole.

Name of Author: The fullest form of the author's name should be given. Unless the work was "made for hire," the individual who actually created the work is its "author." In the case of a work made for hire, the statute provides that "the employer or other person for whom the work was prepared is considered the author."

What is a "Work Made for Hire"? A "work made for hire" is defined as: (1) "a work prepared by an employee within the scope of his or her employment"; or (2) "a work specially ordered or commissioned for use as a contribution to a collective work, as a part of a motion picture or other audiovisual work, as a translation, as a

supplementary work, as a compilation, as an instructional text, as a test, as answer material for a test, or as an atlas, if the parties expressly agree in a written instrument signed by them that the work shall be considered a work made for hire." If you have checked "Yes" to indicate that the work was "made for hire," you must give the full legal name of the employer (or other person for whom the work was prepared). You may also include the name of the employee along with the name of the employer (for example: "Elster Music Co., employer for hire of John Ferguson").

"Anonymous" or "Pseudonymous" Work: An author's contribution to a work is "anonymous" if that author is not identified on the copies or phonorecords of the work. An author's contribution to a work is "pseudonymous" if that author is identified on the copies or phonorecords under a fictitious name. If the work is "anonymous" you may: (1) leave the line blank; or (2) state "anonymous" on the line; or (3) reveal the author's identity. If the work is "pseudonymous" you may: (1) leave the line blank; or (2) give the pseudonym and identify it as such (example: "Huntley Haverstock, pseudonym"); or (3) reveal the author's name, making clear which is the real name and which is the pseudonym (for example: "Judith Barton, whose pseudonym is Madeline Elster"). However, the citizenship or domicile of the author **must** be given in all cases.

Dates of Birth and Death: If the author is dead, the statute requires that the year of death be included in the application unless the work is anonymous or pseudonymous. The author's birth date is optional, but is useful as a form of identification. Leave this space blank if the author's contribution was a "work made for hire."

Author's Nationality or Domicile: Give the country of which the author is a citizen, or the country in which the author is domiciled. Nationality or domicile **must** be given in all cases.

Nature of Authorship: Give a brief general statement of the nature of this particular author's contribution to the work. Examples: "Words"; "Coauthor of Music"; "Words and Music"; "Arrangement"; "Coauthor of Book and Lyrics"; "Dramatization"; "Screen Play"; "Compilation and English Translation"; "Editorial Revisions."

3 SPACE 3: Creation and Publication

General Instructions: Do not confuse "creation" with "publication." Every application for copyright registration must state "the year in which creation of the work was completed." Give the date and nation of first publication only if the work has been published.

Creation: Under the statute, a work is "created" when it is fixed in a copy or phonorecord for the first time. Where a work has been prepared over a period of time, the part of the work existing in fixed form on a particular date constitutes the created work on that date. The date you give here should be the year in which the author completed the particular version for which registration is now being sought, even if other versions exist or if further changes or additions are planned.

Publication: The statute defines "publication" as "the distribution of copies or phonorecords of a work to the public by sale or other transfer of ownership, or by rental, lease, or lending"; a work is also "published" if there has been an "offering to distribute copies or phonorecords to a group of persons for purposes of further distribution, public performance, or public display." Give the full date (month, day, year) when, and the country where, publication first occurred. If first publication took place simultaneously in the United States and other countries, it is sufficient to state "U.S.A."

4 SPACE 4: Claimant(s)

Name(s) and Address(es) of Copyright Claimant(s): Give the name(s) and address(es) of the copyright claimant(s) in this work even if the claimant is the same as the author. Copyright in a work belongs initially to the author of the work (including, in the case of a work made for hire, the employer or other person for whom the work was prepared). The copyright claimant is either the author of the work or a person or organization to whom the copyright initially belonging to the author has been transferred.

Transfer: The statute provides that, if the copyright claimant is not the author, the application for registration must contain "a brief statement of how the claimant obtained ownership of the copyright." If any copyright claimant named in space 4 is not an author named in space 2, give a brief statement explaining how the claimant(s) obtained ownership of the copyright. Examples: "By written contract"; "Transfer of all rights by author"; "Assignment"; "By will." Do not attach transfer documents or other attachments or riders.

5 SPACE 5: Previous Registration

General Instructions: The questions in space 5 are intended to show whether an earlier registration has been made for this work and, if so, whether there is any basis for a new registration. As a general rule, only one basic copyright registration can be made for the same version of a particular work.

Same Version: If this version is substantially the same as the work covered by a previous registration, a second registration is not generally possible unless: (1) the work has been registered in unpublished form and a second registration is now being sought to cover this first published edition; or (2) someone other than the author is identified as copyright claimant in the earlier registration, and the author is now seeking registration in his or her own name. If either of these two exceptions applies, check the appropriate box and give the earlier registration number and date. Otherwise, do not submit Form PA; instead, write the Copyright Office for informa-

tion about supplementary registration or recordation of transfers of copyright ownership.

Changed Version: If the work has been changed and you are now seeking registration to cover the additions or revisions, check the last box in space 5, give the earlier registration number and date, and complete both parts of space 6 in accordance with the instructions below.

Previous Registration Number and Date: If more than one previous registration has been made for the work, give the number and date of the latest registration.

6 SPACE 6: Derivative Work or Compilation

General Instructions: Complete space 6 if this work is a "changed version," "compilation," or "derivative work," and if it incorporates one or more earlier works that have already been published or registered for copyright or that have fallen into the public domain. A "compilation" is defined as "a work formed by the collection and assembling of preexisting materials or of data that are selected, coordinated, or arranged in such a way that the resulting work as a whole constitutes an original work of authorship." A "derivative work" is "a work based on one or more preexisting works." Examples of derivative works include musical arrangements, dramatizations, translations, abridgments, condensations, motion picture versions, or "any other form in which a work may be recast, transformed, or adapted." Derivative works also include works "consisting of editorial revisions, annotations, or other modifications" if these changes, as a whole, represent an original work of authorship.

Preexisting Material (space 6a): Complete this space **and** space 6b for derivative works. In this space identify the preexisting work that has been recast, transformed, or adapted. For example, the preexisting material might be: "French version of Hugo's 'Le Roi s'amuse'." Do not complete this space for compilations.

Material Added to This Work (space 6b): Give a brief, general statement of the **additional** new material covered by the copyright claim for which registration is sought. In the case of a derivative work, identify this new material. Examples: "Arrangement for piano and orchestra"; "Dramatization for television"; "New film version"; "Revisions throughout; Act III completely new." If the work is a compilation, give a brief, general statement describing both the material that has been compiled **and** the compilation itself. Example: "Compilation of 19th Century Military Songs."

7,8,9 SPACE 7, 8, 9: Fee, Correspondence, Certification, Return Address

Deposit Account: If you maintain a Deposit Account in the Copyright Office, identify it in space 7a. Otherwise, leave the space blank and send the fee of $30 (effective through June 30, 2002) with your application and deposit.

Correspondence (space 7b): This space should contain the name, address, area code, telephone number, fax number, and email address (if available) of the person to be consulted if correspondence about this application becomes necessary.

Certification (space 8): The application cannot be accepted unless it bears the date and the **handwritten signature** of the author or other copyright claimant, or of the owner of exclusive right(s), or of the duly authorized agent of the author, claimant, or owner of exclusive right(s).

Address for Return of Certificate (space 9): The address box must be completed legibly since the certificate will be returned in a window envelope.

MORE INFORMATION

How to Register a Recorded Work: If the musical or dramatic work that you are registering has been recorded (as a tape, disk, or cassette), you may choose either copyright application Form PA (Performing Arts) or Form SR (Sound Recordings), depending on the purpose of the registration.

Form PA should be used to register the underlying musical composition or dramatic work. Form SR has been developed specifically to register a "sound recording" as defined by the Copyright Act—a work resulting from the "fixation of a series of sounds," separate and distinct from the underlying musical or dramatic work. Form SR should be used when the copyright claim is limited to the sound recording itself. (In one instance, Form SR may also be used to file for a copyright registration for both kinds of works—see (4) below.) Therefore:

(1) File Form PA if you are seeking to register the musical or dramatic work, not the "sound recording," even though what you deposit for copyright purposes may be in the form of a phonorecord.

(2) File Form PA if you are seeking to register the audio portion of an audiovisual work, such as a motion picture soundtrack; these are considered integral parts of the audiovisual work.

(3) File Form SR if you are seeking to register the "sound recording" itself, that is, the work that results from the fixation of a series of musical, spoken, or other sounds, but not the underlying musical or dramatic work.

(4) File Form SR if you are the copyright claimant for both the underlying musical or dramatic work and the sound recording, *and* you prefer to register both on the same form.

(5) File both forms PA and SR if the copyright claimant for the underlying work and sound recording differ, or you prefer to have separate registration for them.

"Copies" and "Phonorecords": To register for copyright, you are required to deposit "copies" or "phonorecords." These are defined as follows:

Musical compositions may be embodied (fixed) in "copies," objects from which a work can be read or visually perceived, directly or with the aid of a machine or device, such as manuscripts, books, sheet music, film, and videotape. They may also be fixed in "phonorecords," objects embodying fixations of sounds, such as tapes and phonograph disks, commonly known as phonograph records. For example, a song (the work to be registered) can be reproduced in sheet music ("copies") or phonograph records ("phonorecords"), or both.

FORM PA

For a Work of the Performing Arts
UNITED STATES COPYRIGHT OFFICE

REGISTRATION NUMBER

_____

PA   PAU

EFFECTIVE DATE OF REGISTRATION

_____

Month   Day   Year

DO NOT WRITE ABOVE THIS LINE. IF YOU NEED MORE SPACE, USE A SEPARATE CONTINUATION SHEET.

1

TITLE OF THIS WORK ▼

_____

PREVIOUS OR ALTERNATIVE TITLES ▼

_____

NATURE OF THIS WORK ▼ See instructions

2

a

NAME OF AUTHOR ▼

_____

DATES OF BIRTH AND DEATH
Year Born ▼   Year Died ▼

Was this contribution to the work a "work made for hire"?
☐ Yes
☐ No

AUTHOR'S NATIONALITY OR DOMICILE
Name of Country
OR { Citizen of ▶ _____
Domiciled in ▶ _____

WAS THIS AUTHOR'S CONTRIBUTION TO THE WORK
Anonymous?   ☐ Yes ☐ No
Pseudonymous? ☐ Yes ☐ No

If the answer to either of these questions is "Yes," see detailed instructions.

NATURE OF AUTHORSHIP Briefly describe nature of material created by this author in which copyright is claimed. ▼

b

NAME OF AUTHOR ▼

_____

DATES OF BIRTH AND DEATH
Year Born ▼   Year Died ▼

Was this contribution to the work a "work made for hire"?
☐ Yes
☐ No

AUTHOR'S NATIONALITY OR DOMICILE
Name of Country
OR { Citizen of ▶ _____
Domiciled in ▶ _____

WAS THIS AUTHOR'S CONTRIBUTION TO THE WORK
Anonymous?   ☐ Yes ☐ No
Pseudonymous? ☐ Yes ☐ No

If the answer to either of these questions is "Yes," see detailed instructions.

NATURE OF AUTHORSHIP Briefly describe nature of material created by this author in which copyright is claimed. ▼

c

NAME OF AUTHOR ▼

_____

DATES OF BIRTH AND DEATH
Year Born ▼   Year Died ▼

Was this contribution to the work a "work made for hire"?
☐ Yes
☐ No

AUTHOR'S NATIONALITY OR DOMICILE
Name of Country
OR { Citizen of ▶ _____
Domiciled in ▶ _____

WAS THIS AUTHOR'S CONTRIBUTION TO THE WORK
Anonymous?   ☐ Yes ☐ No
Pseudonymous? ☐ Yes ☐ No

If the answer to either of these questions is "Yes," see detailed instructions.

NATURE OF AUTHORSHIP Briefly describe nature of material created by this author in which copyright is claimed. ▼

NOTE

Under the law, the "author" of a "work made for hire" is generally the employer, not the employee (see instructions). For any part of this work that was "made for hire" check "Yes" in the space provided, give the employer (or other person for whom the work was prepared) as "Author" of that part, and leave the space for dates of birth and death blank.

3

a

YEAR IN WHICH CREATION OF THIS WORK WAS COMPLETED
_____ ◀ Year
This information must be given in all cases.

b

DATE AND NATION OF FIRST PUBLICATION OF THIS PARTICULAR WORK
Complete this information ONLY if this work has been published.
Month ▶ _____ Day ▶ _____ Year ▶ _____
◀ Nation

4

See instructions before completing this space.

COPYRIGHT CLAIMANT(S) Name and address must be given even if the claimant is the same as the author given in space 2. ▼

TRANSFER If the claimant(s) named here in space 4 is (are) different from the author(s) named in space 2, give a brief statement of how the claimant(s) obtained ownership of the copyright. ▼

MORE ON BACK ▶
• Complete all applicable spaces (numbers 5-9) on the reverse side of this page.
• See detailed instructions.   • Sign the form at line 8.

DO NOT WRITE HERE

Page 1 of _____ pages

EXAMINED BY _____

CHECKED BY _____

☐ CORRESPONDENCE
  Yes

FORM PA

FOR
COPYRIGHT
OFFICE
USE
ONLY

DO NOT WRITE ABOVE THIS LINE. IF YOU NEED MORE SPACE, USE A SEPARATE CONTINUATION SHEET.

PREVIOUS REGISTRATION Has registration for this work, or for an earlier version of this work, already been made in the Copyright Office?

☐ **Yes** ☐ **No** If your answer is "Yes," why is another registration being sought? (Check appropriate box.) ▼ If your answer is "no," go to space 7.

a. ☐ This is the first published edition of a work previously registered in unpublished form.

b. ☐ This is the first application submitted by this author as copyright claimant.

c. ☐ This is a changed version of the work, as shown by space 6 on this application.

If your answer is "Yes," give: **Previous Registration Number** ▼ _____   **Year of Registration** ▼ _____

5

DERIVATIVE WORK OR COMPILATION   Complete both space 6a and 6b for a derivative work; complete only 6b for a compilation.
Preexisting Material Identify any preexisting work or works that this work is based on or incorporates. ▼

Material Added to This Work Give a brief, general statement of the material that has been added to this work and in which copyright is claimed. ▼

a
b
6

See instructions before completing this space.

DEPOSIT ACCOUNT If the registration fee is to be charged to a Deposit Account established in the Copyright Office, give name and number of Account.
Name ▼   **Account Number** ▼

a
7

CORRESPONDENCE Give name and address to which correspondence about this application should be sent.   Name/Address/Apt/City/State/ZIP ▼

b

Area code and daytime telephone number ▶ (   )   Fax number ▶ (   )

Email ▶

CERTIFICATION* I, the undersigned, hereby certify that I am the

Check only one ▶ {
☐ author
☐ other copyright claimant
☐ owner of exclusive right(s)
☐ authorized agent of _____
   Name of author or other copyright claimant, or owner of exclusive right(s) ▲

of the work identified in this application and that the statements made by me in this application are correct to the best of my knowledge.

8

Typed or printed name and date ▼ If this application gives a date of publication in space 3, do not sign and submit it before that date.

_____   Date ▶ _____

Handwritten signature (X) ▼

x _____

Certificate will be mailed in window envelope to this address:

Name ▼

Number/Street/Apt ▼

City/State/ZIP ▼

YOU MUST:
• Complete all necessary spaces
• Sign your application in space 8
SEND ALL 3 ELEMENTS IN THE SAME PACKAGE:
1. Application form
2. Nonrefundable filing fee in check or money order payable to *Register of Copyrights*
3. Deposit material
MAIL TO:
Library of Congress
Copyright Office
101 Independence Avenue, S.E.
Washington, D.C. 20559-6000

As of July 1, 1999, the filing fee for Form PA is $30.

9

June 1999—200,000
WEB REV: June 1999

♻ PRINTED ON RECYCLED PAPER

☆U.S. GOVERNMENT PRINTING OFFICE: 1999-454-879/68

USE THIS FORM IF—

1. You are the **only** author and copyright owner of this work, *and*
2. The work was **not** made for hire, *and*
3. The work is completely new (does not contain a substantial amount of material that has been previously published or registered or is in the public domain) and is not an audiovisual work.

If any of the above does not apply, you must use standard Form PA.

NOTE: Short Form PA is not appropriate for an anonymous author who does not wish to reveal his or her identity and may not be used for audiovisual works, including motion pictures.

HOW TO COMPLETE SHORT FORM PA

- ■ Type or print in black ink.
- ■ Be clear and legible. (Your certificate of registration will be copied from your form.)
- ■ Give only the information requested.

NOTE: You may use a continuation sheet (Form __/CON) to list individual titles in a collection. Complete Space A and list the individual titles under Space C on the back page. Space B is not applicable to short forms.

---

1 Title of This Work

You must give a title. If there is no title, state "UNTITLED." Alternative title: If the work is known by two titles, you also may give the second title. Or if the work has been published as part of a larger work, give the title of that larger work, in addition to the title of the contribution.

If you are registering an unpublished collection, give the collection title you want to appear in our records (for example: "Songs by Alice, Volume 1"). Be sure to keep a personal record of the songs you have included in the collection. If you want the certificate of registration to list the individual titles as well as the collection title, use a continuation sheet (Form___/CON).

2 Name and Address of Author and Owner of the Copyright

Give your name and mailing address. You may include your pseudonym followed by "pseud." Also, give the nation of which you are a citizen or where you have your domicile (i.e., permanent residence). Please give daytime phone and fax numbers and email address, if available.

3 Year of Creation

Give the latest year in which you completed the work you are registering at this time. A work is "created" when it is written down, recorded, or otherwise "fixed" in a tangible form.

4 Publication

If the work has been published (i.e., if copies have been distributed to the public), give the complete date of publication (month, day, and year) and the nation where the publication first took place.

5 Type of Authorship in This Work

Check the box or boxes that describe the kind of material you are registering. Check *only* the authorship included in the copy, tape, or CD you are sending with the application. For example, if you are registering lyrics and plan to add music later, check only the box for "lyrics."

6 Signature of Author

Sign the application in black ink and check the appropriate box. The person signing the application should be the author or his/her authorized agent.

7 Person to Contact for Rights and Permissions

This space is optional. You may give the name and address of the person or organization to contact for permission to use the work. You may also provide phone, fax, or email information.

8 Certificate Will Be Mailed

This space must be completed. Your certificate of registration will be mailed in a window envelope to this address. Also, if the Copyright Office needs to contact you, we will write to this address.

9 Deposit Account

Complete this space only if you currently maintain a deposit account in the Copyright Office.

MAIL WITH THE FORM—

- ■ A $30 (effective through June 30, 2002) filing fee in the form of a check or money order *(no cash)* payable to "Register of Copyrights," **and**
- ■ One or two copies of the work. If the work is unpublished, send one copy, tape, or CD. If published, send two copies of the best published edition if the work is in printed form, such as sheet music, or one copy of the best published edition if the work is recorded on a tape or disk.

Note: Inquire about special requirements for works first published outside the United States or before 1978. Copies submitted become the property of the U.S. Government.

Mail everything **(application form, copy or copies, and fee)** *in one package* to: Library of Congress, Copyright Office
101 Independence Avenue, S.E.
Washington, D.C. 20559-6000

QUESTIONS? Call (202) 707-3000 [TTY: (202) 707-6737] between 8:30 a.m. and 5:00 p.m. eastern time, Monday through Friday except federal holidays. For forms and informational circulars, call (202) 707-9100 24 hours a day, 7 days a week, or download them from the Internet at www.loc.gov/copyright. Selected informational circulars but not forms are available from Fax-on-Demand at (202) 707-2600.

Registration Number

PA   PAU

Effective Date of Registration

Application Received

Examined By

Deposit Received
One | Two

Correspondence ☐

Fee Received

TYPE OR PRINT IN BLACK INK. DO NOT WRITE ABOVE THIS LINE.

1   **Title of This Work:**

Alternative title or title of larger work in which this work was published:

2   **Name and Address of Author and Owner of the Copyright:**

Nationality or domicile:
Phone, fax, and email:

Phone (   )   Fax (   )

Email:

3   **Year of Creation:**

4   *If work has been published,* **Date and Nation of Publication:**

a. Date _____ _____ _____ *(Month, day, and year all required)*
               Month   Day   Year

b. Nation

5   **Type of Authorship in This Work:**
Check all that this author created.

☐ Music   ☐ Other text (includes dramas, screenplays, etc.)
☐ Lyrics   *(If your work is a motion picture or other audiovisual work, use the Standard Form PA.)*

6   **Signature:**
(Registration cannot be completed without a signature.)

I certify that the statements made by me in this application are correct to the best of my knowledge. Check one:

☐ Author

☐ Authorized agent   **X** _

7   **Name and Address of Person to Contact for Rights and Permissions:**

OPTIONAL

☐ Check here if same as #2 above.

Phone, fax, and email:

Phone (   )   Fax (   )

Email:

8   **Certificate will be mailed in window envelope to this address:**

Name ▼

Number/Street/Apt ▼

City/State/ZIP ▼

Complete this space only if you currently hold a Deposit Account in the Copyright Office.

9   Deposit Account # _____

Name _____

DO NOT WRITE HERE   Page 1 of _____ pages

Application Form VA

Detach and read these instructions before completing this form.
Make sure all applicable spaces have been filled in before you return this form.

BASIC INFORMATION

When to Use This Form: Use Form VA for copyright registration of published or unpublished works of the visual arts. This category consists of "pictorial, graphic, or sculptural works," including two-dimensional and three-dimensional works of fine, graphic, and applied art, photographs, prints and art reproductions, maps, globes, charts, technical drawings, diagrams, and models.

What Does Copyright Protect? Copyright in a work of the visual arts protects those pictorial, graphic, or sculptural elements that, either alone or in combination, represent an "original work of authorship." The statute declares: "In no case does copyright protection for an original work of authorship extend to any idea, procedure, process, system, method of operation, concept, principle, or discovery, regardless of the form in which it is described, explained, illustrated, or embodied in such work."

Works of Artistic Craftsmanship and Designs: "Works of artistic craftsmanship" are registrable on Form VA, but the statute makes clear that protection extends to "their form" and not to "their mechanical or utilitarian aspects." The "design of a useful article" is considered copyrightable "only if, and only to the extent that, such design incorporates pictorial, graphic, or sculptural features that can be identified separately from, and are capable of existing independently of, the utilitarian aspects of the article."

Labels and Advertisements: Works prepared for use in connection with the sale or advertisement of goods and services are registrable if they contain "original work of authorship." Use Form VA if the copyrightable material in the work you are registering is mainly pictorial or graphic; use Form TX if it consists mainly of text. **NOTE :** Words and short phrases such as names, titles, and slogans cannot be protected by copyright, and the same is true of standard symbols, emblems, and other commonly used graphic designs that are in the public domain. When used commercially, material of that sort can sometimes be protected under state laws of unfair competition or under the federal trademark laws. For information about trademark registration, write to the Commissioner of Patents and Trademarks, Washington, D.C. 20231.

Architectural Works: Copyright protection extends to the design of buildings created for the use of human beings. Architectural works created on or after December 1, 1990, or that on December 1, 1990, were unconstructed and embodied only in unpublished plans or drawings are eligible. Request Circular 41 for more information. Architectural works and technical drawings cannot be registered on the same application.

Deposit to Accompany Application: An application for copyright registration must be accompanied by a deposit consisting of copies representing the entire work for which registration is to be made.

    Unpublished Work: Deposit one complete copy.

    Published Work: Deposit two complete copies of the best edition.

    Work First Published Outside the United States: Deposit one complete copy of the first foreign edition.

    Contribution to a Collective Work: Deposit one complete copy of the best edition of the collective work.

The Copyright Notice: Before March 1, 1989, the use of copyright notice was mandatory on all published works, and any work first published before that date should have carried a notice. For works first published on and after March 1, 1989, use of the copyright notice is optional. For more information about copyright notice, see Circular 3, "Copyright Notice."

For Further Information: To speak to an information specialist, call (202) 707-3000 (TTY: (202) 707-6737). Recorded information is available 24 hours a day. Order forms and other publications from the address in space 9 or call the Forms and Publications Hotline at (202) 707-9100. Most circulars (but not forms) are available via fax. Call (202) 707-2600 from a touchtone phone. Access and download circulars, forms, and other information from the Copyright Office Website at:

www.loc.gov/copyright

LINE-BY-LINE INSTRUCTIONS

Please type or print using black ink. The form is used to produce the certificate.

1 SPACE 1: Title

Title of This Work: Every work submitted for copyright registration must be given a title to identify that particular work. If the copies of the work bear a title (or an identifying phrase that could serve as a title), transcribe that wording *completely* and *exactly* on the application. Indexing of the registration and future identification of the work will depend on the information you give here. For an architectural work that has been constructed, add the date of construction after the title; if unconstructed at this time, add "not yet constructed."

Publication as a Contribution: If the work being registered is a contribution to a periodical, serial, or collection, give the title of the contribution in the "Title of This Work" space. Then, in the line headed "Publication as a Contribution," give information about the collective work in which the contribution appeared.

Nature of This Work: Briefly describe the general nature or character of the pictorial, graphic, or sculptural work being registered for copyright. Examples: "Oil Painting"; "Charcoal Drawing"; "Etching"; "Sculpture"; "Map"; "Photograph"; "Scale Model"; "Lithographic Print"; "Jewelry Design"; "Fabric Design."

Previous or Alternative Titles: Complete this space if there are any additional titles for the work under which someone searching for the registration might be likely to look, or under which a document pertaining to the work might be recorded.

2 SPACE 2: Author(s)

General Instruction: After reading these instructions, decide who are the "authors" of this work for copyright purposes. Then, unless the work is a "collective work," give the requested information about every "author" who contributed any appreciable amount of copyrightable matter to this version of the work. If you need further space, request Continuation Sheets. In the case of a collective work, such as a catalog of paintings or collection of cartoons by various authors, give information about the author of the collective work as a whole.

Name of Author: The fullest form of the author's name should be given. Unless the work was "made for hire," the individual who actually created the work is its "author." In the case of a work made for hire, the statute provides that "the employer or other person for whom the work was prepared is considered the author."

What is a "Work Made for Hire"? A "work made for hire" is defined as: (1) "a work prepared by an employee within the scope of his or her employment"; or (2) "a work specially ordered or commissioned for use as a contribution to a collective work, as a part of a motion picture or other audiovisual work, as a translation, as a supplementary work, as a compilation, as an instructional text, as a test, as answer material for a test, or as an atlas, if the parties expressly agree in a written instrument signed by them that the work shall be considered a work made for hire." If you have checked "Yes" to indicate that the work was "made for hire," you must give the full legal name of the employer (or other person for whom the work was prepared). You may also include the name of the employee along with the name of the employer (for example: "Elster Publishing Co., employer for hire of John Ferguson").

"Anonymous" or "Pseudonymous" Work: An author's contribution to a work is "anonymous" if that author is not identified on the copies or phonorecords of the work. An author's contribution to a work is "pseudonymous" if that author is identified on the copies or phonorecords under a fictitious name. If the work is "anonymous" you may: (1) leave the line blank; or (2) state "anonymous" on the line; or (3) reveal the author's identity. If the work is "pseudonymous" you may: (1) leave the line blank; or (2) give the pseudonym and identify it as such (for example: "Huntley Haverstock, pseudonym"); or (3) reveal the author's name, making clear which is the real name and which is the pseudonym (for example: "Henry Leek, whose pseudonym is Priam Farrel"). However, the citizenship or domicile of the author **must** be given in all cases.

Dates of Birth and Death: If the author is dead, the statute requires that the year of death be included in the application unless the work is anonymous or pseudonymous. The author's birth date is optional but is useful as a form of identification. Leave this space blank if the author's contribution was a "work made for hire."

Author's Nationality or Domicile: Give the country of which the author is a citizen or the country in which the author is domiciled. Nationality or domicile **must** be given in all cases.

Nature of Authorship: Catagories of pictorial, graphic, and sculptural authorship are listed below. Check the box(es) that best describe(s) each author's contribution to the work.

3-Dimensional sculptures: fine art sculptures, toys, dolls, scale models, and sculptural designs applied to useful articles.

2-Dimensional artwork: watercolor and oil paintings; pen and ink drawings; logo illustrations; greeting cards; collages; stencils; patterns; computer graphics; graphics appearing in screen displays; artwork appearing on posters, calendars, games, commercial prints and labels, and packaging, as well as 2-dimensional artwork applied to useful articles, and designs reproduced on textiles, lace, and other fabrics; on wallpaper, carpeting, floor tile, wrapping paper, and clothing.

Reproductions of works of art: reproductions of preexisting artwork made by, for example, lithography, photoengraving, or etching.

Maps: cartographic representations of an area, such as state and county maps, atlases, marine charts, relief maps, and globes.

Photographs: pictorial photographic prints and slides and holograms.

Jewelry designs: 3-dimensional designs applied to rings, pendants, earrings, necklaces, and the like.

Technical drawings: diagrams illustrating scientific or technical information in linear form, such as architectural blueprints or mechanical drawings.

Text: textual material that accompanies pictorial, graphic, or sculptural works, such as comic strips, greeting cards, games rules, commercial prints or labels, and maps.

Architectural works: designs of buildings, including the overall form as well as the arrangement and composition of spaces and elements of the design.

NOTE: Any registration for the underlying architectural plans must be applied for on a separate Form VA, checking the box "Technical drawing."

---

3 SPACE 3: Creation and Publication

General Instructions: Do not confuse "creation" with "publication." Every application for copyright registration must state "the year in which creation of the work was completed." Give the date and nation of first publication only if the work has been published.

Creation: Under the statute, a work is "created" when it is fixed in a copy or phonorecord for the first time. Where a work has been prepared over a period of time, the part of the work existing in fixed form on a particular date constitutes the created work on that date. The date you give here should be the year in which the author completed the particular version for which registration is now being sought, even if other versions exist or if further changes or additions are planned.

Publication: The statute defines "publication" as "the distribution of copies or phonorecords of a work to the public by sale or other transfer of ownership, or by rental, lease, or lending"; a work is also "published" if there has been an "offering to distribute copies or phonorecords to a group of persons for purposes of further distribution, public performance, or public display." Give the full date (month, day, year) when, and the country where, publication first occurred. If first publication took place simultaneously in the United States and other countries, it is sufficient to state "U.S.A."

---

4 SPACE 4: Claimant(s)

Name(s) and Address(es) of Copyright Claimant(s): Give the name(s) and address(es) of the copyright claimant(s) in this work even if the claimant is the same as the author. Copyright in a work belongs initially to the author of the work (including, in the case of a work make for hire, the employer or other person for whom the work was prepared). The copyright claimant is either the author of the work or a person or organization to whom the copyright initially belonging to the author has been transferred.

Transfer: The statute provides that, if the copyright claimant is not the author, the application for registration must contain "a brief statement of how the claimant obtained ownership of the copyright." If any copyright claimant named in space 4 is not an author named in space 2, give a brief statement explaining how the claimant(s) obtained ownership of the copyright. Examples: "By written contract"; "Transfer of all rights by author"; "Assignment"; "By will." Do not attach transfer documents or other attachments or riders.

---

5 SPACE 5: Previous Registration

General Instructions: The questions in space 5 are intended to find out whether an earlier registration has been made for this work and, if so, whether there is any basis for a new registration. As a rule, only one basic

---

copyright registration can be made for the same version of a particular work.

Same Version: If this version is substantially the same as the work covered by a previous registration, a second registration is not generally possible unless: (1) the work has been registered in unpublished form and a second registration is now being sought to cover this first published edition; or (2) someone other than the author is identified as a copyright claimant in the earlier registration, and the author is now seeking registration in his or her own name. If either of these two exceptions applies, check the appropriate box and give the earlier registration number and date. Otherwise, do not submit Form VA; instead, write the Copyright Office for information about supplementary registration or recordation of transfers of copyright ownership.

Changed Version: If the work has been changed and you are now seeking registration to cover the additions or revisions, check the last box in space 5, give the earlier registration number and date, and complete both parts of space 6 in accordance with the instruction below.

Previous Registration Number and Date: If more than one previous registration has been made for the work, give the number and date of the latest registration.

---

6 SPACE 6: Derivative Work or Compilation

General Instructions: Complete space 6 if this work is a "changed version," "compilation," or "derivative work," and if it incorporates one or more earlier works that have already been published or registered for copyright, or that have fallen into the public domain. A "compilation" is defined as "a work formed by the collection and assembling of preexisting materials or of data that are selected, coordinated, or arranged in such a way that the resulting work as a whole constitutes an original work of authorship." A "derivative work" is "a work based on one or more preexisting works." Examples of derivative works include reproductions of works of art, sculptures based on drawings, lithographs based on paintings, maps based on previously published sources, or "any other form in which a work may be recast, transformed, or adapted." Derivative works also include works "consisting of editorial revisions, annotations, or other modifications" if these changes, as a whole, represent an original work of authorship.

Preexisting Material (space 6a): Complete this space **and** space 6b for derivative works. In this space identify the preexisting work that has been recast, transformed, or adapted. Examples of preexisting material might be "Grunewald Altarpiece" or "19th century quilt design." Do not complete this space for compilations.

Material Added to This Work (space 6b): Give a brief, general statement of the **additional** new material covered by the copyright claim for which registration is sought. In the case of a derivative work, identify this new material. Examples: "Adaptation of design and additional artistic work"; "Reproduction of painting by photolithography"; "Additional cartographic material"; "Compilation of photographs." If the work is a compilation, give a brief, general statement describing both the material that has been compiled **and** the compilation itself. Example: "Compilation of 19th century political cartoons."

7,8,9 SPACE 7, 8, 9: Fee, Correspondence, Certification, Return Address

Deposit Account: If you maintain a Deposit Account in the Copyright Office, identify it in space 7a. Otherwise, leave the space blank and send the fee of $30 (effective through June 30, 2002) with your application and deposit.

Correspondence (space 7b): This space should contain the name, address, area code, telephone number, email address, and fax number (if available) of the person to be consulted if correspondence about this application becomes necessary.

Certification (space 8): The application cannot be accepted unless it bears the date and the **handwritten signature** of the author or other copyright claimant, or of the owner of exclusive right(s), or of the duly authorized agent of the author, claimant, or owner of exclusive right(s).

Address for Return of Certificate (space 9): The address box must be completed legibly since the certificate will be returned in a window envelope.

FORM VA

For a Work of the Visual Arts
UNITED STATES COPYRIGHT OFFICE

REGISTRATION NUMBER

VA VAU

EFFECTIVE DATE OF REGISTRATION

Month Day Year

DO NOT WRITE ABOVE THIS LINE. IF YOU NEED MORE SPACE, USE A SEPARATE CONTINUATION SHEET.

1

TITLE OF THIS WORK ▼   **NATURE OF THIS WORK ▼** See instructions

PREVIOUS OR ALTERNATIVE TITLES ▼

Publication as a Contribution If this work was published as a contribution to a periodical, serial, or collection, give information about the collective work in which the contribution appeared. **Title of Collective Work ▼**

If published in a periodical or serial give: **Volume ▼** **Number ▼** **Issue Date ▼** **On Pages ▼**

2

a

NAME OF AUTHOR ▼   **DATES OF BIRTH AND DEATH**
Year Born ▼ Year Died ▼

NOTE

Under the law, the "author" of a **"work made for hire"** is generally the employer, not the employee (see instructions). For any part of this work that was "made for hire" check "Yes" in the space provided, give the employer (or other person for whom the work was prepared) as "Author" of that part, and leave the space for dates of birth and death blank.

Was this contribution to the work a "work made for hire"?
☐ Yes
☐ No

Author's Nationality or Domicile
Name of Country
OR { Citizen of ▶
  Domiciled in ▶

Was This Author's Contribution to the Work
Anonymous? ☐ Yes ☐ No
Pseudonymous? ☐ Yes ☐ No
If the answer to either of these questions is "Yes," see detailed instructions.

NATURE OF AUTHORSHIP Check appropriate box(es). **See instructions**
☐ 3-Dimensional sculpture ☐ Map ☐ Technical drawing
☐ 2-Dimensional artwork ☐ Photograph ☐ Text
☐ Reproduction of work of art ☐ Jewelry design ☐ Architectural work

b

NAME OF AUTHOR ▼   **DATES OF BIRTH AND DEATH**
Year Born ▼ Year Died ▼

Was this contribution to the work a "work made for hire"?
☐ Yes
☐ No

Author's Nationality or Domicile
Name of Country
OR { Citizen of ▶
  Domiciled in ▶

Was This Author's Contribution to the Work
Anonymous? ☐ Yes ☐ No
Pseudonymous? ☐ Yes ☐ No
If the answer to either of these questions is "Yes," see detailed instructions.

NATURE OF AUTHORSHIP Check appropriate box(es). **See instructions**
☐ 3-Dimensional sculpture ☐ Map ☐ Technical drawing
☐ 2-Dimensional artwork ☐ Photograph ☐ Text
☐ Reproduction of work of art ☐ Jewelry design ☐ Architectural work

3

a

Year in Which Creation of This Work Was Completed
This information must be given in all cases.
◀ Year

b

Date and Nation of First Publication of This Particular Work
Complete this information ONLY if this work has been published.
Month ▶ Day ▶ Year ▶
◀ Nation

4

See instructions before completing this space.

COPYRIGHT CLAIMANT(S) Name and address must be given even if the claimant is the same as the author given in space 2. ▼

Transfer If the claimant(s) named here in space 4 is (are) different from the author(s) named in space 2, give a brief statement of how the claimant(s) obtained ownership of the copyright. ▼

DO NOT WRITE HERE / OFFICE USE ONLY

APPLICATION RECEIVED

ONE DEPOSIT RECEIVED

TWO DEPOSITS RECEIVED

FUNDS RECEIVED

MORE ON BACK ▶ • Complete all applicable spaces (numbers 5-9) on the reverse side of this page.
 • See detailed instructions. • Sign the form at line 8.

DO NOT WRITE HERE

Page 1 of _____ pages

EXAMINED BY

CHECKED BY

☐ CORRESPONDENCE
   Yes

FORM VA

FOR
COPYRIGHT
OFFICE
USE
ONLY

DO NOT WRITE ABOVE THIS LINE. IF YOU NEED MORE SPACE, USE A SEPARATE CONTINUATION SHEET.

PREVIOUS REGISTRATION Has registration for this work, or for an earlier version of this work, already been made in the Copyright Office?

☐ **Yes** ☐ **No** If your answer is "Yes," why is another registration being sought? (Check appropriate box.) ▼

a. ☐ This is the first published edition of a work previously registered in unpublished form.

b. ☐ This is the first application submitted by this author as copyright claimant.

c. ☐ This is a changed version of the work, as shown by space 6 on this application.

If your answer is "Yes," give: **Previous Registration Number** ▼   **Year of Registration** ▼

5

DERIVATIVE WORK OR COMPILATION Complete both space 6a and 6b for a derivative work; complete only 6b for a compilation.
a. Preexisting Material Identify any preexisting work or works that this work is based on or incorporates. ▼

b. Material Added to This Work Give a brief, general statement of the material that has been added to this work and in which copyright is claimed. ▼

6
a
b

See instructions
before completing
this space.

DEPOSIT ACCOUNT If the registration fee is to be charged to a Deposit Account established in the Copyright Office, give name and number of Account.
Name ▼   **Account Number** ▼

CORRESPONDENCE Give name and address to which correspondence about this application should be sent.   Name/Address/Apt/City/State/ZIP ▼

7
a
b

Area code and daytime telephone number ▶ (   )   Fax number ▶ (   )

Email ▶

CERTIFICATION* I, the undersigned, hereby certify that I am the

check only one ▶ {
☐ author
☐ other copyright claimant
☐ owner of exclusive right(s)
☐ authorized agent of _____
                        Name of author or other copyright claimant, or owner of exclusive right(s) ▲

of the work identified in this application and that the statements made by me in this application are correct to the best of my knowledge.

8

Typed or printed name and date ▼ If this application gives a date of publication in space 3, do not sign and submit it before that date.

_____   Date ▶ _____

Handwritten signature (X) ▼

☞   X _____

**Certificate
will be
mailed in
window
envelope
to this
address:**

Name ▼

Number/Street/Apt ▼

City/State/ZIP ▼

9

YOU MUST:
• Complete all necessary spaces
• Sign your application in space 8

**SEND ALL 3 ELEMENTS
IN THE SAME PACKAGE:**
1. Application form
2. Nonrefundable filing fee in check or money order payable to *Register of Copyrights*
3. Deposit material

As of July 1, 1999, the filing fee for Form VA is $30.

MAIL TO:
Library of Congress
Copyright Office
101 Independence Avenue, S.E.
Washington, D.C. 20559-6000

For pictorial, graphic, and sculptural works

USE THIS FORM IF—

1. You are the **only** author and copyright owner of this work, *and*
2. The work was **not** made for hire, *and*
3. The work is completely new (does not contain a substantial amount of material that has been previously published or registered or is in the public domain).

If any of the above does not apply, you must use standard Form VA.
NOTE: *Short Form VA is not appropriate for an anonymous author who does not wish to reveal his or her identity.*

HOW TO COMPLETE SHORT FORM VA

■ Type or print in black ink.

■ Be clear and legible. (Your certificate of registration will be copied from your form.)

■ Give only the information requested.

NOTE: You may use a continuation sheet (Form ___/CON) to list individual titles in a collection. Complete Space A and list the individual titles under Space C on the back page. Space B is not applicable to short forms.

 ### 1 Title of This Work

You must give a title. If there is no title, state "UNTITLED." If you are registering an unpublished collection, give the collection title you want to appear in our records (for example: "Jewelry by Josephine, 1995 Volume"). Alternative title: If the work is known by two titles, you also may give the second title. If the work has been published as part of a larger work (including a periodical), give the title of that larger work instead of an alternative title, in addition to the title of the contribution.

 ### 2 Name and Address of Author and Owner of the Copyright

Give your name and mailing address. You may include your pseudonym followed by "pseud." Also, give the nation of which you are a citizen or where you have your domicile (i.e., permanent residence).
Please give daytime phone, fax numbers, and email address, if available.

 ### 3 Year of Creation

Give the latest year in which you completed the work you are registering at this time. A work is "created" when it is "fixed" in a tangible form. Examples: drawn on paper, molded in clay, stored in a computer.

4 Publication

If the work has been published (i.e., if copies have been distributed to the public), give the complete date of publication (month, day, and year) and the nation where the publication first took place.

 ### 5 Type of Authorship in This Work

Check the box or boxes that describe your authorship in the material you are sending. For example, if you are registering illustrations but have not written the story yet, check only the box for "2-dimensional artwork."

6 Signature of Author

Sign the application in black ink and check the appropriate box. The person signing the application should be the author or his/her authorized agent.

7 Person to Contact for Rights/Permissions

This space is optional. You may give the name and address of the person or organization to contact for permission to use the work. You may also provide phone, fax, or email information.

8 Certificate Will Be Mailed

This space must be completed. Your certificate of registration will be mailed in a window envelope to this address. Also, if the Copyright Office needs to contact you, we will write to this address.

9 Deposit Account

Complete this space only if you currently maintain a deposit account in the Copyright Office.

MAIL WITH THE FORM

■ A $30 filing fee (effective through June 30, 2002) in the form of a check or money order (*no cash*) payable to "Register of Copyrights," **and**

■ One or two copies of the work or identifying material consisting of photographs or drawings showing the work. See table (right) for the requirements for most works. **Note:** Request Circular 40a for more information about the requirements for other works. Copies submitted become the property of the U.S. Government.

Mail everything **(application form, copy or copies, and fee)** *in one package* to:

Library of Congress
Copyright Office
101 Independence Avenue, S.E.
Washington, D.C. 20559-6000

QUESTIONS? Call (202) 707-3000 [TTY: (202) 707-6737] between 8:30 a.m. and 5:00 p.m. eastern time, Monday through Friday. For forms and informational circulars, call (202) 707-9100 24 hours a day, 7 days a week, or download them from the Internet at www.loc.gov/copyright. Selected informational circulars but not forms are available from Fax-on-Demand at (202) 707-2600.

If you are registering:	And the work is *unpublished/published* send:
• 2-dimensional artwork in a book, map, poster, or print	**a.** And the work is *unpublished*, **send** one complete copy or identifying material **b.** And the work is *published*, **send** two copies of the best published edition
• 3-dimensional sculpture, • 2-dimensional artwork applied to a T-shirt	**a.** And the work is *unpublished*, **send** identifying material **b.** And the work is *published*, **send** identifying material
• a greeting card, pattern, commercial print or label, fabric, wallpaper	**a.** And the work is *unpublished*, **send** one complete copy or identifying material **b.** And the work is *published*, **send** one copy of the best published edition

Registration Number

VA   VAU

Effective Date of Registration

Application Received

Deposit Received
One | Two

Examined By

Correspondence ☐

Fee Received

TYPE OR PRINT IN BLACK INK. DO NOT WRITE ABOVE THIS LINE.

1 **Title of This Work:**

Alternative title or title of larger work in which this work was published:

2 **Name and Address of Author and Owner of the Copyright:**

Nationality or domicile:
Phone, fax, and email:

Phone ( )   Fax ( )

Email

3 **Year of Creation:**

4 *If work has been published,* **Date and Nation of Publication:**

a. Date _____ _____ _____ *(Month, day, and year all required)*
     Month   Day   Year

b. Nation

5 **Type of Authorship in This Work:**
Check all that this author created.

☐ 3-Dimensional sculpture   ☐ Photograph   ☐ Map
☐ 2-Dimensional artwork   ☐ Jewelry design   ☐ Text
☐ Technical drawing

6 **Signature:**

Registration cannot be completed without a signature.

*I certify that the statements made by me in this application are correct to the best of my knowledge.** Check one:

☐ Author   ☐ Authorized agent

X _

OPTIONAL

7 **Name and Address of Person to Contact for Rights and Permissions:**
Phone, fax, and email:

☐ Check here if same as #2 above.

Phone ( )   Fax ( )

Email

8
Certificate will be mailed in window envelope to this address:

Name ▼

Number/Street/Apt ▼

City/State/ZIP ▼

Complete this space only if you currently hold a Deposit Account in the Copyright Office.

9
Deposit Account #_____

Name _____

_____

_____

DO NOT WRITE HERE   Page 1 of _____ pages

June 1999—100,000
WEB REV: June 1999

♻ PRINTED ON RECYCLED PAPER

☆U.S. GOVERNMENT PRINTING OFFICE: 1999-454-879/54

Application Form SR

Detach and read these instructions before completing this form.
Make sure all applicable spaces have been filled in before you return this form.

BASIC INFORMATION

When to Use This Form: Use Form SR for registration of published or unpublished sound recordings. It should be used when the copyright claim is limited to the sound recording itself, and it may also be used where the same copyright claimant is seeking simultaneous registration of the underlying musical, dramatic, or literary work embodied in the phonorecord.

With one exception, "sound recordings" are works that result from the fixation of a series of musical, spoken, or other sounds. The exception is for the audio portions of audiovisual works, such as a motion picture soundtrack or an audio cassette accompanying a filmstrip. These are considered a part of the audiovisual work as a whole.

Deposit to Accompany Application: An application for copyright registration must be accompanied by a deposit consisting of phonorecords representing the entire work for which registration is to be made.

Unpublished Work: Deposit one complete phonorecord.

Published Work: Deposit two complete phonorecords of the best edition, together with "any printed or other visually perceptible material" published with the phonorecords.

Work First Published Outside the United States: Deposit one complete phonorecord of the first foreign edition.

Contribution to a Collective Work: Deposit one complete phonorecord of the best edition of the collective work.

The Copyright Notice: Before March 1, 1989, the use of copyright notice was mandatory on all published works, and any work first published before that date should have carried a notice. For works first published on and after March 1, 1989, use of the copyright notice is optional. For more information about copyright notice, see Circular 3, "Copyright Notices."

For Further Information: To speak to an information specialist, call (202) 707-3000 (TTY: (202) 707-6737). Recorded information is available 24 hours a day. Order forms and other publications from Library of Congress, Copyright Office, 101 Independence Avenue, S.E., Washington, D.C. 20559-6000 or call the Forms and Publications Hotline at (202) 707-9100. Most circulars (but not forms) are available via fax. Call (202) 707-2600 from a touchtone phone. Access and download circulars, forms, and other information from the Copyright Office Website at www.loc.gov/copyright.

LINE-BY-LINE INSTRUCTIONS

Please type or print neatly using black ink. The form is used to produce the certificate.

1 SPACE 1: Title

Title of This Work: Every work submitted for copyright registration must be given a title to identify that particular work. If the phonorecords or any accompanying printed material bears a title (or an identifying phrase that could serve as a title), transcribe that wording completely and exactly on the application. Indexing of the registration and future identification of the work may depend on the information you give here.

Previous, Alternative, or Contents Titles: Complete this space if there are any previous or alternative titles for the work under which someone searching for the registration might be likely to look, or under which a document pertaining to the work might be recorded. You may also give the individual contents titles, if any, in this space or you may use a Continuation Sheet. Circle the term that describes the titles given.

2 SPACE 2: Author(s)

General Instructions: After reading these instructions, decide who are the "authors" of this work for copyright purposes. Then, unless the work is a "collective work," give the requested information about every "author" who contributed any appreciable amount of copyrightable matter to this version of the work. If you need further space, request additional Continuation Sheets. In the case of a collective work such as a collection of previously published or registered sound recordings, give information about the author of the collective work as a whole. If you are submitting this Form SR to cover the recorded musical, dramatic, or literary work as well as the sound recording itself, it is important for space 2 to include full information about the various authors of all of the material covered by the copyright claim, making clear the nature of each author's contribution.

Name of Author: The fullest form of the author's name should be given. Unless the work was "made for hire," the individual who actually created the work is its "author." In the case of a work made for hire, the statute provides that "the employer or other person for whom the work was prepared is considered the author."

What is a "Work Made for Hire"? A "work made for hire" is defined as: (1) "a work prepared by an employee within the scope of his or her employment"; or (2)

"a work specially ordered or commissioned for use as a contribution to a collective work, as a part of a motion picture or other audiovisual work, as a translation, as a supplementary work, as a compilation, as an instructional text, as a test, as answer material for a test, or as an atlas, if the parties expressly agree in a written instrument signed by them that the work shall be considered a work made for hire." If you have checked "Yes" to indicate that the work was "made for hire," you must give the full legal name of the employer (or other person for whom the work was prepared). You may also include the name of the employee along with the name of the employer (for example: "Elster Record Co., employer for hire of John Ferguson").

"Anonymous" or "Pseudonymous" Work: An author's contribution to a work is "anonymous" if that author is not identified on the copies or phonorecords of the work. An author's contribution to a work is "pseudonymous" if that author is identified on the copies or phonorecords under a fictitious name. If the work is "anonymous" you may: (1) leave the line blank; or (2) state "anonymous" on the line; or (3) reveal the author's identity. If the work is "pseudonymous" you may: (1) leave the line blank; or (2) give the pseudonym and identify it as such (for example: "Huntley Haverstock, pseudonym"); or (3) reveal the author's name, making clear which is the real name and which is the pseudonym (for example: "Judith Barton, whose pseudonym is Madeline Elster"). However, the citizenship or domicile of the author **must** be given in all cases.

Dates of Birth and Death: If the author is dead, the statute requires that the year of death be included in the application unless the work is anonymous or pseudonymous. The author's birth date is optional, but is useful as a form of identification. Leave this space blank if the author's contribution was a "work made for hire."

Author's Nationality or Domicile: Give the country in which the author is a citizen, or the country in which the author is domiciled. Nationality or domicile **must** be given in all cases.

Nature of Authorship: Sound recording authorship is the performance, sound production, or both, that is fixed in the recording deposited for registration. Describe this authorship in space 2 as "sound recording." If the claim also covers the underlying work(s), include the appropriate authorship terms for each author, for example, "words," "music," "arrangement of music," or "text."

Generally, for the claim to cover both the sound recording and the underlying work(s), every author should have contributed to both the sound recording **and** the underlying work(s). If the claim includes artwork or photographs, include the appropriate term in the statement of authorship.

3 SPACE 3: Creation and Publication

General Instructions: Do not confuse "creation" with "publication." Every application for copyright registration must state "the year in which creation of the work was completed." Give the date and nation of first publication only if the work has been published.

Creation: Under the statute, a work is "created" when it is fixed in a copy or phonorecord for the first time. Where a work has been prepared over a period of time, the part of the work existing in fixed form on a particular date constitutes the created work on that date. The date you give here should be the year in which the author completed the particular version for which registration is now being sought, even if other versions exist or if further changes or additions are planned.

Publication: The statute defines "publication" as "the distribution of copies or phonorecords of a work to the public by sale or other transfer of ownership, or by rental, lease, or lending"; a work is also "published" if there has been an "offering to distribute copies or phonorecords to a group of persons for purposes of further distribution, public performance, or public display." Give the full date (month, date, year) when, and the country where, publication first occurred. If first publication took place simultaneously in the United States and other countries, it is sufficient to state "U.S.A."

4 SPACE 4: Claimant(s)

Name(s) and Address(es) of Copyright Claimant(s): Give the name(s) and address(es) of the copyright claimant(s) in the work even if the claimant is the same as the author. Copyright in a work belongs initially to the author of the work (including, in the case of a work made for hire, the employer or other person for whom the work was prepared). The copyright claimant is either the author of the work or a person or organization to whom the copyright initially belonging to the author has been transferred.

Transfer: The statute provides that, if the copyright claimant is not the author, the application for registration must contain "a brief statement of how the claimant obtained ownership of the copyright." If any copyright claimant named in space 4a is not an author named in space 2, give a brief statement explaining how the claimant(s) obtained ownership of the copyright. Examples: "By written contract"; "Transfer of all rights by author"; "Assignment"; "By will." Do not attach transfer documents or other attachments or riders.

5 SPACE 5: Previous Registration

General Instructions: The questions in space 5 are intended to show whether an earlier registration has been made for this work and, if so, whether there is any basis for a new registration. As a rule, only one basic copyright registration can be made for the same version of a particular work.

Same Version: If this version is substantially the same as the work covered by a previous registration, a second registration is not generally possible unless: (1) the work has been registered in unpublished form and a second registration is now being sought to cover this first published edition; or (2) someone other than the author is identified as copyright claimant in the earlier registration and the author is now seeking registration in his or her own name. If either of these two exceptions applies, check the appropriate box and give the earlier registration number and date. Otherwise, do not submit Form SR. Instead, write the Copyright Office for information about supplementary registration or recordation of transfers of copyright ownership.

Changed Version: If the work has been changed and you are now seeking registration to cover the additions or revisions, check the last box in space 5, give the earlier registration number and date, and complete both parts of space 6 in accordance with the instructions below.

Previous Registration Number and Date: If more than one previous registration has been made for the work, give the number and date of the latest registration.

6 SPACE 6: Derivative Work or Compilation

General Instructions: Complete space 6 if this work is a "changed version," "compilation," or "derivative work," and if it incorporates one or more earlier works that have already been published or registered for copyright, or that have fallen into the public domain, or sound recordings that were fixed before February 15, 1972. A "compilation" is defined as "a work formed by the collection and assembling of preexisting materials or of data that are selected, coordinated, or arranged in such a way that the resulting work as a whole constitutes an original work of authorship." A "derivative work" is "a work based on one or more preexisting works." Examples of derivative works include recordings reissued with substantial editorial revisions or abridgments of the recorded sounds, and recordings republished with new recorded material, or "any other form in which a work may be recast, transformed, or adapted." Derivative works also include works "consisting of editorial revisions, annotations, or other modifications" if these changes, as a whole, represent an original work of authorship.

Preexisting Material (space 6a): Complete this space **and** space 6b for derivative works. In this space identify the preexisting work that has been recast, transformed, or adapted. The preexisting work may be material that has been previously published, previously registered, or that is in the public domain. For example, the preexisting material might be: "1970 recording by Sperryville Symphony of Bach Double Concerto."

Material Added to This Work (space 6b): Give a brief, general statement of the **additional** new material covered by the copyright claim for which registration is sought. In the case of a derivative work, identify this new material. Examples: "Recorded performances on bands 1 and 3"; "Remixed sounds from original multitrack sound sources"; "New words, arrangement, and additional sounds." If the work is a compilation, give a brief, general statement describing both the material that has been compiled **and** the compilation itself. Example: "Compilation of 1938 Recordings by various swing bands."

7,8,9 SPACE 7,8,9: Fee, Correspondence, Certification, Return Address

Deposit Account: If you maintain a Deposit Account in the Copyright Office, identify it in space 7a. Otherwise, leave the space blank and send the filing fee of $30 (effective through June 30, 2002) with your application and deposit. (See space 8 on form.)

Correspondence (space 7b): This space should contain the name, address, area code, telephone number, fax number, and email address (if available) of the person to be consulted if correspondence about this application becomes necessary.

Certification (space 8): This application cannot be accepted unless it bears the date and the **handwritten signature** of the author or other copyright claimant, or of the owner of exclusive right(s), or of the duly authorized agent of the author, claimant, or owner of exclusive right(s).

Address for Return of Certificate (space 9): The address box must be completed legibly since the certificate will be returned in a window envelope.

MORE INFORMATION

"Works": "Works" are the basic subject matter of copyright; they are what authors create and copyright protects. The statute draws a sharp distinction between the "work" and "any material object in which the work is embodied."

"Copies" and "Phonorecords": These are the two types of material objects in which "works" are embodied. In general, **"copies"** are objects from which a work can be read or visually perceived, directly or with the aid of a machine or device, such as manuscripts, books, sheet music, film, and videotape. **"Phonorecords"** are objects embodying fixations of sounds, such as audio tapes and phonograph disks. For example, a song (the "work") can be reproduced in sheet music ("copies") or phonograph disks ("phonorecords"), or both.

"Sound Recordings": These are "works," not "copies" or "phonorecords." "Sound recordings" are "works that result from the fixation of a series of musical, spoken, or other sounds, but not including the sounds accompanying a motion picture or other audiovisual work." Example: When a record company issues a new release, the release will typically involve two distinct "works": the "musical work" that has been recorded, and the "sound recording" as a separate work in itself. The material objects that the record company sends out are "phonorecords": physical reproductions of both the "musical work" and the "sound recording."

Should You File More Than One Application? If your work consists of a recorded musical, dramatic, or literary work and if both that "work" and the sound recording as a separate "work" are eligible for registration, the application form you should file depends on the following:

File Only Form SR if: The copyright claimant is the same for both the musical, dramatic, or literary work and for the sound recording, and you are seeking a single registration to cover both of these "works."

File Only Form PA (or Form TX) if: You are seeking to register only the musical, dramatic, or literary work, not the sound recording. Form PA is appropriate for works of the performing arts; Form TX is for nondramatic literary works.

Separate Applications Should Be Filed on Form PA (or Form TX) and on Form SR if: (1) The copyright claimant for the musical, dramatic, or literary work is different from the copyright claimant for the sound recording; or (2) You prefer to have separate registrations for the musical, dramatic, or literary work and for the sound recording.

FORM SR

For a Sound Recording
UNITED STATES COPYRIGHT OFFICE

REGISTRATION NUMBER

| SR | SRU |

EFFECTIVE DATE OF REGISTRATION

_____ _____ _____
Month   Day   Year

DO NOT WRITE ABOVE THIS LINE. IF YOU NEED MORE SPACE, USE A SEPARATE CONTINUATION SHEET.

1

TITLE OF THIS WORK ▼

PREVIOUS, ALTERNATIVE, OR CONTENTS TITLES (CIRCLE ONE) ▼

2

a

NAME OF AUTHOR ▼

DATES OF BIRTH AND DEATH
Year Born ▼   Year Died ▼

Was this contribution to the work a "work made for hire"?
☐ Yes
☐ No

AUTHOR'S NATIONALITY OR DOMICILE
Name of Country
OR { Citizen of ▶ _____
Domiciled in ▶ _____

WAS THIS AUTHOR'S CONTRIBUTION TO THE WORK
Anonymous?   ☐ Yes   ☐ No
Pseudonymous?   ☐ Yes   ☐ No

If the answer to either of these questions is "Yes," see detailed instructions.

NATURE OF AUTHORSHIP Briefly describe nature of material created by this author in which copyright is claimed. ▼

NOTE

Under the law, the "author" of a "work made for hire" is generally the employer, not the employee (see instructions). For any part of this work that was made for hire," check "Yes" in the space provided, give the employer (or other person for whom the work was prepared) as "Author" of that part, and leave the space for dates of birth and death blank.

b

NAME OF AUTHOR ▼

DATES OF BIRTH AND DEATH
Year Born ▼   Year Died ▼

Was this contribution to the work a "work made for hire"?
☐ Yes
☐ No

AUTHOR'S NATIONALITY OR DOMICILE
Name of Country
OR { Citizen of ▶ _____
Domiciled in ▶ _____

WAS THIS AUTHOR'S CONTRIBUTION TO THE WORK
Anonymous?   ☐ Yes   ☐ No
Pseudonymous?   ☐ Yes   ☐ No

If the answer to either of these questions is "Yes," see detailed instructions.

NATURE OF AUTHORSHIP Briefly describe nature of material created by this author in which copyright is claimed. ▼

c

NAME OF AUTHOR ▼

DATES OF BIRTH AND DEATH
Year Born ▼   Year Died ▼

Was this contribution to the work a "work made for hire"?
☐ Yes
☐ No

AUTHOR'S NATIONALITY OR DOMICILE
Name of Country
OR { Citizen of ▶ _____
Domiciled in ▶ _____

WAS THIS AUTHOR'S CONTRIBUTION TO THE WORK
Anonymous?   ☐ Yes   ☐ No
Pseudonymous?   ☐ Yes   ☐ No

If the answer to either of these questions is "Yes," see detailed instructions.

NATURE OF AUTHORSHIP Briefly describe nature of material created by this author in which copyright is claimed. ▼

3

a **YEAR IN WHICH CREATION OF THIS WORK WAS COMPLETED**

This information must be given in all cases.
◀ Year

b **DATE AND NATION OF FIRST PUBLICATION OF THIS PARTICULAR WORK**

Complete this information ONLY if this work has been published.

Month ▶ _____ Day ▶ _____ Year ▶ _____
_____ ◀ Nation

4

a

COPYRIGHT CLAIMANT(S) Name and address must be given even if the claimant is the same as the author given in space 2. ▼

See instructions before completing this space.

b

TRANSFER If the claimant(s) named here in space 4 is (are) different from the author(s) named in space 2, give a brief statement of how the claimant(s) obtained ownership of the copyright. ▼

DO NOT WRITE HERE OFFICE USE ONLY

APPLICATION RECEIVED

ONE DEPOSIT RECEIVED

TWO DEPOSITS RECEIVED

FUNDS RECEIVED

MORE ON BACK ▶
• Complete all applicable spaces (numbers 5-9) on the reverse side of this page.
• See detailed instructions.
• Sign the form at line 8.

DO NOT WRITE HERE

Page 1 of _____ pages

DO NOT WRITE ABOVE THIS LINE. IF YOU NEED MORE SPACE, USE A SEPARATE CONTINUATION SHEET.

PREVIOUS REGISTRATION Has registration for this work, or for an earlier version of this work, already been made in the Copyright Office?

❑ Yes   ❑ No   If your answer is "Yes," why is another registration being sought? (Check appropriate box) ▼

a. ❑ This work was previously registered in unpublished form and now has been published for the first time.

b. ❑ This is the first application submitted by this author as copyright claimant.

c. ❑ This is a changed version of the work, as shown by space 6 on this application.

If your answer is "Yes," give: **Previous Registration Number** ▼   **Year of Registration** ▼

5

DERIVATIVE WORK OR COMPILATION

Preexisting Material Identify any preexisting work or works that this work is based on or incorporates. ▼

a

Material Added to This Work Give a brief, general statement of the material that has been added to this work and in which copyright is claimed. ▼

b

6

See instructions
before completing
this space.

DEPOSIT ACCOUNT If the registration fee is to be charged to a Deposit Account established in the Copyright Office, give name and number of Account.

Name ▼   **Account Number** ▼

a

7

CORRESPONDENCE Give name and address to which correspondence about this application should be sent.   Name/Address/Apt/City/State/ZIP ▼

b

Area code and daytime telephone number ▶   Fax number ▶

Email ▶

CERTIFICATION* I, the undersigned, hereby certify that I am the

Check only one ▼

❑ author   ❑ owner of exclusive right(s)

❑ other copyright claimant   ❑ authorized agent of _____

Name of author or other copyright claimant, or owner of exclusive right(s) ▲

of the work identified in this application and that the statements made by me in this application are correct to the best of my knowledge.

Typed or printed name and date ▼ If this application gives a date of publication in space 3, do not sign and submit it before that date.

_____   Date▶ _____

Handwritten signature (x) ▼

X _

8

*17 U.S.C. § 506(e): Any person who knowingly makes a false representation of a material fact in the application for copyright registration provided for by section 409, or in any written statement filed in connection with the application, shall be fined not more than $2,500.

June 1999—50,000
WEB REV: June 1999

♺ PRINTED ON RECYCLED PAPER

☆U.S. GOVERNMENT PRINTING OFFICE: 1999-454-879/48

Detach and read these instructions before completing this form.
Make sure all applicable spaces have been filled in before you return this form.

BASIC INFORMATION

How to Register a Renewal Claim:

First: Study the information on this page and make sure you know the answers to two questions:
(1) What is the renewal filing period in your case?
(2) Who can claim the renewal?

Second: Read through the instructions for filling out Form RE. Before completing the form, make sure that the copyright is now eligible for renewal, that you are authorized to file a renewal claim, and that you have all needed information about the copyright.

Third: Complete all applicable spaces on Form RE, following the line-by-line instructions. Use typewriter or print in black ink.

Fourth: Detach this sheet and send your completed Form RE to: Library of Congress, Copyright Office, 101 Independence Avenue, S.E., Washington, D.C. 20559-6000. Unless you have a Copyright Office Deposit Account, your application must be accompanied by a check or money order for $45, payable to: *Register of Copyrights.* Do not send copies, phonorecords, or supporting documents with your renewal application unless specifically requested to do so by the Copyright Office.

What Is Renewal of Copyright?
For works copyrighted before January 1, 1978, the copyright law provides a first term of copyright protection lasting 28 years followed by a second term of protection known as the renewal term. However, these works were required to be renewed within strict time limits to obtain a second term of copyright protection. If copyright was originally secured before January 1, 1964, and was not renewed at the proper time, copyright protection expired permanently at the end of the 28th year of the first term and could not be renewed. **Public Law 102-307, enacted on June 26, 1992,** amended the copyright law with respect to works copyrighted between January 1, 1964, and December 31, 1977, to secure *automatically* the second term of copyright and to make renewal registration optional. The renewal term automatically vests in the party entitled to claim renewal on December 31 of the 28th year of the first term. **Public Law 105-298, enacted on October 27, 1998,** extended the renewal term an additional 20 years for all works still under copyright, whether in their first term or renewal term at the time the law became effective. The 1992 and 1998 amendments do not retroactively restore copyright to U.S. works that are in the public domain. For information concerning the restoration of copyright in certain foreign works under the 1994 Uruguay Round Agreements Act, request Circular 38b.

Some Basic Points About Renewal:

(1) A work is eligible for renewal registration at the beginning of the 28th year of the first term of copyright.
(2) There is no requirement to make a renewal filing in order to extend the original 28-year copyright term to the full term of 95 years; however, there are benefits from making a renewal registration during the 28th year of the original term. For more information, request Circular 15, "Renewal of Copyright."
(3) Only certain persons who fall into specific categories named in the law can claim renewal.

(4) For works originally copyrighted on or after January 1, 1978, the copyright law has eliminated all renewal requirements and established a single copyright term and different methods for computing the duration of a copyright. For further information, request Circular 15a, "Duration of Copyright."

Renewal Filing Period:
The amended copyright statute provides that, in order to register a renewal copyright, the renewal application and fee must be received in the Copyright Office
—within the last (28th) calendar year before the expiration of the original term of copyright or
—at any time during the renewed and extended term of 67 years.

To determine the filing period for renewal in your case:
(1) First, find out the date of original copyright for the work. In the case of works originally registered in unpublished form, the date of copyright is the date of registration; for published works, copyright begins on the date of first publication.
(2) Then add 28 years to the year the work was originally copyrighted. Your answer will be the calendar year during which the copyright will become eligible for renewal. Example: A work originally copyrighted on April 19, 1972, will be eligible for renewal in the calendar year 2000.

To renew a copyright during the original copyright term, the renewal application and fee **must** be received in the Copyright Office within 1 year prior to the expiration of the original copyright. All terms of the original copyright run through the end of the 28th calendar year making the period for renewal registration during the original term from December 31st of the 27th year of the copyright through December 31st of the following year.

Who May Claim Renewal:
Renewal copyright may be claimed only by those persons specified in the law. Except in the case of four specific types of works, the law gives the right to claim renewal to the individual author of the work, regardless of who owned the copyright during the original term. If the author is dead, the statute gives the right to claim renewal to certain of the author's beneficiaries (widow and children, executors, or next of kin, depending on the circumstances). The present owner (proprietor) of the copyright is entitled to claim renewal only in four specified cases as explained in more detail on the reverse of this page.

For Further Information:
To speak to an information specialist, call (202)707-3000 (TTY:(202)707-6737). Recorded information is available 24 hours a day. Order forms and other publications from the address in space 8 or call the Forms and Publications Hotline at (202)707-9100 24 hours a day. Obtain circulars by fax by using a touchtone phone to call (202)707-2600. Access and download circulars, forms, and other information from the Copyright Office Website at www.loc.gov/copyright.
Helpful publications include Circular 96 202.20, "Deposit of Copies and Phonorecords for Copyright Registration"; Circular 96 202.21 "Deposit of Identifying Material Instead of Copies"; Circular 96 202.17, "Renewals"; Circular 15, "Renewal of Copyright"; and Circular 15a, "Duration of Copyright."

LINE-BY-LINE INSTRUCTIONS

Please type or print neatly using black ink. The form is used to produce the certificate.

SPACE 1: Renewal Claimant(s)

General Instructions: For this application to result in a valid renewal, space 1 must identify one or more of the persons who are entitled to renew the copyright under the statute. Give the full name and address of each claimant, with a statement of the basis of each claim, using the wording given in these instructions.

For registration in the 28th year of the original copyright term, the renewal claimant is the individual(s) or entity who is entitled to claim renewal copyright on the date filed.

For registration after the 28th year of the original copyright term, the renewal claimant is the individual(s) or entity who is entitled to claim renewal copyright on December 31st of the 28th year.

Persons Entitled to Renew:
A. The following persons may claim renewal in all types of works except those enumerated in Paragraph B below:

1. The author, if living. State the claim as: *the author*

2. The widow, widower, and/or children of the author, if the author is not living.

State the claim as:

the widow (widower) of the author . . . .
(Name of author)

and/or the child (children) of the deceased author . . . .
(Name of author)

3. The author's executor(s), if the author left a will and if there is no surviving widow, widower, or child. State the claim as:
the executor(s) of the author . . . .
(Name of author)

4. The next of kin of the author, if the author left no will and if there is no surviving widow, widower, or child. State the claim as:
the next of kin of the deceased author . . . .*there being no will.*
(Name of author)

B. In the case of the following four types of works, the proprietor (owner of the copyright at the time of renewal registration) may claim renewal:

1. Posthumous work (a work published after the author's death as to which no copyright assignment or other contract for exploitation has occurred during the author's lifetime). State the claim as: *proprietor of copyright in a posthumous work.*

2. Periodical, cyclopedic, or other composite work. State the claim as: *proprietor of copyright in a composite work.*

3. "Work copyrighted by a corporate body otherwise than as assignee or licensee of the individual author." State the claim as: *proprietor of copyright in a work copyrighted by a corporate body otherwise than as assignee or licensee of the individual author.* This type of claim is considered appropriate in relatively few cases.

4. Work copyrighted by an employer for whom such work was made for hire. State the claim as: *proprietor of copyright in a work made for hire.*

SPACE 2: Work Renewed

General Instructions: This space is to identify the particular work being renewed. The information given here should agree with that appearing in the certificate of original registration.

Title: Give the full title of the work, together with any subtitles or descriptive wording included with the title in the original registration. In the case of a musical composition, give the specific instrumentation of the work.

Renewable Matter: Copyright in a new version of a previously published or copyrighted work such as an arrangement, translation, dramatization, compilation, or work republished with new matter covers only the additions, changes, or other new material appearing for the first time in that version. If this work was a new version, state in general the new matter upon which copyright was claimed.

Contribution to Periodical, Serial, or other Composite Work: Separate renewal registration is possible for a work published as a contribution to a periodical, serial, or other composite work, whether the contribution was copyrighted independently or as part of the larger work in which it appeared. Each contribution published in a separate issue ordinarily requires a separate renewal registration. However, the law provides an alternative, permitting groups of periodical contributions by the same individual author to be combined under a single renewal application and fee in certain cases.

If this renewal application covers a single contribution, give all of the requested information in space 2. If you are seeking to renew a group of contributions, include a reference such as "See space 5" in space 2 and give the requested information about all of the contributions in space 5.

SPACE 3: Author(s)

General Instructions: The copyright secured in a new version of a work is independent of any copyright protection in material published earlier. The only "authors" of a new version are those who contributed copyrightable matter to it. Thus, for renewal purposes, the person who wrote the original version on which the new work is based cannot be regarded as an "author" of the new version, unless that person also contributed to the new matter.

Authors of Renewable Matter: Give the full names of all authors who contributed copyrightable matter to this particular version of the work.

Space 4: Facts of Original Registration

General Instructions: Each item in space 4 should agree with the information appearing in the original registration for the work. If the work being renewed is a single contribution to a periodical or composite work that was not separately registered, give information about the particular issue in which the contribution appeared. You may leave this space blank if you are completing space 5.

Original Registration Number: Give the full registration number, which appears in the upper right hand corner of the front of the certificate of registration.

Original Copyright Claimant: Give the name in which ownership of the copyright was claimed in the original registration.

Date of Publication or Registration: Give only one date. If the original registration gave a publication date, it should be transcribed here; otherwise the registration was for an unpublished work, and the date of registration should be given. See Note below.

SPACE 5: Group Renewals

General Instructions: A renewal registration using a single application and $45 fee can be made for a group of works if **all** the following statutory conditions are met: (1) all the works were written by the same author, who is named in space 3 and who is or was an individual (not an employer for hire); (2) all the works were first published as contributions to periodicals (including newspapers) and were copyrighted on their first publication either through separate copyright notice and registration or by virtue of a general copyright notice in the periodical issue as a whole; (3) the renewal claimant or claimants and the basis of claim or claims, as stated in space 1, are the same for all the works; (4) the renewal application and fee are received not less than 27 years after the 31st day of December of the calendar year in which all the works were first published (See following Note); and (5) the renewal application identifies each work separately, including the periodical containing it and the date of first publication.

Note: During the 28th year of the original term and during the extended 67-year renewal term, renewal registration may be made for a single work or a group of works without having made an original registration. This option requires the filing of a renewal application Form RE accompanied by a Form RE Addendum, a copy of the work as first published or appropriate identifying material in accordance with the requirements of 37 CFR 202.17, and a total $60 filing fee.

Time Limits for Group Renewals: To be renewed as a group, all the contributions must have been first published during the same calendar year. For example, suppose six contributions by the same author were published on April 1, 1968, July 1, 1968, November 1, 1968, February 1, 1969, July 1, 1969, and March 1, 1970. The three 1968 copyrights can be combined and renewed at any time during 1996, and the two 1969 copyrights can be renewed as a group during 1997, but the 1970 copyright must be renewed by itself in 1998.

Identification of Each Work: Give all the requested information for each contribution. The registration number should be that for the contribution itself if it was separately registered, and the registration number for the periodical issue if it was not.

SPACE 6,7,8: Deposit Account (Fee), Correspondence, Certification, Return Address

Deposit Account (Fee): If you maintain a Deposit Account in the Copyright Office, identify it in space 6. Otherwise, leave the space blank and send the fee of $45 for Form RE or $60 for Form RE accompanied by Form RE Addendum with your application and deposit.

Correspondence: This space should contain the name, address, area code, telephone number, fax number, and email address of the person to be consulted if correspondence about this application becomes necessary.

Certification (Space 7): The renewal application is not acceptable unless it bears the date and the handwritten signature of the renewal claimant or the duly authorized agent of the renewal claimant.

Address for Return of Certificate (Space 8): The address box must be completed legibly since the certificate will be returned in a window envelope.

FORM RE
For Renewal of a Work
UNITED STATES COPYRIGHT OFFICE

REGISTRATION NUMBER

_____

EFFECTIVE DATE OF RENEWAL REGISTRATION

_____

Month   Day   Year

DO NOT WRITE ABOVE THIS LINE. IF YOU NEED MORE SPACE, USE A SEPARATE CONTINUATION SHEET (FORM RE/CON).

1

RENEWAL CLAIMANT(S), ADDRESS(ES), AND STATEMENT OF CLAIM ▼   (See Instructions)

a
Name ....
Address ....
Claiming as ....
(Use appropriate statement from instructions)

b
Name ....
Address ....
Claiming as ....

c
Name ....
Address ....
Claiming as ....

2

TITLE OF WORK IN WHICH RENEWAL IS CLAIMED ▼

RENEWABLE MATTER ▼

PUBLICATION AS A CONTRIBUTION If this work was published as a contribution to a periodical, serial, or other composite work, give information about the collective work in which the contribution appeared.   **Title of Collective Work ▼**

If published in a periodical or serial give: **Volume ▼**   **Number ▼**   **Issue Date ▼**

3

AUTHOR(S) OF RENEWABLE MATTER ▼

4

ORIGINAL REGISTRATION NUMBER ▼   **ORIGINAL COPYRIGHT CLAIMANT ▼**

ORIGINAL DATE OF COPYRIGHT

If the original registration for this work was made in published form, give:

DATE OF PUBLICATION: _____

(Month)   (Day)   (Year)

OR

If the original registration for this work was made in unpublished form, give:

DATE OF REGISTRATION: _____

(Month)   (Day)   (Year)

MORE ON BACK ▶   • Complete all applicable spaces (numbers 5-8) on the reverse side of this page.
• See detailed instructions.   • Sign the form at space 7.

DO NOT WRITE HERE

Page 1 of _____ pages

DO NOT WRITE ABOVE THIS LINE. IF YOU NEED MORE SPACE, USE A SEPARATE CONTINUATION SHEET (FORM RE/CON).

RENEWAL FOR GROUP OF WORKS BY SAME AUTHOR: To make a single registration for a group of works by the same individual author published as contributions to periodicals (see instructions), give full information about each contribution. If more space is needed, request continuation sheet (Form RE/CON).

5

a
Title of Contribution: . . . .

Title of Periodical: . . . . Vol: . . . . No: . . . . Issue Date:. . . . .

Date of Publication: . . . . Registration Number: . . . .
　　　　　　　　　　(Month)　　　(Day)　　　(Year)

b
Title of Contribution: . . . .

Title of Periodical: . . . . Vol: . . . . No: . . . . Issue Date:. . . . .

Date of Publication: . . . . Registration Number: . . . .
　　　　　　　　　　(Month)　　　(Day)　　　(Year)

c
Title of Contribution: . . . .

Title of Periodical: . . . . Vol: . . . . No: . . . . Issue Date:. . . . .

Date of Publication: . . . . Registration Number: . . . .
　　　　　　　　　　(Month)　　　(Day)　　　(Year)

d
Title of Contribution: . . . .

Title of Periodical: . . . . Vol: . . . . No: . . . . Issue Date:. . . . .

Date of Publication: . . . . Registration Number: . . . .
　　　　　　　　　　(Month)　　　(Day)　　　(Year)

6

DEPOSIT ACCOUNT: If the registration fee is to be charged to a Deposit Account established in the Copyright Office, give name and number of Account.

Name _____

_____

Account Number _____

Area code and daytime telephone number ▶ _____

CORRESPONDENCE: Give name and address to which correspondence about this application should be sent.

Name _____

Address _____
　　　　　　　　　　　　　　　　　　　　(Apt)

_____
(City)　　　　　　(State)　　　(ZIP)

Fax number ▶ _____ Email Address ▶ _____

7

CERTIFICATION* I, the undersigned, hereby certify that I am the: (Check one)
❏ renewal claimant　　❏ duly authorized agent of _____
　　　　　　　　　　　　　　　　　　(Name of renewal claimant) ▲
of the work identified in this application and that the statements made by me in this application are correct to the best of my knowledge.

Typed or printed name ▼ _____　　Date ▼ _____

☞　Handwritten signature (X) ▼

8

Certificate will be mailed in window envelope to this address:

Name ▼

Number/Street/Apt ▼

City/State/ZIP ▼

*17 U.S.C. § 506(e): Any person who knowingly makes a false representation of a material fact in the application for copyright registration provided for by section 409, or in any written statement filed in connection with the application, shall be fined not more than $2,500.

December 1999—20,000
WEB REV: December 1999

✪ PRINTED ON RECYCLED PAPER

☆U.S. GOVERNMENT PRINTING OFFICE: 2000-461-113/87

CONTINUATION SHEET FOR APPLICATION FORM RE

⊘ **FORM RE /CON**
UNITED STATES COPYRIGHT OFFICE

REGISTRATION NUMBER

INSTRUCTIONS

- Use this continuation sheet **only** in conjunction with basic Form RE.

- Use this sheet only if you need more space to continue the listing started in Space 1 and/or Space 5 of Form RE. Use as many additional continuation sheets as you need.

- Use the continuation of Space 5 on this sheet only for contributions to periodicals by the same individual author that were published in the same calendar year.

- Follow instructions accompanying Form RE in filling out this continuation sheet. Number each line in Spaces B and C consecutively.

- Submit this continuation sheet with the basic Form RE and the other continuation sheets, if any. Clip (do not tape or staple) and fold all sheets together before submitting them.

- Type or clearly print all information in **black ink.**

EFFECTIVE DATE OF RENEWAL REGISTRATION

| (Month) | (Day) | (Year) |

CONTINUATION SHEET RECEIVED

Page _____ of _____ pages

DO NOT WRITE ABOVE THIS LINE. FOR COPYRIGHT OFFICE USE ONLY.

A
Identification of Application

IDENTIFICATION OF CONTINUATION: This sheet is a continuation of Space 1 and Space 5 of the application for renewal registration on Form RE, submitted for the following:

- TITLE AT SPACE 2 OR TITLE OF FIRST OF GROUP OF WORKS IN WHICH RENEWAL IS CLAIMED: Give first title as given in Space 5 of Form RE.
....
- RENEWAL CLAIMANT AND ADDRESS: Give the name and address of at least one renewal claimant as given in Space 1 of Form RE.
....

B
Continuation of Space 1

RENEWAL CLAIMANT(S), ADDRESS(ES), AND STATEMENT OF CLAIM: See Instructions on basic Form RE.

☐ Name ....
Address ....
Claiming as ....

☐ Name ....
Address ....
Claiming as ....

☐ Name ....
Address ....
Claiming as ....

☐ Name ....
Address ....
Claiming as ....

☐ Name ....
Address ....
Claiming as ....

☐ Name ....
Address ....
Claiming as ....

Use the reverse side of this sheet if you need more space for continuation of Space 5 of the basic form.

	Title of Contribution:		**C**
☐	Title of Periodical: .... Vol. ...... No. ..... Issue Date		
	Date of Publication: .... Registration Number:		**Continuation**
	(Month) (Day) (Year)		**of**
	Title of Contribution:		**Space 5**
☐	Title of Periodical: .... Vol. ...... No. ..... Issue Date		
	Date of Publication: .... Registration Number:		
	(Month) (Day) (Year)		

☐ Title of Contribution: ....
Title of Periodical: .... Vol. ...... No. ..... Issue Date ....
Date of Publication: .... Registration Number: ....
(Month)   (Day)   (Year)

☐ Title of Contribution: ....
Title of Periodical: .... Vol. ...... No. ..... Issue Date ....
Date of Publication: .... Registration Number: ....
(Month)   (Day)   (Year)

☐ Title of Contribution: ....
Title of Periodical: .... Vol. ...... No. ..... Issue Date ....
Date of Publication: .... Registration Number: ....
(Month)   (Day)   (Year)

☐ Title of Contribution: ....
Title of Periodical: .... Vol. ...... No. ..... Issue Date ....
Date of Publication: .... Registration Number: ....
(Month)   (Day)   (Year)

☐ Title of Contribution: ....
Title of Periodical: .... Vol. ...... No. ..... Issue Date ....
Date of Publication: .... Registration Number: ....
(Month)   (Day)   (Year)

☐ Title of Contribution: ....
Title of Periodical: .... Vol. ...... No. ..... Issue Date ....
Date of Publication: .... Registration Number: ....
(Month)   (Day)   (Year)

☐ Title of Contribution: ....
Title of Periodical: .... Vol. ...... No. ..... Issue Date ....
Date of Publication: .... Registration Number: ....
(Month)   (Day)   (Year)

☐ Title of Contribution: ....
Title of Periodical: .... Vol. ...... No. ..... Issue Date ....
Date of Publication: .... Registration Number: ....
(Month)   (Day)   (Year)

☐ Title of Contribution: ....
Title of Periodical: .... Vol. ...... No. ..... Issue Date ....
Date of Publication: .... Registration Number: ....
(Month)   (Day)   (Year)

☐ Title of Contribution: ....
Title of Periodical: .... Vol. ...... No. ..... Issue Date ....
Date of Publication: .... Registration Number: ....
(Month)   (Day)   (Year)

Certificate will be mailed in window envelope to this address:

Name ▼

Number/Street/Apt ▼

City/State/ZIP ▼

YOU MUST:
• Complete all necessary spaces
• Sign your application in Space 7

SEND ALL 3 ELEMENTS IN THE SAME PACKAGE:
1. Application form
2. Nonrefundable $45 filing fee in check or money order payable to *Register of Copyrights*

MAIL TO:
Library of Congress, Copyright Office
101 Independence Avenue, S.E.
Washington, D.C. 20559-6000

D

As of July 1, 1999, the filing fee for form RE is $45.

December 1999–20,000
WEB REV: December 1999

✪ PRINTED ON RECYCLED PAPER

☆U.S.GOVERNMENT PRINTING OFFICE: 2000-461-113/89

Addendum to Form RE

Read these instructions before completing this form.
Make sure all applicable spaces have been filled in before you return this form.

BASIC INFORMATION

When to Complete the Addendum: The Addendum to Form RE must be completed when registration of the work for which renewal registration is sought was not completed during the first 28-year term of copyright. If registration was made during the first term of copyright, complete space 4 of the Form RE instead.

Fee: As of July 1, 1999, the nonrefundable filing fee for the addendum to Form RE is $15. This fee is in addition to the $45 fee for Form RE, which must accompany the addendum.

PRIVACY ACT ADVISORY STATEMENT
Required by the Privacy Act of 1974 (Public Law 93-579)

AUTHORITY FOR REQUESTING THIS INFORMATION:
● Title 17, U.S.C., Sec. 304

FURNISHING THE REQUESTED INFORMATION IS:
● Voluntary

BUT IF THE INFORMATION IS NOT FURNISHED:
● It may be necessary to delay or refuse renewal registration
● If renewal registration is not made before expiration of the original copyright term, ownership of the renewal term may be affected

PRINCIPAL USES OF REQUESTED INFORMATION:
● Establishment and maintenance of a public record
● Examination of the application for compliance with registration requirements of the copyright code

OTHER ROUTINE USES:
● Public inspection and copying
● Preparation of public indexes
● Preparation of public catalogs of copyright registrations
● Preparation of search reports upon request

NOTE:
● No other advisory statement will be given you in connection with this application
● Please keep this statement and refer to it if we contact you regarding this application

---

LINE-BY-LINE INSTRUCTIONS

Please type or print using black ink.

SPACE 1: Title of the Work

Give the title as of the time of first publication.

SPACE 2: Name of the Author(s)

Name at least one author of the work.

SPACE 3:   Citizenship and/or Domicile of the Author(s)

Give the nation of citizenship and/or domicile for at least one author of the work at the time the work was first published.

SPACE 4: Date and Nation of First Publication

Give the exact date of publication in this space. If the exact date is not known and must be estimated, it is still necessary to enter a month, day, and year. The earliest possible date should be used. Also, give the nation where the work was first published.

SPACE 5: Manufacture

This space must be completed if the work is a nondramatic literary work with or without accompanying illustrations. In part A, identify the nation(s) where the mechanical processes in the manufacture of the work—typesetting, printing, and binding—were done. In part B, describe the processes by which the work was manufactured. This space also applies to certain two-dimensional prints.

SPACE 6: Deposit

If copies of the work as first published are available, you must send one such copy along with your application and fee. Check Box A in this case. Check Box B if no copy can be procured to send with the application and fee; explain fully why you are unable to obtain a copy. You will be contacted by the Renewals Section to determine a suitable deposit.

SPACE 7: Verification of Notice

The statement in this space requires the handwritten signature of the applicant and constitutes an affidavit of publication with notice.

SPACE 8: Certification

This space also requires the handwritten signature of the applicant, along with the date of signing. Providing the Copyright Office with a daytime telephone number, email address, and FAX number, if any, will facilitate resolution of any problems or questions concerning your application for renewal registration.

Why Does the Copyright Office Need the Information Requested in This Addendum?

Works published prior to January 1, 1978, were subject to the 1909 copyright law. This law was stricter than the law currently in effect. Certain formalities had to be met in order for a work of authorship to secure copyright protection. The use of a copyright notice in a prescribed form and location was required. For most works, the notice had to include the word "Copyright," its abbreviation "Copr.," or the symbol "©;" the name of the copyright owner; and the date of first publication. Eligibility had to be established for both published and unpublished works based on the citizenship or domicile of the author(s) or the nation where the work was first published. Certain literary and artistic works had to be manufactured in the United States in order to qualify for full-term copyright protection in this country. The information appearing in this form will determine whether the work is currently under copyright protection in the United States. If the work is in the public domain in this country, having failed to meet one or more of the preceding requirements, renewal registration will be denied.

ADDENDUM TO FORM RE

THIS FORM MUST BE COMPLETED FOR ALL WORKS
PUBLISHED BETWEEN JANUARY 1, 1964, AND
DECEMBER 31, 1977, *THAT WERE NOT REGISTERED
DURING THEIR FIRST 28-YEAR TERM.*

DO NOT WRITE ABOVE THIS LINE.

1 TITLE OF WORK IN WHICH RENEWAL IS CLAIMED: ▼

2 NAME OF THE AUTHOR(S): ▼

3 CITIZENSHIP AND/OR DOMICILE OF THE AUTHOR(S) AT THE TIME THE WORK WAS FIRST PUBLISHED: ▼

4 DATE AND NATION OF FIRST PUBLICATION:

Month▼   Day▼   Year▼   Nation▼

5 Manufacture:
A. If this is a nondramatic literary work or a two-dimensional print or label, the country in which the work was manufactured:▼

B. The processes by which the work was manufactured:▼

6 DEPOSIT: (Check one)
❑ A. One complete copy of this work as first published is deposited with this application.

❑ B. A complete copy of this work as first published cannot be deposited for the following

reason:▼

7 VERIFICATION OF NOTICE:
I hereby aver that all copies of this work as first published bore the copyright notice as it appears in the accompanying deposit materials and said copyright notice appeared on all copies of the work published in the United States until December 31, 1977.

Signature of applicant: _____

8 CERTIFICATION:
I certify under penalty of perjury under the laws of the United States of America that the foregoing is true and correct.

Signature of applicant: _____

Date signed: _____

Daytime telephone number: _____

FAX number if any: _____

Email address: _____

DO NOT WRITE HERE
OFFICE USE ONLY

ADDENDUM RECEIVED

DEPOSIT RECEIVED

December 1999 —20,000
WEB REV: December 1999   ✿ PRINTED ON RECYCLED PAPER   ☆U.S. GOVERNMENT PRINTING OFFICE: 2000-461-113/88

 Application Form CA

Detach and read these instructions before completing this form.
Make sure all applicable spaces have been filled in before you return this form.

BASIC INFORMATION

Use Form CA When:
- An earlier registration has been completed in the Copyright Office; and
- Some of the facts given in that registration are incorrect or incomplete; and
- You want to place the correct or complete facts on record.

Purpose of Supplementary Copyright Registration: As a rule, only one basic copyright registration can be made for the same work. To take care of cases where information in the basic registration turns out to be incorrect or incomplete, section 408(d) of the copyright law provides for "the filing of an application for supplementary registration, to correct an error in a copyright registration or to amplify the information given in a registration."

Who May File: Once basic registration has been made for a work, any author or other copyright claimant or owner of any exclusive right in the work or the duly authorized agent of any such author, other claimant, or owner who wishes to correct or amplify the information given in the basic registration may submit Form CA.

Please Note: Do not use Form CA to correct errors in statements on the copies or phonorecords of the work in question or to reflect changes in the content of the work. If the work has been changed substantially, you should consider making an entirely new registration for the revised version to cover the additions or revisions.

Do not use Form CA as a substitute for renewal registration. Renewal of copyright cannot be accomplished by using Form CA. For information on renewal of copyright, request Circular 15, "Renewal of Copyright," from the Copyright Office. Do not use Form CA to correct an error regarding publication when the work was registered as an unpublished work.

Do not use Form CA as a substitute for recording a transfer of copyright or other document pertaining to rights under a copyright. Recording a document under section 205 of the statute gives all persons constructive notice of the facts stated in the document and may have other important consequences in cases of infringement or conflicting transfers. Supplementary registration does not have that legal effect.

For information on recording a document, request Circular 12, "Recordation of Transfers and Other Documents," from the Copyright Office. To record a document in the Copyright Office, request the Document Cover Sheet.

How to Apply for Supplementary Registration:
First: Study the information on this page to make sure that filing an application on Form CA is the best procedure to follow in your case.
Second: Read the back of this page for specific instructions on filling out Form CA. Before starting to complete the form, make sure that you have all the necessary detailed information from the certificate of the basic registration.

Third: Complete all applicable spaces on the form following the line-by-line instructions on the back of this page. Use a typewriter or print the information in black ink.
Fourth: Detach this sheet and send your completed Form CA along with a **photocopy** of the front and back of the certificate of registration being amended to:

> Library of Congress
> Copyright Office
> 101 Independence Avenue, S.E.
> Washington, D.C. 20559-6000

Fee: Unless you have a Deposit Account in the Copyright Office, your application must be accompanied by a nonrefundable filing fee in the form of a check or money order for $65 (effective through June 30, 2002) payable to: *Register of Copyrights*. Do not send copies, phonorecords, or supporting documents other than the photocopied certificate with your application. They cannot be made part of the record of a supplementary registration.

What Happens When a Supplementary Registration Is Made? When a supplementary registration is completed, the Copyright Office will assign it a new registration number in the appropriate registration category and will issue a certificate of supplementary registration under that number. The basic registration will not be cancelled. The two registrations will stand in the Copyright Office records. The supplementary registration will have the effect of calling the public's attention to a possible error or omission in the basic registration and of placing the correct facts or the additional information on official record.

> Fees are effective through June 30, 2002. After that date, check the Copyright Office Website at **www.loc.gov/copyright** or call (202) 707-3000 for current fee information.

For Further Information
- **Internet:** Circulars, application forms, announcements, regulations, and other related materials are available at **www.loc.gov/copyright**
- **Fax:** Circulars are available from Fax-on-Demand at (202) 707-2600.
- **Telephone:** To speak to an information specialist, call the Public Information Office at (202) 707-3000 (TTY (202) 707-6737). Recorded information is available 24 hours a day. If you know which application forms and circulars you want, call the Forms and Publications Hotline at (202) 707-9100 24 hours a day.
- **Regular Mail:** Write to:
> Library of Congress
> Copyright Office
> Public Information Office
> 101 Independence Avenue, S.E.
> Washington, D.C. 20599-6000

LINE-BY-LINE INSTRUCTIONS

Please type or print neatly using black ink. The certificate of registration is created by copying your CA application form.

 SPACE A: Identification of Basic Registration

General Instructions: The information in this part identifies the basic registration that will be corrected or amplified. Even if the purpose of filing Form CA is to change one of these items, each item must agree exactly with the information as it already appears in the basic registration, that is, as it appears in the registration you wish to correct. Do not give any new information in this part.

Title of Work: Give the title as it appears in the basic registration.

Registration Number: Give the registration number (the series of numbers preceded by one or more letters) that appears in the upper right-hand corner of the certificate of registration. Give only one basic registration number since one CA form may correct or amend only one basic registration.

Registration Date: Give the year when the basic registration was completed.

Name(s) of Author(s) and Copyright Claimant(s): Give all the names as they appear in the basic registration.

B **SPACE B: Correction**

General Instructions: Complete this part **only** if information in the basic registration **was incorrect at the time that basic registration was made.** Leave this part blank and complete Part C instead if your purpose is to add, update, or clarify information rather than to rectify an actual error.

Location and Nature of Incorrect Information: Give the line number and the heading or description of the space in the basic registration where the error occurs. Example: Line number 2…Citizenship of author.

Incorrect Information as It Appears in Basic Registration: Transcribe the incorrect statement exactly as it appears in the basic registration, even if you have already given this information in Part A.

Corrected Information: Give the statement as it should have appeared in the application of the basic registration.

Explanation of Correction: You may need to add an explanation to clarify this correction.

C **SPACE C: Amplification**

General Instructions: Complete this part if you want to provide any of the following: (1) information that was omitted at the time of basic registration; (2) changes in facts other than ownership but including changes such as title or address of claimant that have occurred since the basic registration; or (3) explanations clarifying information in the basic registration.

Location and Nature of Information to be Amplified: Give the line number and the heading or description of the space in the basic registration where the information to be amplified appears.

Amplified Information: Give a statement of the additional, updated, or explanatory information as clearly and succinctly as possible. You should add an explanation of the amplification if it is necessary.

 **SPACES D,E,F,G: Continuation, Fee, Certification, Return Address**

Continuation (Part D): Use this space if you do not have enough room in Parts B or C.

Deposit Account and Mailing Instructions (Part E): If you maintain a Deposit Account in the Copyright Office, identify it in Part E. Otherwise, you will need to send the nonrefundable filing fee with your form. The space headed "Correspondence" should contain the name, address, telephone number with area code, and fax and email numbers, if available, of the person to be consulted if correspondence about the form becomes necessary.

Certification (Part F): The application is not acceptable unless it bears the handwritten signature of the author, or other copyright claimant, or of the owner of exclusive right(s), or of the duly authorized agent of such author, claimant, or owner.

Address for Return of Certificate (Part G): The address box must be completed legibly, since a reproduced image of that space will appear in the window of the mailing envelope.

| TX | TXU | PA | PAU | VA | VAU | SR | SRU | RE |

EFFECTIVE DATE OF SUPPLEMENTARY REGISTRATION

_____ _____ _____
Month   Day   Year

DO NOT WRITE ABOVE THIS LINE. IF YOU NEED MORE SPACE, USE A SEPARATE CONTINUATION SHEET.

A

Title of Work ▼

_____

Registration Number of the Basic Registration ▼

Year of Basic Registration ▼

Name(s) of Author(s) ▼

Name(s) of Copyright Claimant(s) ▼

B

Location and Nature of Incorrect Information in Basic Registration ▼

Line Number _____ Line Heading or Description _____

Incorrect Information as It Appears in Basic Registration ▼

Corrected Information ▼

Explanation of Correction ▼

C

Location and Nature of Information in Basic Registration to be Amplified ▼

Line Number _____ Line Heading or Description _____

Amplified Information and Explanation of Information ▼

MORE ON BACK ▶ • Complete all applicable spaces (D-G) on the reverse side of this page.
 • See detailed instructions. • Sign the form at Space F.

DO NOT WRITE HERE

Page 1 of _____ pages

DO NOT WRITE ABOVE THIS LINE. IF YOU NEED MORE SPACE, USE A SEPARATE CONTINUATION SHEET.

Continuation of: ❏ Part B *or* ❏ Part C   **D**

Correspondence: Give name and address to which correspondence about this application should be sent.   **E**

Phone (_____)_____ Fax (_____)_____ Email _____

Deposit Account: If the registration fee is to be charged to a Deposit Account established in the Copyright Office, give name and number of Account.

Name _____

Account Number _____

Certification* I, the undersigned, hereby certify that I am the: (Check only one)   **F**

❏ author   ❏ owner of exclusive right(s)
❏ other copyright claimant   ❏ duly authorized agent of _____
Name of author or other copyright claimant, or owner of exclusive right(s) ▲

of the work identified in this application and that the statements made by me in this application are correct to the best of my knowledge.

Typed or printed name ▼   **Date ▼**

Handwritten signature (X) ▼

Certificate will be mailed in window envelope to this address:	Name ▼
	Number/Street/Apt ▼
	City/State/ZIP ▼

YOU MUST:
• Complete all necessary spaces
• Sign your application in Space F

SEND ALL ELEMENTS IN THE SAME PACKAGE:
1. Application form
2. Nonrefundable filing fee in check or money order payable to *Register of Copyrights*

MAIL TO:
Library of Congress
Copyright Office
101 Independence Avenue, S.E.
Washington, D.C. 20559-6000

As of July 1, 1999, the fee for filing Form CA is $65.

G

Adjunct Application Form GR/CP

Detach and read these instructions before completing this form.
Make sure all applicable spaces have been filled in before you return this form.

BASIC INFORMATION

When to Use This Form: Form GR/CP is the appropriate adjunct application form to use when you are submitting a basic application on Form TX, Form PA, or Form VA for a group of works that qualify for a single registration under section 408(c)(2) of the copyright statute.

This Form:

- Can be used solely as an adjunct to a basic application for copyright registration.
- Is not acceptable unless submitted together with Form TX, Form PA, or Form VA.
- Is acceptable only if the group of works listed on it all qualify for a single copyright registration under 17 U.S.C. § 408 (c)(2).

When Does a Group of Works Qualify for a Single Registration Under 17 U.S.C. §408 (c)(2)?

For all works first published on or after March 1, 1989, a single copyright registration for a group of works can be made if **all** of the following conditions are met:

(1) All of the works are by the same author, who is an individual (not an employer for hire); and

(2) All of the works were first published as contributions to periodicals (including newspapers) within a 12-month period; and

(3) All of the works have the same copyright claimant; and

(4) One copy of the entire periodical issue or newspaper section in which each contribution was first published; or a photocopy of the contribution itself; or a photocopy of the entire page containing the contribution; or the entire page containing the contribution cut or torn from the collective work; or the contribution cut or torn from the collective work; or photographs or photographic slides of the contribution or entire page containing the contribution as long as all contents of the contributions are clear and legible are (is) deposited with the application; and

(5) The application identifies each contribution separately, including the periodical containing it and the date of its first publication.

> **NOTE:** For contributions that were first published prior to March 1, 1989, in addition to the conditions listed above, each contribution as first published must have borne a separate copyright notice, and the name of the owner of copyright in the work (or an abbreviation or alternative designation of the owner) must have been the same in each notice.

How to Apply for Group Registration:

First: Study the information on this page to make sure that all of the works you want to register together as a group qualify for a single registration.

Second: Read through the **Procedure for Group Registration** in the next column. Decide which form you should use for the basic registration (Form TX for nondramatic literary works; Form PA for musical, dramatic, and other works of the performing arts; or Form VA for pictorial and graphic works). Be sure that you have all of the information you need before you start filling out both the basic and the adjunct application forms.

Third: Complete the basic application form, following the detailed instructions accompanying it **and the special instructions on the reverse of this page.**

Fourth: Complete the adjunct application on Form GR/CP and mail it, together with the basic application form and the required copy of each contribution, to:

> Library of Congress
> Copyright Office
> 101 Independence Avenue, S.E.
> Washington, D.C. 20559-6000

Unless you have a Deposit Account in the Copyright Office, your application and copies must be accompanied by a check or money order payable to *Register of Copyrights.*

Procedure for Group Registration

Two Application Forms Must Be Filed

When you apply for a single registration to cover a group of contributions to periodicals, you must submit two application forms:

(1) A basic application on either Form TX, Form PA, or Form VA. It must contain all of the information required for copyright registration except the titles and information concerning publication of the contributions.

(2) An adjunct application on Form GR/CP. The purpose of this form is to provide separate identification for each of the contributions and to give information about their first publication, as required by the statute.

Which Basic Application Form To Use

The basic application form you choose to submit should be determined by the nature of the contributions you are registering. As long as they meet the statutory qualifications for group registration (outlined above), the contributions can be registered together even if they are entirely different in nature, type, or content. However, you must choose which of three forms is generally the most appropriate on which to submit your basic application:

Form TX: for nondramatic literary works consisting primarily of text. Examples are fiction, verse, articles, news stories, features, essays, reviews, editorials, columns, quizzes, puzzles, and advertising copy.

Form PA: for works of the performing arts. Examples are music, drama, choreography, and pantomimes.

Form VA: for works of the visual arts. Examples are photographs, drawings, paintings, prints, art reproductions, cartoons, comic strips, charts, diagrams, maps, pictorial ornamentation, and pictorial or graphic material published as advertising.

If your contributions differ in nature, choose the form most suitable for the majority of them.

Registration Fee for Group Registration

If a published serial has not been assigned an ISSN, application forms and additional information my be obtained from Library of Congress, National Serials Data Program, Serial Record Division, Washington, D.C. 20540-4160. Call (202) 707-6452. Or obtain information via the Internet at www.loc.gov/issn/. Unless you maintain a Deposit Account in the Copyright Office, the registration fee must accompany your application forms and copies. Make your remittance payable to: *Register of Copyrights.*

What Copies Should Be Deposited for Group Registration?

The application forms you file for group registration must be accompanied by one complete copy of each published contribution listed on Form GR/CP. The deposit may consist of the entire issue of the periodical containing the contribution. Or, if the contribution was first published in a newspaper, the deposit may consist of the entire section in which the contribution appeared. Tear sheets or proof copies are also acceptable for deposit. Additional acceptable deposits for a GR/CP registration include a photocopy of the contribution itself; a photocopy of the entire page containing the contribution; the entire page containing the contribution cut or torn from the collective work; the contribution cut or torn from the collective work; and photographs or photographic slides of the contribution or entire page containing the contribution as long as all contents of the contributions are clear and legible.

> **NOTE:** Since these deposit alternatives differ from the current regulations, the Office will automatically grant special relief upon receipt. There is no need for the applicant to request such relief in writing. This is being done to facilitate registration pending a change in the regulations.

The Copyright Notice: Before March 1, 1989, the use of a copyright notice was mandatory on all published works, and any work first published before that date should have carried a notice. Furthermore, among the conditions for group registration of contributions to periodicals for works first published prior to March 1, 1989, the statute establishes two requirements involving the copyright notice: (1) Each of the contributions as first published must have borne a separate copyright notice; and (2) "The name of the owner of copyright in the works, or an abbreviation by which the name can be recognized, or a generally known alternative designation of the owner" must have been the same in each notice. For works first published on and after

continued ▶

March 1, 1989, use of the copyright notice is optional. For more information about copyright notice, request Circular 3, "Copyright Notice."

For Further Information: To speak to an information specialist, call (202) 707-3000 (TTY: (202) 707-6737). Recorded information is available 24 hours a day. Order forms and other publications from Library of Congress, Copyright Office, 101 Independence Avenue, S.E., Washington, D.C. 20559-6000 or call the Forms and Publications Hotline at (202) 707-9100. Most circulars (but not forms) are available via fax. Call (202) 707-2600 from a touchtone phone. Access and download circulars, forms, and other information from the Copyright Office Website at **www.loc.gov/copyright.**

> **NOTE:** The advantage of group registration is that it allows any number of works published within a 12-month period to be registered "on the basis of a single deposit, application, and registration fee." On the other hand, group registration may also have disadvantages under certain circumstances. If infringement of a published work begins before the work has been registered, the copyright owner can still obtain the ordinary remedies for copyright infringement (including injunctions, actual damages and profits, and impounding and disposition of infringing articles). However, in that situation—where the copyright in a published work is infringed before registration is made—the owner cannot obtain special remedies (statutory damages and attorney's fees) unless registration was made within 3 months after first publication of the work.

▓▓ INSTRUCTIONS FOR THE BASIC APPLICATION FOR GROUP REGISTRATION ▓▓

In general, the instructions for filling out the basic application (Form TX, Form PA, or Form VA) apply to group registrations. In addition, please observe the following specific instructions:

 SPACE 1: Title

Do not give information concerning any of the contributions in space 1 of the basic application. Instead, in the block headed "Title of this Work," state: "See Form GR/CP, attached." Leave the other blocks in space 1 blank.

 SPACE 2: Author

Give the name and other information concerning the author of all of the contributions listed in Form GR/CP. To qualify for group registration, all of the contributions must have been written by the same individual author.

3 **SPACE 3: Creation and Publication**

In the block calling for the year of creation, give the year of creation of the last of the contributions to be completed. Leave the block calling for the date and nation of first publication blank.

4 **SPACE 4: Claimant**

Give all of the requested information, which must be the same for all of the contributions listed on Form GR/CP.

Other Spaces

Complete all of the applicable spaces and be sure that the form is signed in the certification space.

▓▓ HOW TO FILL OUT FORM GR/CP ▓▓
Please type or print using black ink.

 **PART A: Identification of Application**

• **Identification of Basic Application:** Indicate, by checking one of the boxes, which of the basic application forms (Form TX, Form PA, or Form VA) you are filing for registration.

• **Identification of Author and Claimant:** Give the name of the individual author exactly as it appears in line 2 of the basic application, and give the name of the copyright claimant exactly as it appears in line 4. These must be the same for all of the contributions listed in Part B of Form GR/CP.

B **PART B: Registration for Group of Contributions**

General Instructions: Under the statute, a group of contributions to periodicals will qualify for a single registration only if the application "identifies each work separately, including the periodical containing it and its date of first publication." Part B of the Form GR/CP provides enough lines to list 19 separate contributions; if you need more space, use additional Forms GR/CP. If possible, list the contributions in the order of their publication, giving the earliest first. Number each line consecutively.

• **Important:** All of the contributions listed on Form GR/CP must have been published within a single 12-month period. This does not mean that all of the contributions must have been published during the same calendar year, but it does mean that, to be grouped in a single application, the earliest and latest contributions must not have been published more than 12 months apart. Example: Contributions published on April 1, 1978, July 1, 1978, and March 1, 1979, could be grouped together, but a contribution published on April 15, 1979, could not be registered with them as part of the group.

• **Title of Contribution:** Each contribution must be given a title that identifies that particular work and can distinguish it from others. If the contribution as published in the periodical bears a title (or an identifying phrase that could serve as a title), transcribe its wording completely and exactly.

• **Identification of Periodical:** Give the overall title of the periodical in which the contribution was first published, together with the volume and issue number (if any) and the issue date.

• **Pages:** Give the number of the page of the periodical issue on which the contribution appeared. If the contribution covered more than one page, give the inclusive pages, if possible.

• **First Publication:** The statute defines "publication" as "the distribution of copies or phonorecords of a work to the public by sale or other transfer of ownership, or by rental, lease, or lending"; a work is also "published" if there has been an "offering to distribute copies or phonorecords to a group of persons for purposes of further distribution, public performance, or public display." Give the full date (month, day, and year) when, and the country where, publication of the periodical issue containing the contribution first occurred. If first publication took place simultaneously in the United States and other countries, it is sufficient to state "U.S.A."

ADJUNCT APPLICATION
for Copyright Registration for a
Group of Contributions to Periodicals

- Use this adjunct form only if you are making a single registration for a group of contributions to periodicals, and you are also filing a basic application on Form TX, Form PA, or Form VA. Follow the instructions, attached.
- Number each line in Part B consecutively. Use additional Forms GR/CP if you need more space.
- Submit this adjunct form with the basic application form. Clip (do not tape or staple) and fold all sheets together before submitting them.
- **Fees are effective through June 30, 2002. After that date, check the Copyright Office Website at www.loc.gov/copyright or call (202) 707-3000 for current fee information.**

FORM GR/CP
For a Group of Contributions to Periodicals
UNITED STATES COPYRIGHT OFFICE

REGISTRATION NUMBER

TX	PA	VA

EFFECTIVE DATE OF REGISTRATION

Month	Day	Year

FORM GR/CP RECEIVED

Page _____ of _____ pages

DO NOT WRITE ABOVE THIS LINE. FOR COPYRIGHT OFFICE USE ONLY

A — Identification of Application

IDENTIFICATION OF BASIC APPLICATION:
- This application for copyright registration for a group of contributions to periodicals is submitted as an adjunct to an application filed on: (Check which)

  ☐ Form TX   ☐ Form PA   ☐ Form VA

IDENTIFICATION OF AUTHOR AND CLAIMANT: (Give the name of the author and the name of the copyright claimant in all of the contributions listed in Part B of this form. The names should be the same as the names given in spaces 2 and 4 of the basic application.)

Name of Author _____

Name of Copyright Claimant _____

B — Registration for Group of Contributions

COPYRIGHT REGISTRATION FOR A GROUP OF CONTRIBUTIONS TO PERIODICALS: (To make a single registration for a group of works by the same individual author, all first published as contributions to periodicals within a 12-month period (see instructions), give full information about each contribution. If more space is needed, use additional Forms GR/CP.)

☐ Title of Contribution _____
Title of Periodical _____ Vol.____ No._____ Issue Date _____ Pages _____
Date of First Publication _____ Nation of First Publication _____
(Month)   (Day)   (Year)   (Country)

☐ Title of Contribution _____
Title of Periodical _____ Vol.____ No._____ Issue Date _____ Pages _____
Date of First Publication _____ Nation of First Publication _____
(Month)   (Day)   (Year)   (Country)

☐ Title of Contribution _____
Title of Periodical _____ Vol.____ No._____ Issue Date _____ Pages _____
Date of First Publication _____ Nation of First Publication _____
(Month)   (Day)   (Year)   (Country)

☐ Title of Contribution _____
Title of Periodical _____ Vol.____ No._____ Issue Date _____ Pages _____
Date of First Publication _____ Nation of First Publication _____
(Month)   (Day)   (Year)   (Country)

☐ Title of Contribution _____
Title of Periodical _____ Vol.____ No._____ Issue Date _____ Pages _____
Date of First Publication _____ Nation of First Publication _____
(Month)   (Day)   (Year)   (Country)

☐ Title of Contribution _____
Title of Periodical _____ Vol.____ No._____ Issue Date _____ Pages _____
Date of First Publication _____ Nation of First Publication _____
(Month)   (Day)   (Year)   (Country)

☐ Title of Contribution _____
Title of Periodical _____ Vol.____ No._____ Issue Date _____ Pages _____
Date of First Publication _____ Nation of First Publication _____
(Month)   (Day)   (Year)   (Country)

DO NOT WRITE ABOVE THIS LINE. FOR COPYRIGHT OFFICE USE ONLY.

☐ Title of Contribution _____
  Title of Periodical _____ Vol.____ No._____ Issue Date _____ Pages _____
  Date of First Publication _____ Nation of First Publication _____
               (Month)   (Day)   (Year)   (Country)

B
Continued

☐ Title of Contribution _____
  Title of Periodical _____ Vol.____ No._____ Issue Date _____ Pages _____
  Date of First Publication _____ Nation of First Publication _____
               (Month)   (Day)   (Year)   (Country)

☐ Title of Contribution _____
  Title of Periodical _____ Vol.____ No._____ Issue Date _____ Pages _____
  Date of First Publication _____ Nation of First Publication _____
               (Month)   (Day)   (Year)   (Country)

☐ Title of Contribution _____
  Title of Periodical _____ Vol.____ No._____ Issue Date _____ Pages _____
  Date of First Publication _____ Nation of First Publication _____
               (Month)   (Day)   (Year)   (Country)

☐ Title of Contribution _____
  Title of Periodical _____ Vol.____ No._____ Issue Date _____ Pages _____
  Date of First Publication _____ Nation of First Publication _____
               (Month)   (Day)   (Year)   (Country)

☐ Title of Contribution _____
  Title of Periodical _____ Vol.____ No._____ Issue Date _____ Pages _____
  Date of First Publication _____ Nation of First Publication _____
               (Month)   (Day)   (Year)   (Country)

☐ Title of Contribution _____
  Title of Periodical _____ Vol.____ No._____ Issue Date _____ Pages _____
  Date of First Publication _____ Nation of First Publication _____
               (Month)   (Day)   (Year)   (Country)

☐ Title of Contribution _____
  Title of Periodical _____ Vol.____ No._____ Issue Date _____ Pages _____
  Date of First Publication _____ Nation of First Publication _____
               (Month)   (Day)   (Year)   (Country)

☐ Title of Contribution _____
  Title of Periodical _____ Vol.____ No._____ Issue Date _____ Pages _____
  Date of First Publication _____ Nation of First Publication _____
               (Month)   (Day)   (Year)   (Country)

☐ Title of Contribution _____
  Title of Periodical _____ Vol.____ No._____ Issue Date _____ Pages _____
  Date of First Publication _____ Nation of First Publication _____
               (Month)   (Day)   (Year)   (Country)

☐ Title of Contribution _____
  Title of Periodical _____ Vol.____ No._____ Issue Date _____ Pages _____
  Date of First Publication _____ Nation of First Publication _____
               (Month)   (Day)   (Year)   (Country)

☐ Title of Contribution _____
  Title of Periodical _____ Vol.____ No._____ Issue Date _____ Pages _____
  Date of First Publication _____ Nation of First Publication _____
               (Month)   (Day)   (Year)   (Country)

June 1999–20,000
WEB REV: June 1999

♻ PRINTED ON RECYCLED PAPER

☆U.S. GOVERNMENT PRINTING OFFICE: 1999-454-879

CONTINUATION SHEET
FOR APPLICATION FORMS

Ⓔ**FORM _____ /CON**

UNITED STATES COPYRIGHT OFFICE

REGISTRATION NUMBER

PA	PAU	SE	SEG	SEU	SR	SRU	TX	TXU	VA	VAU

EFFECTIVE DATE OF REGISTRATION

_____

(Month)   (Day)   (Year)

CONTINUATION SHEET RECEIVED

Page _____ of _____ pages

- This Continuation Sheet is used in conjunction with Forms CA, PA, SE, SR, TX, and VA, **only**. Indicate which basic form you are continuing in the space in the upper right-hand corner.
- If at all possible, try to fit the information called for into the spaces provided on the basic form.
- If you do not have enough space for all the information you need to give on the basic form, use this Continuation Sheet and submit it with the basic form.
- If you submit this Continuation Sheet, clip (do not tape or staple) it to the basic form and fold the two together before submitting them.
- **Space A of this sheet is intended to identify the basic application.**
  Space B is a continuation of Space 2 on the basic application. Space B is not applicable to Short forms.
  Space C (on the reverse side of this sheet) is for the continuation of Spaces 1, 4, or 6 on the basic application or for the continuation of Space 1 on any of the three Short Forms PA, TX, or VA.

DO NOT WRITE ABOVE THIS LINE. FOR COPYRIGHT OFFICE USE ONLY

A
Identification of Application

IDENTIFICATION OF CONTINUATION SHEET: This sheet is a continuation of the application for copyright registration on the basic form submitted for the following work:
- TITLE: (Give the title as given under the heading "Title of this Work" in Space 1 of the basic form.)

. . . .

- NAME(S) AND ADDRESS(ES) OF COPYRIGHT CLAIMANT(S) : (Give the name and address of at least one copyright claimant as given in Space 4 of the basic form or Space 2 of any of the Short Forms PA, TX, or VA.)

B
Continuation of Space 2

d

NAME OF AUTHOR ▼

DATES OF BIRTH AND DEATH
Year Born▼   Year Died▼

Was this contribution to the work a "work made for hire"?
☐ Yes
☐ No

AUTHOR'S NATIONALITY OR DOMICILE
Name of Country
OR { Citizen of ▶ _____
{ Domiciled in ▶ _____

WAS THIS AUTHOR'S CONTRIBUTION TO THE WORK
Anonymous? ☐ Yes ☐ No
Pseudonymous? ☐ Yes ☐ No

If the answer to either of these questions is "Yes," see detailed instructions.

NATURE OF AUTHORSHIP Briefly describe nature of the material created by the author in which copyright is claimed. ▼

e

NAME OF AUTHOR ▼

DATES OF BIRTH AND DEATH
Year Born▼   Year Died▼

Was this contribution to the work a "work made for hire"?
☐ Yes
☐ No

AUTHOR'S NATIONALITY OR DOMICILE
Name of Country
OR { Citizen of ▶ _____
{ Domiciled in ▶ _____

WAS THIS AUTHOR'S CONTRIBUTION TO THE WORK
Anonymous? ☐ Yes ☐ No
Pseudonymous? ☐ Yes ☐ No

If the answer to either of these questions is "Yes," see detailed instructions.

NATURE OF AUTHORSHIP Briefly describe nature of the material created by the author in which copyright is claimed. ▼

f

NAME OF AUTHOR ▼

DATES OF BIRTH AND DEATH
Year Born▼   Year Died▼

Was this contribution to the work a "work made for hire"?
☐ Yes
☐ No

AUTHOR'S NATIONALITY OR DOMICILE
Name of Country
OR { Citizen of ▶ _____
{ Domiciled in ▶ _____

WAS THIS AUTHOR'S CONTRIBUTION TO THE WORK
Anonymous? ☐ Yes ☐ No
Pseudonymous? ☐ Yes ☐ No

If the answer to either of these questions is "Yes," see detailed instructions.

NATURE OF AUTHORSHIP Briefly describe nature of the material created by the author in which copyright is claimed. ▼

Use the reverse side of this sheet if you need more space for continuation of Spaces 1, 4, or 6 of the basic form or for the continuation of Space 1 on any of the Short Forms PA, TX, or VA.

CONTINUATION OF (Check which): ☐ Space 1 ☐ Space 4 ☐ Space 6

C

**Continuation
of other
Spaces**

**Certificate
will be
mailed in
window
envelope
to this
address:**

Name ▼

Number/Street/Apt ▼

City/State/ZIP ▼

YOU MUST:
• Complete all necessary spaces
• Sign your application

**SEND ALL 3 ELEMENTS
IN THE SAME PACKAGE:**
1. Application form
2. Nonrefundable fee in check or
money order payable to *Register
of Copyrights*
3. Deposit Material
MAIL TO:
Library of Congress, Copyright Office
101 Independence Avenue, S.E.
Washington, D.C. 20559-6000

D

Fees are effective
through June 30,
2002. After that date,
check the Copyright
office Website at
www.loc.gov/copy-
right or call (202)
707-3000 for current
fee information.

November 1999—30,000
WEB REV: June 1999

♲ PRINTED ON RECYCLED PAPER

☆U.S. GOVERNMENT PRINTING OFFICE: 2000-461-113/78

Form MW should be used for registration of a claim for protection in a mask work which is fixed in a semiconductor chip product, by or under the authority of the owner of the mask work.

A "mask work" is a series of related images, however fixed or encoded, having or representing the predetermined, three-dimensional pattern of metallic, insulating, or semiconductor material present or removed from the layers of a semiconductor chip product, and in which the relation of the images to one another is such that each image has the pattern of the surface of one form of the semiconductor chip product. To be protected, a mask work must be original. If the mask work consists of designs that are staple, commonplace, or familiar in the semiconductor industry, any variation or combination of such designs must, considered as a whole, be original to be protected. In no case does protection for a mask work extend to any idea, procedure, process, system, method of operation, concept, discovery, or the like embodied or illustrated in a mask work. Nor is a design protectible if it is dictated by a particular electronic function or is one of only a few available design choices that will accomplish that function.

Protection for a mask work begins on the date on which the mask work is registered, or the date of first commercial exploitation anywhere in the world, whichever occurs first, and lasts for a term of 10 years. During such time, the owner has the exclusive rights to: 1) reproduce the mask work by any means; 2) import or distribute semiconductor chip products embodying the mask work; and 3) authorize or induce others to reproduce, to import, or to distribute.

Statutory protection for a mask work which has been commercially exploited anywhere in the world is terminated if application for registration of a claim for protection is not made within 2 years after the date of first commercial exploitation.

DEPOSIT TO ACCOMPANY APPLICATION: The Act requires the deposit of identifying material as specified in the Copyright Office Regulations. (37 C.F.R. §211). For further information, request Circular 96 Part 211.

MASK WORK PROTECTION DIFFERENT FROM COPYRIGHT: Both the Copyright Act and the Semiconductor Chip Protection Act are administered by the Copyright Office and involve protection for intellectual property. However, they differ from each other in most respects, including term, ownership, eligibility, scope of exclusive rights, limitations on exclusive rights, remedies, and registration procedures.

FOR FORMS OR INFORMATION: For information, write or call the Copyright Office, Library of Congress, Washington, D.C. 20559-6000, (202) 707-3000. For forms call (202) 707-9100 or download them from http://www.loc.gov/copyright. You may photocopy blank application forms; **however**, photocopies of Form MW submitted to the Copyright Office must be clear, legible, on a good grade of 8 1/2-inch by 11-inch (preferably blue) paper, suitable for automatic feeding through a photocopier. **Forms not meeting these requirements will be returned.**

MASK WORK NOTICE: The owner of a protected mask work may affix a notice to the mask work or to the semiconductor chip product embodying the mask work in such a way as to give reasonable notice of such protection. The notice consists of two elements: 1) the words "mask work," the symbol *M*, or the letter M in a circle Ⓜ; and 2) the name of the owner or owners of the mask work or an abbreviation by which the name is recognized or is generally known. The affixation of a notice is not a condition of protection under the law, but provides certain benefits.

SPACE BY SPACE INSTRUCTIONS

Space 1: TITLE.
Every work submitted for registration must be given a title for purposes of cataloging and identification. This title may include the name of the semiconductor chip product in which the mask work is embodied, e.g., "ASTRA 2014," "Memory Cell 5522," or "Register X22."

Space 2: NATURE OF DEPOSIT.
Give a short description of the object deposited as identifying material, e.g., "chips plus seven of nine acetate layers," "acetate color overlay sheets," or "composite plot."

Spaces 3, 4, and 5: INFORMATION ABOUT CURRENT OWNER(S).
The owner of a mask work is: 1) the person who created the mask work; 2) the legal representative of that person if that person is deceased or under a legal incapacity; 3) the employer for whom a person created the mask work within the scope of his or her employment; or 4) the party to whom all the rights of such a person, employer or representative are transferred. Give the name(s) and address(es) of the current owner(s) of the mask work which is the subject matter of this application. Use a continuation sheet if additional space is needed.

Give the citizenship or domicile of the current owner in space 4.

If the current owner is not the person who created the mask work which is the subject matter of this application, check the appropriate box in space 5 to explain how the owner acquired the right to claim protection in this mask work. NOTE: If the current owner is a company or organization, one of the boxes must be checked.

Space 6: DATE AND NATION OF FIRST COMMERCIAL EXPLOITATION.
To "commercially exploit" a mask work is to distribute to the public for commercial purposes a semiconductor chip product embodying the mask work. The offering to sell or transfer a semiconductor chip product is a commercial exploitation only when the offer is in writing and occurs after the fixation of a mask work in a semiconductor chip product.

If this mask work has been commercially exploited anywhere in the world, give the exact date (month, day and year) and the nation of first commercial exploitation. If the work has not yet been commercially exploited, leave this space blank.

Space 7: CITIZENSHIP OR DOMICILE OF OWNER AT TIME OF FIRST COMMERCIAL EXPLOITATION.
Eligibility for protection may depend on the nationality or domicile of the owner of a commercially exploited mask work at the time of first commercial exploitation. Complete this space if the mask work which is the subject of this application was commercially exploited, and if the nationality or domicile of the owner at the time of first commercial exploitation is different from that given in space 4.

Space 8: NATURE OF CONTRIBUTION.
Mask works generally contain preexisting material that is common in the semiconductor industry. Such material is not protectible. However, if staple designs are combined in a way that is original, the new authorship may be protected. Further, portions of a work that may have been previously commercially exploited or previously registered for protection may not be included in the claim.

Give a brief, general statement that describes the new protectible contribution that is the basis of this claim. This statement may, if appropriate, refer to any previous mask work upon which the mask work being registered is based, as an aid in distinguishing the new contribution from the preexisting material. NOTE: Protection does not extend to the functions of the semiconductor chip product.

Spaces 9, 10, 11, and 12: CORRESPONDENCE. In space 9, give the name, address, and daytime telephone number of the contact person if further information about this claim is needed.
DEPOSIT ACCOUNT. Complete space 10 if an existing deposit account is to be charged for the filing fee.
CERTIFICATION. Give the handwritten signature of a person authorized to certify the facts asserted in this application. **The application must be signed.**
ADDRESS FOR RETURN OF CERTIFICATE. The name and address must be completed legibly; the certificate will be mailed in a window envelope.

FEE CHANGES

Mask works filing fees are effective through June 30, 2002. For information on the fee changes, write the Copyright Office, check http://www.loc.gov/copyright, or call (202) 707-3000. Beginning as early as January 1, 2000, the Copyright Office may impose a service charge when insufficient fees are received.

FORM MW
For Mask Works
UNITED STATES COPYRIGHT OFFICE

REGISTRATION NUMBER

MW

EFFECTIVE DATE OF REGISTRATION

| Month | Day | Year |

APPLICATION RECEIVED

DEPOSIT RECEIVED

SEE SPACE-BY-SPACE INSTRUCTIONS ON OTHER SIDE. DO NOT WRITE ABOVE THIS LINE. IF YOU NEED MORE SPACE, USE FORM MW/CON.

1. TITLE OF THIS WORK _____

2. NATURE OF DEPOSIT _____

3. NAME AND ADDRESS OF CURRENT OWNER(S) _____

4. CITIZENSHIP OR DOMICILE OF CURRENT OWNER(S)
Citizen of: _____
or
Domiciled in: _____

5. DERIVATION OF OWNERSHIP: If the person who created the mask work which is subject matter of this application is NOT named as the owner, check one: (Note: If a company or organization is named as the current owner, one of the following boxes *must* be checked.)
☐ a. The owner is the employer of a person who created such mask work within the scope of his/her employment.
☐ b. The owner has acquired the rights by transfer from the creator, employer or representative.
☐ c. The owner is the legal representative of the deceased or legally incapacitated creator.

6. DATE AND NATION OF FIRST COMMERCIAL EXPLOITATION
Month _____ Day _____ Year _____
Nation _____

7. CITIZENSHIP OR DOMICILE OF OWNER AT THE TIME OF FIRST COMMERCIAL EXPLOITATION (See instructions)
Citizen of: _____
Domiciled in: _____

8. NATURE OF CONTRIBUTION: Mask works generally contain designs that are staple, commonplace, or familiar in the semiconductor industry, or are variations of such designs, or are variations of designs that have been previously commercially exploited or previously registered for protection. Describe the new, original contribution in this mask work for which statutory protection is sought: _____

9. CONTACT PERSON FOR CORRESPONDENCE ABOUT THIS CLAIM
Name: _____
Daytime telephone number: (   ) _____
Address (if other than given at space 12): _____
FAX: (   ) _____ Email: _____

10. DEPOSIT ACCOUNT
Name of Account: _____
Account Number: _____

11. CERTIFICATION: I, the undersigned, hereby certify that I have the authority to submit this application and that the statements made herein are correct to the best of my knowledge.*

☞ **HANDWRITTEN SIGNATURE (X)** _____
(This application MUST be signed.)

TYPED SIGNATURE _____

12.
Certificate will be mailed in window envelope to this address:

Name _____

Number/Street/Apt Number _____

City/State/ZIP _____

PLEASE BE SURE THAT YOU HAVE:
• Signed the application at space 11.
• Enclosed a check or money order for the nonrefundable filing fee of $75, payable to **Register of Copyrights.**
• Enclosed deposit, application, and fee.

MAIL TO:
Library of Congress
Department MW
101 Independence Avenue, S.E.
Washington, DC 20540

*Any person who knowingly makes a false representation of a material fact in the application for registration as provided in 18 USC 1001 shall be fined not more than $10,000.

July 1998 — 15,000

☆U.S. GOVERNMENT PRINTING OFFICE: 1998: 432-381/80,015

CONTINUATION SHEET FOR FORM MW

- This sheet should be used to complete information appearing on Form MW.

- Identify the work by completing the first section.

- Spaces are provided to identify two additional owners.

- Other information may be provided in the last space.

	Month	Day	Year

CONTINUATION SHEET RECEIVED

DO NOT WRITE ABOVE THIS LINE. FOR COPYRIGHT OFFICE USE ONLY.

Page   of   pages

IDENTIFICATION OF CONTINUATION SHEET: This sheet is a continuation of the application for registration on Form MW filed for the following work:

- **TITLE:** Give the title as given under the heading "Title of This Work" in space 1 of Form MW.

_____

- **NAME AND ADDRESS OF CURRENT OWNER(S):** Give the name and address of at least one of the owners named at space 3 of Form MW.

NAME AND ADDRESS OF CURRENT OWNER(S) _____

_____

_____

_____

CITIZENSHIP OR DOMICILE OF CURRENT OWNER(S)

Citizen of: _____
or
Domiciled in: _____

DERIVATION OF OWNERSHIP: If the person who created the mask work which is subject matter of this application is NOT named as the owner, check one: (Note: If a company or organization is named as the current owner, one of the following boxes *must* be checked.)

☐ a. The owner is the employer of a person who created such mask work within the scope of his/her employment.

☐ b. The owner has acquired the rights by transfer from the creator, employer or representative.

☐ c. The owner is the legal representative of the deceased or legally incapacitated creator.

NAME AND ADDRESS OF CURRENT OWNER(S) _____

_____

_____

_____

CITIZENSHIP OR DOMICILE OF CURRENT OWNER(S)

Citizen of: _____
or
Domiciled in: _____

DERIVATION OF OWNERSHIP: If the person who created the mask work which is subject matter of this application is NOT named as the owner, check one: (Note: If a company or organization is named as the current owner, one of the following boxes *must* be checked.)

☐ a. The owner is the employer of a person who created such mask work within the scope of his/her employment.

☐ b. The owner has acquired the rights by transfer from the creator, employer or representative.

☐ c. The owner is the legal representative of the deceased or legally incapacitated creator.

ADDITIONAL INFORMATION: Indicate the Heading and the Space Number from the basic Form MW being amplified, followed by the added facts.

_____

_____

_____

_____

_____

_____

_____

_____

This page intentionally left blank.

Document Cover Sheet

*Read these instructions carefully before completing this form. Make sure all applicable spaces
have been properly filled in before you return this form. Otherwise, the form cannot be used.*

BASIC INFORMATION

When to Use This Form: Use the Document Cover Sheet when you are submitting a document for recordation in the U.S. Copyright Office.

Mailing Requirements: It is important that you send **two** copies of the Document Cover Sheet, any additional sheets, the document, and the fee together in the same envelope or package. The Copyright Office cannot process them unless they are received together. Send to: *Library of Congress, Copyright Office, Documents Recordation Section, LM-462, 101 Independence Avenue, S.E., Washington, D.C. 20559-6000.*

Two copies of this Document Cover Sheet should be submitted with each document. Cover sheets should be typed or printed and should contain the information requested so the Copyright Office can process the document and return it. Be sure to complete the return address space. The Copyright Office will process the document based on the information in the document. Therefore, parties and titles should be clearly identified in the document or an attachment to it. Information for indexing will not be taken from the Document Cover Sheet. To be recordable, a document must satisfy the recordation requirements of the copyright code and Copyright Office regulations.

The person(s) submitting a document with a cover sheet is (are) solely responsible for verifying the correctness of the cover sheet and the sufficiency of the document. Recording a document submitted with or without a cover sheet does not constitute a determination by the Copyright Office of the document's validity or effect. Only a court may make such determinations.

Any cover sheets submitted will be recorded with the document as part of the official recordation.

> **PRIVACY ACT ADVISORY STATEMENT**
> **Required by the Privacy Act of 1974 (P.L. 93-579)**
> The authority for requesting this information is title 17 U.S.C., sec. 205. Furnishing the requested information is voluntary. But if the information is not provided, it may be necessary to delay recordation.
> The principal uses of the requested information are the establishment and maintenance of a public record and the evaluation for compliance with the recordation requirements of section 205 of the copyright code. Other routine uses include public inspection and copying, preparation of public indexes, preparation of public catalogs of copyright recordations, and preparation of search reports upon request.
> NOTE: No other advisory statement will be given in connection with this application. Please keep this statement and refer to it if we communicate with you regarding this cover sheet.

SPACE-BY-SPACE INSTRUCTIONS

SPACE 1: Name of Party or Parties to the Document

List up to the first three (3) parties to this document.

SPACE 2: Date of Execution

Give the date the accompanying document (not this Cover Sheet) was executed and/or became effective.

SPACE 3: Completeness of Document

Check a box. All documents recorded under section 205 of the copyright code must be complete by their own terms in order to be recordable. Examples of section 205 documents include transfers of copyright ownerships and other documents pertaining to a copyright, such as exclusive and nonexclusive licenses, contracts, mortgages, powers of attorney, certificates of change of corporate name or title, wills, and decrees of distribution.

SPACE 4: Description of Document

Check a box that describes the document.

SPACE 5: Title of First Work

List the title of the first work included in the document.

SPACE 6: Number of Titles in Document

The total number of titles determines the recordation fee. In the case of multiple title documents, titles that are repeated in documents will be counted as a single title, except where the document lists different issues, volumes, chapters, or installments following the title. Each such entry will be regarded as a separate title and will be indexed separately and counted separately for purposes of computing the recordation fee. The Copyright Office will verify title counts.

SPACE 7: Amount of Fee

The fee for a document of any length containing one title is $50. Additional titles are $15 for each group of 10 or fewer. Calculate the fee from the information given in Space 6. Fees are effective through June 30, 2002.

SPACE 8: Fee Enclosed

Check a box. If a Copyright Office Deposit Account is to be charged, give the Copyright Office Deposit Account number and name.

SPACE 9: Affirmation

This space must be completed by all applicants. The party to the document submitting it for recordation or his/her authorized agent should sign the affirmation and authorization contained in this space. This affirmation and authorization is not a substitute for the certification required for documents containing a photocopy signature. (See Certification, Space 10.) The affirmation must be signed even if you are signing Space 10.

SPACE 10: Certification

Complete this section only if submitting photocopied documents in lieu of a document bearing the actual signature.

Certification: Any transfer of copyright ownership or other document pertaining to a copyright (section 205) may be recorded in the Copyright Office if the document bears the actual signature of the person or persons who executed (signed) the documents. If a photocopy of the original signed document is submitted, it must be accompanied by a sworn or official certification. A sworn certification signed by at least one of the parties to the document or their authorized representative (who is identified as such) at Space 10 will satisfy that requirement. **Copies of documents on file in a federal, state, or local government office must be accompanied by an official certification.**

If you sign Space 10, you must also have signed Space 9.

Fees are effective through June 30, 2002. After that date, check the Copyright Office Website at www.loc.gov/copyright or call (202) 707-3000 for current fee information.

DOCUMENT COVER SHEET

For Recordation of Documents
UNITED STATES COPYRIGHT OFFICE

DATE OF RECORDATION
(Assigned by Copyright Office)

Month _____ Day _____ Year _____

Volume _____ Page _____

Volume _____ Page _____

FUNDS RECEIVED _____

Do not write above this line.

To the Register of Copyrights:

Please record the accompanying original document or copy thereof.

FOR OFFICE USE ONLY

1 Name of the party or parties to the document spelled as they appear in the document (List up to the first three)

_____
_____
_____

2 Date of execution and/or effective date of the accompanying document
_____ _____ _____
(month)   (day)   (year)

3 Completeness of document
❏ Document is complete by its own terms.
❏ Document is not complete. Record "as is."

4 Description of document
❏ Transfer of Copyright
❏ Security Interest
❏ Change of Name of Owner
❏ Termination of Transfer(s) [Section 304]
❏ Shareware
❏ Life, Identity, Death Statement [Section 302]
❏ Transfer of Mask Works
❏ Other _____
_____

5 Title of first work as given in the document _____
_____

6 Total number of titles in document _____

7 Amount of fee calculated
$ _____

8 Fee enclosed
❏ Check
❏ Money Order

❏ Fee authorized to be charged to :
Copyright Office
Deposit Account number _____

Account name _____

9 **Affirmation:** * I hereby affirm to the Copyright Office that the information given on this form is a true and correct representation of the accompanying document. This affirmation will not suffice as a certification of a photocopy signature on the document.
(Affirmation *must* be signed even if you are also signing Space 10.)

_____
Signature

_____
Date

_____
Phone Number   Fax Number

10 **Certification:** * Complete this certification in addition to the Affirmation if a photocopy of the original signed document is substituted for a document bearing the actual signature.
NOTE: This space *may not* be used for an official certification.
I certify under penalty of perjury under the laws of the United States of America that the accompanying document is a true copy of the original document.

_____
Signature

_____
Duly Authorized Agent of:

_____
Date

Recordation will be mailed in window envelope to this address:

Name▼ _____

Number/Street/Apt▼ _____

City/State/ZIP▼ _____

YOU MUST:
• Complete all necessary spaces
• Sign your Cover Sheet in Space 9
SEND ALL 3 ELEMENTS TOGETHER:
1. Two copies of the Document Cover Sheet
2. Check/money order payable to *Register of Copyrights*
3. Document
MAIL TO:
Library of Congress, Copyright Office
Documents Recordation Section, LM-462
101 Independence Avenue, S.E.
Washington, D.C. 20559-6000

The recordation fee for the Document Cover Sheet is $50 and $15 for each group of 10 additional titles as of July 1, 1999.

request for
special handling

1

SPECIAL HANDLING IS NOT FOR CONVENIENCE ONLY!
NOTE: The special handling of a registration application or other fee service severely disrupts the entire registration process and workflow of the Copyright Office. It is granted only in the most urgent of cases. A request for special handling is subject to the approval of the Chief of the Receiving and Processing Division, who takes into account the workload situation of the office at the time the request is made. A minimum period of five working days is required to process a registration application under special handling procedures.

Why is there an urgent need for special handling?

☐ Litigation   ☐ Contractual/Publishing Deadlines

☐ Customs Matter   ☐ Other, Specify

2

If you must have the requested action to go forward with the litigation, please answer the following questions.

a.   Is the litigation actual or prospective?

Unless all blanks are completed your request cannot be processed.

b.   Are you (or your client) the plaintiff or defendant in the action? Please specify.

c.   What are the names of the parties and what is the name of the court where the action is pending or expected?

I certify that the statements made above are correct to the best of my knowledge.

(Signature)

(Address)

(Phone)   (Date)

FOR COPYRIGHT OFFICE USE ONLY

Information Specialist handling matter

remarks

This page intentionally left blank.

Work Made-for-Hire Agreement

This Agreement is made the _____ day of _____, 20___, between _____ as Owner and_____ as Author/Artist.

Whereas _____ wishes to commission a Work called_____ which shall consist of _____
_____
_____
_____ and

Whereas _____ has represented that he/she can create said work according to the specifications provided by Owner,

It is agreed between the parties hereto that in consideration of the sum of $_____, to be paid by Owner to Author/Artist within thirty days of satisfactory completion of the work, Author/Artist shall create the Work as specified. Upon payment, Owner shall acquire all rights to the commissioned Work including copyright.

Author/Artist warrants that the Work will be original and will not infringe or plagiarize any other work; will not libel any person or invade any person's right to privacy; and will not contain any unlawful materials. Author/Artist shall indemnify and save Owner harmless from any loss or liability due to any breach of these warranties, including reasonable attorney fees.

Author/Artist shall be responsible for all costs in creation of the Work unless otherwise agreed in writing by the Owner.

This Agreement shall not be modified or terminated except in writing signed by the parties hereto.

In witness whereof, the Owner and Author/Artist have executed this Agreement the date above written.

_____
Owner

_____
Author/Artist

This page intentionally left blank.

Work Made-for-Hire Employment Agreement

This Agreement is made the _____ day of _____, 20___, between _____ as Employer and _____ _____ as Employee.

Whereas Employer wishes to have a Work created which shall consist of _____ _____ _____ _____ _____ and

Whereas Employee has represented that he/she can create said work according to the specifications previously provided by Employer,

It is agreed between the parties hereto that in consideration of the sum of $_____, to be paid by Employer to Employee at a rate of $_____ per _____, Employee shall create the Work as specified. In consideration of this payment, Employer shall be entitled to all rights to said work, including the copyright.

The parties agree that Employer shall have the right to control the manner and means by which the Work is created and

Employee warrants that the Work will be original and will not infringe or plagiarize any other work; will not libel any person or invade any person's right to privacy; and will not contain any unlawful materials. Employee shall indemnify and save Employer harmless from any loss or liability due to any breach of these warranties, including reasonable attorney fees.

Employee will not disclose to any parties outside of Employer's business any trade secrets or confidential information of Employer.

This Agreement shall not be modified or terminated except in writing signed by the parties hereto.

In witness whereof, the Employer and Employee have executed this Agreement the date above written.

_____
Employer

_____
Employee

This page intentionally left blank.

Independent Contractor Agreement

This Agreement is made the _____ day of _____, 20___, between _____ as Purchaser and_____ as Author/Artist.

Whereas Purchaser wishes to purchase a Work called _____ which shall consist of _____ _____ and and shall be used for _____ and

Whereas Author/Artist has represented that he/she can create said work according to the specifications provided by Owner.

It is agreed between the parties hereto that in consideration of the sum of $_____, to be paid by Purchaser to Author/Artist upon completion of the work, Author/Artist shall create the Work according to the specifications agreed to between Purchaser and Author/Artist. It is understood that while Purchaser shall own the work itself, Author/Artist retains the copyright to the Work, including the right to reproduce the work and license the Work to others.

Author/Artist warrants that the Work will be original and will not infringe or plagiarize any other work; will not libel any person or invade any person's right to privacy; and will not contain any unlawful materials. Author/Artist shall indemnify and save Purchaser harmless from any loss or liability due to any breach of these warranties, including reasonable attorney fees.

Author/Artist shall be responsible for all costs in creation of the Work unless otherwise agreed in writing by the Purchaser.

This Agreement shall not be modified or terminated except in writing signed by the parties hereto.

In witness whereof, the Purchaser and Author/Artist have executed this Agreement the date above written.

_____
Purchaser

_____
Author/Artist

This page intentionally left blank.

Collaboration Agreement

This Agreement is made the _____ day of _____, 20___, between and among the following Collaborators:

_____   _____

_____   _____

Whereas the parties hereto wish to collaborate on a Work to be known as _____ which shall consist of _____
_____ and

Whereas the parties have agreed that they will contribute to the work as follows:

Party: Contribution:

_____   _____

_____   _____

_____   _____

_____   _____

Their names shall appear on any attribution of the work in the order appearing next to their contribution.

It is agreed between the parties hereto that in consideration of their mutual agreements they shall each contribute as stated in this agreement and shall own the resulting work in the following percentages:

Party: Ownership:

_____   _____%

_____   _____%

_____   _____%

_____   _____%

The parties agree that they shall each complete their share of the work as follows:

Party: Date:

_____   _____

_____   _____

_____   _____

_____   _____

Each party warrants that their contribution to the Work will be original and will not infringe or plagiarize any other work; will not libel any person or invade any person's right to privacy; and will not contain any unlawful materials. Each party shall indemnify and save other parties harmless from any loss or liability due to his or her breach of these warranties, including reasonable attorney fees.

The parties to this agreement are independent of each other and do not intend to create a partnership or joint venture. Each shall be responsible for his or her own debts and expenses.

No party shall transfer his or her interest in this agreement without the consent of the other collaborators.

This Agreement shall not be modified or terminated except in writing signed by the parties hereto.

In witness whereof, the parties have executed this Agreement the date above written.

_____

_____

_____

_____

Assignment of Copyright

This Assignment is made the _____ day of _____, 20___, between
_____ as Owner of the copyright on the Work known as

_____

_____,

and _____ Purchaser.

Whereas Owner is sole owner of all rights in the Work and whereas Purchaser is desirous of purchasing all such rights,

It is agreed between the parties hereto that in consideration of the sum of $_____, the receipt of which is hereby acknowledged, the Owner hereby assigns to Purchaser all of his/her interest in the Work and the copyright thereon, which interest shall be held for the full term of said copyright.

In witness whereof, the Owner has executed this Assignment the date above written.

_____

State of _____)

County of _____)

Acknowledgment

Before me, a Notary Public in and for the said state and county, personally appeared _____ who acknowledged that he/she did sign the foregoing Assignment as his/her free act and deed.

In testimony whereof, I have hereunto affixed my name and official seal this _____ day of _____, 20_____.

_____

Notary Public

My commission expires:

Note: In some states the notary paragraph must be worded according to the local law to be valid.

This page intentionally left blank.

Copyright License

This License is made the _____ day of _____, 20____, between _____ as Owner of the copyright on the Work known as

_____

_____,

and _____ as Licensee.

    Whereas _____ is sole owner of all rights in the Work and whereas _____ is desirous of purchasing rights in said Work,

    It is agreed between the parties hereto that in consideration of the sum of $_____, the receipt of which is hereby acknowledged, the Owner hereby licenses the Licensee to use the copyrighted Work as follows:

_____

_____

_____

_____

_____

_____

    It is understood between the parties that this License covers only those uses listed above for the time period stated. All other rights in and to the copyrighted work shall remain the property of the Owner.

    In witness whereof, the Owner has executed this Copyright License the date above written.

_____
Owner

_____
Licensee

This page intentionally left blank.

Application Form D-VH

Detach and read these instructions before completing this form.
Make sure all applicable spaces have been filled in before you return this form.

Form D-VH should be used for the registration of an original design of a vessel hull which makes the hull attractive or distinctive in appearance to the purchasing or using public. A vessel hull includes the design of a plug or mold used to manufacture the vessel hull.

Definition: A "vessel" is a craft designed to navigate on water, but does not include any such craft that exceeds 200 feet in length. A "hull" is the frame or body of a vessel, including the deck of a vessel, exclusive of masts, sails, yards, and rigging. A "plug" is a device or model used to make a mold for the purpose of exact duplication, regardless of whether the device or model has an intrinsic utilitarian function that is not only to portray the appearance of the product or to convey information. A "mold" is a matrix or form in which a substance for material is used, regardless of whether the matrix or form has an intrinsic utilitarian function that is not only to portray the appearance of the product or to convey information.

Design Protection: Design protection for vessel hulls is available only for original designs that are embodied in an actual vessel hull: no protection is available for designs that exist only in models, drawings or representations. Staple or commonplace designs, such as a standard geometric figure, a familiar symbol, an emblem, or a motif, or another shape, pattern, or configuration which has become standard, common, prevalent, or ordinary, are not protected. Designs that are different from staple or commonplace designs only in insignificant details or in elements which are variants commonly used in the relevant trades are also not protectible. Designs which are embodied in a vessel hull that were made public by the designer or owner in the United States or a foreign country more than 1 year before the date of this application are also not eligible for protection. Finally, no protection is available for designs which were made public prior to October 28, 1998.

Design protection afforded under chapter 13 of title 17, United States Code, commences upon publication of the registration by the Copyright Office, or upon the date the design is first made public, whichever date is earlier. Design protection is for a period of ten years, terminating at the end of the calendar year in which the ten year period expires. However, the provisions of chapter 13 are scheduled to expire on October 27, 2000, and design protection will terminate at that time unless the law is renewed by Congress.

Drawings or Photographs to Accompany Application: The drawings or photographs of the design are a critical element of a design protection application. Because the drawings or photographs constitute the entire visual disclosure of the design, it is of the utmost importance that they be clear and complete, and that they include a sufficient number of views so that the appearance of the design is adequately shown. All drawings or photographs must be submitted on plain white, 8 1/2" x 11" unruled paper. Such paper should be flexible, strong, smooth, non-shiny and durable. All sheets must be free from cracks, creases, and folds. Only one side of a sheet may be used for drawings or photographs.

> **IMPORTANT NOTE:** Because the certificate of registration requires reproduction of the drawings or photographs of the design, a charge of $20 per sheet of depictions of the design, beyond three pages, is required in addition to the basic $75 application fee.

The Views: The drawings or photographs should contain a sufficient number of views to completely disclose the appearance of the design, i.e. front, rear, right and left sides, top and bottom. While not required, it is suggested that perspective views be submitted to show clearly the appearance and shape of three dimensional designs. No more than two drawings or photographs of the design may appear on a single sheet. In addition, no combinations of drawings and photographs may be submitted on a single sheet.

It is extremely important that the drawings or photographs that accompany the application reveal all aspects of the design for which protection is claimed. The registration extends only to those aspects of the design that are adequately shown in the drawings or photographs.

Drawings. Drawings are required to be in black ink on white 8 1/2" x 11" unruled paper. A drawing of a design should be provided with appropriate surface shading which shows clearly the character and contour of all surfaces of any 3-dimensional aspects of the design. Surface shading is also necessary to distinguish between any open and solid areas of the design. Solid black surface shading is not permitted except when used to represent the black color as well as color contrast.

The use of broken lines in drawings depicting the design is understood to be for illustrative purposes only and forms no part of the claimed design. Structure that is not part of the design, but that is considered necessary to show the environment in which the design is used, may be represented in the drawing by broken lines. This includes any portion of the vessel hull in which the design is embodied or applied that is not considered part of the design. When the claimed design is only surface ornamentation to the vessel hull, the vessel hull in which it is embodied must be shown in broken lines.

In general, when broken lines are used, they should not intrude upon or cross the image of the design and should not be of heavier weight than the lines used in depicting the design. Where a broken line depiction of environmental structure must necessarily cross or intrude upon the representation of the design and obscures a clear understanding of the design, such an illustration should be included as a separate figure, in addition to other figures which fully disclose the subject matter of the design.

Photographs. The Copyright Office will accept high quality black and white or color photographs provided that they are mounted on plain white 8 1/2" x 11" unlined paper, not to exceed two photographs per sheet. Photographs must be developed on double weight photographic paper and must be of sufficient quality so that all the details of the design are plainly visible and are capable of reproduction on the registration certificate, if issued.

Design Protection Different from Copyright Protection: Although design protection and copyright protection under title 17 of the United States Code are both administered by the Register of Copyrights, they are not identical. Design protection differs significantly in most respects, including term of protection, ownership, eligibility, scope of protection and registration procedures. While some designs that are eligible for design protection may also be eligible for copyright protection, design registration does not include a copyright registration. Copyright registration must be made separately.

Design Protection Not Available for Patented Designs: Design protection under chapter 13 of title 17, United States Code, is not available, and registration may not be made, for designs that have received patent protection under title 35 of the United States Code.

For Forms or Information: For information, write or call the Copyright Office, Library of Congress, Washington, D.C. 20559-6000, (202) 707-3000. For forms call (202) 707-9100. You may copy blank application forms; however, photocopies of Form D-VH submitted to the Copyright Office must be clear, legible, on a good grade of 8 1/2 inch by 11 inch paper, suitable for automatic feeding through a photocopier. Forms not meeting these requirements will be returned.

> **PRIVACY ACT ADVISORY STATEMENT**
> Consistent with the Privacy Act of 1974 (P.L. 93-579):
> The authority for requesting the information on this application form is 17 U.S.C. §1301 et. seq., which provide for registration of designs of vessel hulls for which design protection is claimed. Furnishing of the information is voluntary, but if the information is not furnished, it is probable that registration will be refused. Unless a judicial appeal should result in an order compelling registration, any inchoate rights in the design would be forfeited at the expiration of one year from the date the design embodied in the useful article was made public by the designer or owner in the United States or a foreign country.
> The principal uses of the requested information are the examination of the application for registration to determine compliance with legal requirements and the establishment and maintenance of a public record of claims of protection.
> Other routine uses include public inspection and copying, preparation of public indexes, preparation of public catalogues of designs, preparation of search reports upon request, and on-line publication of registrations.
> NOTE: No other advisory statement will be given in connection with this application. Please keep this statement and refer to it if the Office communicates with you regarding this application.

1 SPACE 1: Title

The make and model of the vessel which embodies the design for which protection is sought must be provided for purposes of identification and cataloging. If a design is used for more than one make and model, list each make and model in this space. The make and model will typically include the name of the manufacturer and the model identification given the vessel, including any descriptive information, such as the general categorization or type of the vessel, that is useful to the identification. Examples: "Tracker Tahoe Q 5 runabout;" "Ranger Commanche 518VX bass boat."

2 SPACE 2: Design

Space 2a requires identification of the type or style of the design for which protection is sought. The identification of the type or style should be general and, where possible, conform with accepted industry classifications. Examples: "fiberglass tri-hull;" or "aluminum pontoon."

Space 2b requests a brief description of the salient features of the design. While the description should be brief, it should be sufficiently descriptive to allow easy identification of the design for which protection is sought (examples: "design of transom," or "configuration of deck"), and to assist in the determination of the originality of the design. Space 2-b is optional. Although it is desirable that such a description be provided, the absence of a description shall not prevent registration.

If the design is derived from a prior design, Space 2-c should be completed. The description of the revisions, adaptations or rearrangements that make the new design original should be sufficiently detailed to enable identification of the new design from the prior design.

Use a continuation sheet, FORM D-VH\CON, if additional space for Space 2 is required.

IMPORTANT NOTE: A single application may be used for more than one design embodied in a vessel provided that the information contained in all spaces of the application other than Space 2 is the same for each design. If the information is different in one or more of the spaces (e.g., registration is sought for two designs in the same vessel and the name of the designer in Space 3 is different for each design), then separate applications should be used. The $75 application fee applies to each design submitted, regardless of whether the designs are submitted on one or more applications.

For applications for registration of multiple designs, Form D-VH/CON must be used to identify each design beyond the design specified in the basic Form D-VH. Use an additional Form D-VH/CON for each design included in the registration, and attach the deposit material identifying each design to the corresponding Form D-VH/CON. The space on Form D-VH/CON stating "Design ___ of ___ designs" should be completed (e.g., "Design 2 of 3 designs"), and the same information (e.g., "Design 2 of 3 designs") should be placed on each page of drawings or photographs of the corresponding design.

SPACE 3: Designer(s)

The designer is the person or persons whose creative endeavors have resulted in the creation of the design. The name of the owner of the design may be substituted for that of the designer if the design was made within the regular scope of the designer's employment and the individual authorship of the design is difficult or impossible to ascribe due to the number of employee designers who contributed to the creation of the design.

SPACE 4: Owner

Space 4 must be completed if the owner of the design is not the designer and the owner was not identified in Space 3.

SPACE 5: Priority Claim

If an application for registration of a design is filed with the Copyright Office by any person who has, or whose representative or predecessor or successor in title has, previously filed an application for registration of the same design in a foreign country, then protection under chapter 13 of the Copyright Act commences on the date that the application was first filed in the foreign country, provided that such date was within 6 months of the filing of the application for the design with the Copyright Office. The benefit of the earlier date of registration in the foreign country only applies where the law of the foreign country (1) extends to designs of owners who are citizens of the United States; and (2) the law of the foreign country affords similar protection to the design as that found in chapter 13 of the Copyright Act. Applicants must submit additional information and documents; see the Copyright Office regulations at 37 CFR §212.3(h)

SPACE 6: Date Made Public

Applications will not be accepted for designs that were made public prior to October 28, 1998 because the law provides that such designs are not subject to protection. A design is generally considered to be "made public" if it is anywhere publicly exhibited, publicly distributed, or offered for sale or sold to the public by the owner of the design or with the owner's consent. Protection for a design commences on the earlier of the date of publication of the registration or the date the design was first made public.

SPACE 7: Contact Person

Give the name, address, e-mail address (if any), daytime phone number and facsimile number (if any) of the person to contact if further information regarding the application is needed

SPACE 8: Deposit Account

Complete Space 8 if an existing deposit account is to be charged for the filing fee.

SPACE 9: Certification and Sworn Statements

In order to obtain a registration of a vessel hull design, the applicant, or the applicant's duly appointed agent or representative, must complete the declaration in Space 9. Applicants, or their duly appointed agents or representatives, should read the declaration very closely before signing it. Willfully making false statements is punishable by fine or imprisonment, or both, and may jeopardize the validity of the application and any resulting registration. The declaration contained in Space 9 need not be notarized.

If the design has been made public with a design notice as prescribed in 17 U.S.C. §1306, then the form and location of the notice must be disclosed. The affixation of a notice is not a condition of protection under the law, but omission of the notice can affect an owner's recovery and relief in the event of an infringement action. The notice consists of three elements: 1) the words "Protected Design", the abbreviation "Prot'd Des.", or the letter "D" with a circle, or the symbol *D*; 2) the year of the date on which protection for the design commenced; and 3) the name of the owner of the design, an abbreviation by which the name can be recognized, or a generally accepted alternative designation of the owner. A distinctive identification of the owner may be used in lieu of the name if the distinctive identification has been recorded with the Copyright Office before the design marked with such identification is registered. Contact the Copyright Office for information regarding recordation of distinctive identifications.

In addition to the form of the design notice, its location on the vessel must also be disclosed. The design notice must be located and applied in such a fashion as to give reasonable notice of design protection while the vessel is passing through normal channels of commerce. Only a single notice is required to appear on the vessel, although multiple locations are acceptable. Acceptable locations for a design notice include, but are not limited to, the following: in close proximity to the hull identification number required by the Coast Guard Regulations set forth at 33 C.F.R. §181.23; in close proximity of the driver's console such that it is in plain view; if the vessel is twenty feet in length or less and is governed by the Coast Guard's regulations set forth at 33 C.F.R. §183.21, in close proximity to the capacity marking; or in close proximity to the make and model designation of the vessel. The notice should be affixed to the vessel in such a manner that it is not easily removable or likely to become detached. Engraving of the notice into the hull or deck of the vessel is not required.

ADDRESS FOR RETURN OF CERTIFICATE

The name and address must be completed legibly; the certificate will be mailed in a window envelope.

DATE OF REGISTRATION/PUBLICATION

Month	Day	Year

DO NOT WRITE ABOVE THIS LINE. IF YOU NEED MORE SPACE, USE A SEPARATE CONTINUATION SHEET. (Form D-VH/CON)

1 TITLE

Please give the make and model of the vessel that embodies the design.

2 DESIGN

(a) What is the type or style of the design for which registration is sought?

(b) Provide a brief general statement setting forth the salient features of the design.

❑ Check here if this is a **single** design.

❑ Check here if registering **more than** one design. Use Form D-VH/CON for additional designs.

(c) If this design is derived from an earlier design, describe how that design has been revised, adapted, or rearranged.

3 DESIGNER(S)

Provide the name and address of the designer(s). The name of the employer may be given instead of the designer(s) if, (1) the design was made within the regular scope of employment of the designer(s) and (2) the individual authorship of the design is difficult or impossible to ascribe.

❑ Please check here if those conditions are satisfied and you are providing the employer's name.

Name: _____   Name: _____

Address: _____   Address: _____

4 OWNER, IF NOT DESIGNER(S)

If the owner is different from the designer(s) or employer named above, provide the name and address of the owner:

Name: _____

Address: _____

5 PRIORITY CLAIM

(a) Was an application for registration of this design identified in an application filed in a foreign country that extends to designs of owners who are citizens of the United States, or to persons filing applications in the United States, similar protection to that afforded in 17 U.S.C. chapter 13?
❑ Yes ❑ No

(b) If yes, identify the country and date of application:
Country: _____

Date of application: _____

Serial No: _____

6 DATE MADE PUBLIC

Was this design made public before the date of application? ❑ Yes ❑ No

If yes, on what date? _____
Month   Day   Year

DO NOT WRITE HERE OFFICE USE ONLY

APPLICATION RECEIVED _____

DESIGN COPIES RECEIVED _____

FUNDS RECEIVED _____

MORE ON BACK ▶
• Complete all applicable spaces (numbers 7 -9) on the reverse side of this page.
• See detailed instructions.
• Sign the form at section 9.

DO NOT WRITE HERE
Page 1 of _____ pages

EXAMINED BY

CHECKED BY

CORRESPONDENCE
☐ Yes

FORM D-VH

FOR
COPYRIGHT
OFFICE
USE
ONLY

DO NOT WRITE ABOVE THIS LINE. IF YOU NEED MORE SPACE, USE A SEPARATE CONTINUATION SHEET. (Form D-VH/CON)

7 CONTACT PERSON

Please provide the name and address of the person to whom correspondence regarding this application may be directed:

Name: _____

Address: _____

_____ E-mail address _____

FAX number _____ Daytime phone: (   ) _____

8 DEPOSIT ACCOUNT

Give the name and account number if the registration fee is to be charged to a Deposit Account established in the Copyright Office:

Name of Account: _____

Account number: _____

9 CERTIFICATION AND SWORN STATEMENTS

DECLARATION: The undersigned, as the applicant or the applicant's duly appointed agent or representative, being hereby warned that willful false statements are punishable by fine or imprisonment, or both, under 18 U.S.C. §1001, and that such willful false statements may jeopardize the validity of this application or any resulting registration, hereby declares to the best of his/her knowledge and belief:

(1) that the design has been fixed in a useful article;
(2) that the design is original and was created by the designer(s), or employer if applicable, named in the application;
(3) that those aspects of the design for which registration is sought are not protected by a design patent;
(4) that the design has not previously been registered on behalf of the applicant or applicant's predecessor in title; and
(5) that the applicant is the person entitled to protection and to registration under chapter 13 of title 17, United States Code.

Complete if applicable:
The design has been made public with a design notice as prescribed by 17 U.S.C. §1306.
Following is the exact form of the design notice:

_____

Where on the useful article is the design notice located?

_____

If the undersigned is not the applicant, he/she is properly authorized to execute this application on behalf of the applicant.

☞ **X** _____   _____
Signature   Date

_____   _____
Print or type name   Position or Title

_____   _____
Telephone number   FAX number   E-mail address

As of July 1, 1999, the fee is $75.00. For current fee information, please write the Copyright Office, check the Copyright Office Website at http://www.loc.gov/copyright, or call (202) 707-3000.

Mail certificate to:	Name ▼	YOU MUST:
		• Complete all necessary spaces
		• Sign your application in space 9
Certificate will be mailed in window envelope	Number/Street/Apt ▼	**SEND ALL 3 ELEMENTS IN THE SAME PACKAGE:**
		1. Application form
		2. Nonrefundable filing fee in check or money order payable to *Register of Copyrights*
	City/State/ZIP ▼	3. Design material
		MAIL TO: Dept. D-VH Vessel Hull Registration P.O. Box 71380 Washington, D.C. 20024-1380

INDEX

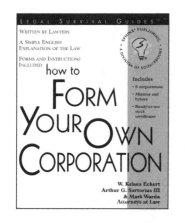
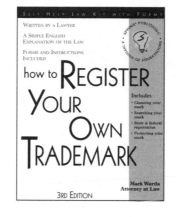

SPHINX® PUBLISHING'S NATIONAL TITLES

Valid in All 50 States

LEGAL SURVIVAL IN BUSINESS

The Complete Book of Corporate Forms	$24.95
How to Form a Delaware Corporation from Any State	$24.95
How to Form a Limited Liability Company	$22.95
Incorporate in Nevada from Any State	$24.95
How to Form a Nonprofit Corporation	$24.95
How to Form Your Own Corporation (3E)	$24.95
How to Form Your Own Partnership	$22.95
How to Register Your Own Copyright (4E)	$24.95
How to Register Your Own Trademark (3E)	$21.95
Most Valuable Business Legal Forms You'll Ever Need (3E)	$21.95

LEGAL SURVIVAL IN COURT

Crime Victim's Guide to Justice (2E)	$21.95
Grandparents' Rights (3E)	$24.95
Help Your Lawyer Win Your Case (2E)	$14.95
Jurors' Rights (2E)	$12.95
Legal Research Made Easy (2E)	$16.95
Winning Your Personal Injury Claim (2E)	$24.95
Your Rights When You Owe Too Much	$16.95

LEGAL SURVIVAL IN REAL ESTATE

Essential Guide to Real Estate Contracts	$18.95
Essential Guide to Real Estate Leases	$18.95
How to Buy a Condominium or Townhome (2E)	$19.95

LEGAL SURVIVAL IN PERSONAL AFFAIRS

Cómo Hacer su Propio Testamento	$16.95
Guía de Inmigración a Estados Unidos (3E)	$24.95
Guía de Justicia para Víctimas del Crimen	$21.95
Cómo Solicitar su Propio Divorcio	$24.95
How to File Your Own Bankruptcy (5E)	$21.95
How to File Your Own Divorce (4E)	$24.95
How to Make Your Own Will (2E)	$16.95
How to Write Your Own Living Will (2E)	$16.95
How to Write Your Own Premarital Agreement (3E)	$24.95
How to Win Your Unemployment Compensation Claim	$21.95
Living Trusts and Simple Ways to Avoid Probate (2E)	$22.95
Manual de Beneficios para el Seguro Social	$18.95
Most Valuable Personal Legal Forms You'll Ever Need	$24.95
Neighbor v. Neighbor (2E)	$16.95
The Nanny and Domestic Help Legal Kit	$22.95
The Power of Attorney Handbook (3E)	$19.95
Repair Your Own Credit and Deal with Debt	$18.95
The Social Security Benefits Handbook (3E)	$18.95
Unmarried Parents' Rights	$19.95
U.S.A. Immigration Guide (3E)	$19.95
Your Right to Child Custody, Visitation and Support (2E)	$24.95

Legal Survival Guides are directly available from Sourcebooks, Inc., or from your local bookstores.
Prices are subject to change without notice.

For credit card orders call 1–800–432–7444, write P.O. Box 4410, Naperville, IL 60567-4410
or fax 630-961-2168

SPHINX® PUBLISHING ORDER FORM

BILL TO:		SHIP TO:	
Phone #	Terms	F.O.B. Chicago, IL	Ship Date

Charge my: ☐ VISA ☐ MasterCard ☐ American Express

☐ **Money Order or Personal Check**

Credit Card Number   Expiration Date

Qty	ISBN	Title	Retail	Ext.
		SPHINX PUBLISHING NATIONAL TITLES		
___	1-57248-148-X	Cómo Hacer su Propio Testamento	$16.95	___
___	1-57248-147-1	Cómo Solicitar su Propio Divorcio	$24.95	___
___	1-57248-166-8	The Complete Book of Corporate Forms	$24.95	___
___	1-57248-163-3	Crime Victim's Guide to Justice (2E)	$21.95	___
___	1-57248-159-5	Essential Guide to Real Estate Contracts	$18.95	___
___	1-57248-160-9	Essential Guide to Real Estate Leases	$18.95	___
___	1-57248-139-0	Grandparents' Rights (3E)	$24.95	___
___	1-57248-160-9	Guía de Inmigración a Estados Unidos (3E)	$24.95	___
___	1-57248-187-0	Guía de Justicia para Víctimas del Crimen	$21.95	___
___	1-57248-103-X	Help Your Lawyer Win Your Case (2E)	$14.95	___
___	1-57248-164-1	How to Buy a Condominium or Townhome (2E)	$19.95	___
___	1-57248-191-1	How to File Your Own Bankruptcy (5E)	$21.95	___
___	1-57248-132-3	How to File Your Own Divorce (4E)	$24.95	___
___	1-57248-100-5	How to Form a DE Corporation from Any State	$24.95	___
___	1-57248-083-1	How to Form a Limited Liability Company	$22.95	___
___	1-57248-099-8	How to Form a Nonprofit Corporation	$24.95	___
___	1-57248-133-1	How to Form Your Own Corporation (3E)	$24.95	___
___	1-57071-343-X	How to Form Your Own Partnership	$22.95	___
___	1-57248-119-6	How to Make Your Own Will (2E)	$16.95	___
___	1-57248-200-1	How to Register Your Own Copyright (4E)	$24.95	___
___	1-57248-104-8	How to Register Your Own Trademark (3E)	$21.95	___
___	1-57071-349-9	How to Win Your Unemployment Compensation Claim	$21.95	___
___	1-57248-118-8	How to Write Your Own Living Will (2E)	$16.95	___
___	1-57248-156-0	How to Write Your Own Premarital Agreement (3E)	$24.95	___
___	1-57248-158-7	Incorporate in Nevada from Any State	$24.95	___
___	1-57071-333-2	Jurors' Rights (2E)	$12.95	___
___	1-57071-400-2	Legal Research Made Easy (2E)	$16.95	___
___	1-57071-336-7	Living Trusts and Simple Ways to Avoid Probate (2E)	$22.95	___
___	1-57248-186-2	Manual de Beneficios para el Seguro Social	$18.95	___
___	1-57248-167-6	Most Valuable Bus. Legal Forms You'll Ever Need (3E)	$21.95	___
___	1-57248-130-7	Most Valuable Personal Legal Forms You'll Ever Need	$24.95	___
___	1-57248-098-X	The Nanny and Domestic Help Legal Kit	$22.95	___
___	1-57248-089-0	Neighbor v. Neighbor (2E)	$16.95	___
___	1-57071-348-0	The Power of Attorney Handbook (3E)	$19.95	___
___	1-57248-149-8	Repair Your Own Credit and Deal with Debt	$18.95	___
___	1-57248-168-4	The Social Security Benefits Handbook (3E)	$18.95	___
___	1-57071-399-5	Unmarried Parents' Rights	$19.95	___
___	1-57071-354-5	U.S.A. Immigration Guide (3E)	$19.95	___
___	1-57248-138-2	Winning Your Personal Injury Claim (2E)	$24.95	___
___	1-57248-162-5	Your Right to Child Custody, Visitation and Support (2E)	$24.95	___
___	1-57248-157-9	Your Rights When You Owe Too Much	$16.95	___
		CALIFORNIA TITLES		
___	1-57248-150-1	CA Power of Attorney Handbook (2E)	$18.95	___
___	1-57248-151-X	How to File for Divorce in CA (3E)	$26.95	___
___	1-57071-356-1	How to Make a CA Will	$16.95	___
___	1-57248-145-5	How to Probate and Settle an Estate in California	$26.95	___
___	1-57248-146-3	How to Start a Business in CA	$18.95	___
___	1-57071-358-8	How to Win in Small Claims Court in CA	$16.95	___
___	1-57071-359-6	Landlords' Rights and Duties in CA	$21.95	___
		FLORIDA TITLES		
___	1-57071-363-4	Florida Power of Attorney Handbook (2E)	$16.95	___
___	1-57248-176-5	How to File for Divorce in FL (7E)	$26.95	___
___	1-57248-177-3	How to Form a Corporation in FL (5E)	$24.95	___
___	1-57248-086-6	How to Form a Limited Liability Co. in FL	$22.95	___
___	1-57071-401-0	How to Form a Partnership in FL	$22.95	___
___	1-57248-113-7	How to Make a FL Will (6E)	$16.95	___

Form Continued on Following Page   **SUBTOTAL**

To order, call Sourcebooks at 1-800-432-7444 or FAX (630) 961-2168 (Bookstores, libraries, wholesalers—please call for discount)

Prices are subject to change without notice.

SPHINX® PUBLISHING ORDER FORM

Qty	ISBN	Title	Retail	Ext.
_____	1-57248-088-2	How to Modify Your FL Divorce Judgment (4E)	$24.95	_____
_____	1-57248-144-7	How to Probate and Settle an Estate in FL (4E)	$26.95	_____
_____	1-57248-081-5	How to Start a Business in FL (5E)	$16.95	_____
_____	1-57071-362-6	How to Win in Small Claims Court in FL (6E)	$16.95	_____
_____	1-57248-123-4	Landlords' Rights and Duties in FL (8E)	$21.95	_____
		GEORGIA TITLES		
_____	1-57248-137-4	How to File for Divorce in GA (4E)	$21.95	_____
_____	1-57248-180-3	How to Make a GA Will (4E)	$21.95	_____
_____	1-57248-140-4	How to Start a Business in Georgia (2E)	$16.95	_____
		ILLINOIS TITLES		
_____	1-57071-405-3	How to File for Divorce in IL (2E)	$21.95	_____
_____	1-57248-170-6	How to Make an IL Will (3E)	$16.95	_____
_____	1-57071-416-9	How to Start a Business in IL (2E)	$18.95	_____
_____	1-57248-078-5	Landlords' Rights & Duties in IL	$21.95	_____
		MASSACHUSETTS TITLES		
_____	1-57248-128-5	How to File for Divorce in MA (3E)	$24.95	_____
_____	1-57248-115-3	How to Form a Corporation in MA	$24.95	_____
_____	1-57248-108-0	How to Make a MA Will (2E)	$16.95	_____
_____	1-57248-106-4	How to Start a Business in MA (2E)	$18.95	_____
_____	1-57248-107-2	Landlords' Rights and Duties in MA (2E)	$21.95	_____
		MICHIGAN TITLES		
_____	1-57071-409-6	How to File for Divorce in MI (2E)	$21.95	_____
_____	1-57248-182-X	How to Make a MI Will (3E)	$16.95	_____
_____	1-57248-183-8	How to Start a Business in MI (3E)	$18.95	_____
		MINNESOTA TITLES		
_____	1-57248-142-0	How to File for Divorce in MN	$21.95	_____
_____	1-57248-179-X	How to Form a Corporation in MN	$24.95	_____
_____	1-57248-178-1	How to Make a MN Will (2E)	$16.95	_____
		NEW YORK TITLES		
_____	1-57248-141-2	How to File for Divorce in NY (2E)	$26.95	_____
_____	1-57248-105-6	How to Form a Corporation in NY	$24.95	_____
_____	1-57248-095-5	How to Make a NY Will (2E)	$16.95	_____
_____	1-57071-185-2	How to Start a Business in NY	$18.95	_____
_____	1-57071-187-9	How to Win in Small Claims Court in NY	$16.95	_____
_____	1-57071-186-0	Landlords' Rights and Duties in NY	$21.95	_____

Qty	ISBN	Title	Retail	Ext.
_____	1-57071-188-7	New York Power of Attorney Handbook	$19.95	_____
_____	1-57248-122-6	Tenants' Rights in NY	$21.95	_____
		NORTH CAROLINA TITLES		
_____	1-57248-185-4	How to File for Divorce in NC (3E)	$22.95	_____
_____	1-57248-129-3	How to Make a NC Will (3E)	$16.95	_____
_____	1-57248-184-6	How to Start a Business in NC (3E)	$18.95	_____
_____	1-57248-091-2	Landlords' Rights & Duties in NC	$21.95	_____
		OHIO TITLES		
_____	1-57248-190-0	How to File for Divorce in OH (2E)	$24.95	_____
_____	1-57248-174-9	How to Form a Corporation in OH	$24.95	_____
_____	1-57248-173-0	How to Make an OH Will	$16.95	_____
		PENNSYLVANIA TITLES		
_____	1-57248-127-7	How to File for Divorce in PA (2E)	$24.95	_____
_____	1-57248-094-7	How to Make a PA Will (2E)	$16.95	_____
_____	1-57248-112-9	How to Start a Business in PA (2E)	$18.95	_____
_____	1-57071-179-8	Landlords' Rights and Duties in PA	$19.95	_____
		TEXAS TITLES		
_____	1-57248-171-4	Child Custody, Visitation, and Support in TX	$22.95	_____
_____	1-57248-172-2	How to File for Divorce in TX (3E)	$24.95	_____
_____	1-57248-114-5	How to Form a Corporation in TX (2E)	$24.95	_____
_____	1-57071-417-7	How to Make a TX Will (2E)	$16.95	_____
_____	1-57071-418-5	How to Probate an Estate in TX (2E)	$22.95	_____
_____	1-57071-365-0	How to Start a Business in TX (2E)	$18.95	_____
_____	1-57248-111-0	How to Win in Small Claims Court in TX (2E)	$16.95	_____
_____	1-57248-110-2	Landlords' Rights and Duties in TX (2E)	$21.95	_____

SUBTOTAL THIS PAGE _____

SUBTOTAL PREVIOUS PAGE _____

Shipping — $5.00 for 1st book, $1.00 each additional _____

Illinois residents add 6.75% sales tax _____

Connecticut residents add 6.00% sales tax _____

TOTAL _____

To order, call Sourcebooks at 1-800-432-7444 or FAX (630) 961-2168 (Bookstores, libraries, wholesalers—please call for discount)

Prices are subject to change without notice.